Seventh Edition   *Form A*

Inside
Writing

A Writer's Workbook

William Salomone
Palomar College

Stephen McDonald
Palomar College

WADSWORTH
CENGAGE Learning

Australia • Brazil • Japan • Korea • Mexico • Singapore • Spain • United Kingdom • United States

WADSWORTH
CENGAGE Learning

Inside Writing: A Writer's Workbook, Form A, Seventh Edition
William Salomone, Stephen McDonald

Publisher: Lyn Uhl

Director: Annie Todd

Development Editor: Cathlynn Richard Dodson

Associate Editor: Janine Tangney

Editorial Assistant: Melanie Opacki

Managing Media Editor: Cara Douglass-Graff

Senior Marketing Manager: Kirsten Stoller

Marketing Assistant: Ryan Ahern

Marketing Communications Manager: Martha Pfeiffer

Art Director: Jill Ort

Print Buyer: Denise Powers

Permissions Editor: Margaret Chamberlain-Gaston

Production Service/Compositor: Pre-PressPMG

Cover Designer: Robert Doron

Cover Image: © Getty Images

For product information and technology assistance, contact us at
Cengage Learning Customer & Sales Support, 1-800-354-9706
For permission to use material from this text or product,
submit all requests online at **www.cengage.com/permissions**
Further permissions questions can be emailed to
permissionrequest@cengage.com

Library of Congress Control Number: 2009940470

ISBN-13: 978-0-495-80250-1

ISBN-10: 0-495-80250-6

Wadsworth
20 Channel Center Street
Boston, MA 02210
USA

Cengage Learning is a leading provider of customized learning solutions with office locations around the globe, including Singapore, the United Kingdom, Australia, Mexico, Brazil, and Japan. Locate your local office at: **international.cengage.com/region**

Cengage Learning products are represented in Canada by Nelson Education, Ltd.

For your course and learning solutions, visit **www.cengage.com**

Purchase any of our products at your local college store or at our preferred online store **www.CengageBrain.com**

Printed in Canada
2 3 4 5 6 7 13 12 11 10

To Rosemary and Marlyle

Contents

Chapter Three Improving Sentence Patterns   151

Chapter Five Using Punctuation and Capitalization   277

Preface

Inside Writing was constructed on the premise that there is really only one reason for learning the essential rules of English grammar—to become better writers. In this text, we constantly stress that all college students are writers and that the aim of any college writing course—developmental or otherwise—is to improve writing. To this purpose, *Inside Writing* has been created with clear and simple organization, a friendly, non-threatening tone, thorough integration of grammar sections with writing sections, and unique thematic exercises.

The Reason for This Text

We are all aware of widespread disagreement about what should be presented in a first-semester developmental writing course. *Inside Writing* was written to address the resulting diversity of course content with a union of grammar and writing instruction. In it, we teach basic grammar and sentence structure, yet we also provide extensive practice in sentence combining and paragraph writing.

Moving Beyond a Traditional Approach. The traditional approach to developmental writing has been to review the rules of grammar, punctuation, and usage and then to test the students' understanding of those rules through a series of chapter tests. However, as research and experience have demonstrated, there is no necessary correlation between the study of grammar and the development of competent writers. As a result, many English departments have restructured their developmental courses to focus on the process of writing, developing courses that have very little in common with each other from one campus to the next. Today, some developmental writing instructors teach the traditional exercises in grammar, others focus on journal and expressive writing, others emphasize sentence combining, and still others teach the writing of paragraphs and short essays.

Using an Integrated Approach. Inside Writing responds to this spectrum of course content by integrating grammar instruction and writing practice. Certainly the practice of writing is important in a first-semester developmental class. Yet the study of traditional grammar, punctuation, and usage is also important because it provides a fundamental knowledge of sentence structure—knowledge that writers need not only to revise their own writing but also to discuss their writing with others. The writing practices in this text are specifically designed to support, not merely to supplement, the grammar instruction. As soon as students have mastered a particular grammatical principle, they are asked to put their knowledge into practice in the writing sections of each chapter. This immediate reinforcement makes it more likely that students will improve their writing as well as retain the rules of grammar, usage, and mechanics.

Text Organization and Features

Inside Writing is presented in six chapters and an appendix. Each chapter consists of five sections that cover major principles of basic grammar, sentence construction, and paragraph writing. The appendix provides a review of common ESL issues. Throughout the text, the instruction is kept as simple as possible, giving the students only the information that is absolutely essential.

- Each chapter's grammar instruction is broken into three sections so that the students are not presented with too much at once.

- Each of the three grammar sections includes various practices and ends with three exercises that give the students an opportunity to apply the concepts and rules they have learned.

- Each chapter is followed by a practice test covering the material presented in the first three sections of the chapter, and the text closes with a practice final examination.

- The fourth section of each chapter presents both instruction and exercises in sentence combining, based on the specific concepts and rules covered in the three grammar sections. For example, in the chapter covering participial phrases and adjective clauses, the sentence-combining section instructs the students to combine sentences by using participial phrases and adjective clauses.

- The fifth section of each chapter includes instruction in writing paragraphs and essays and a choice of several writing assignments, again designed to reinforce the grammar sections of the chapter by leading students to employ in their own writing the rules for sentence structure they have studied.

- The appendix, "Working with ESL Issues," discusses common challenges faced by the ESL writer, including the correct use of count and noncount nouns, articles, subjects and verbs, and adjectives.

- At the end of the text, answers to the practices—but not to the exercises—are provided. These answers allow the students to check their understanding of the material as they read the text. The extensive exercises without answers permit the instructor to determine where more explanation or study is needed.

- Many of the practices and exercises develop thematic ideas or contain a variety of cultural, mythological, and historical allusions. Some exercises, for example, explain the origin of the names of our weekdays, tell the story of the Native-American character Woodpecker, or illustrate common urban legends. In addition, individual sentences within practices and exercises often provoke questions and discussion when they refer to characters and events from history, mythology, or contemporary culture. This feature of *Inside Writing* encourages developmental writing students to look beyond grammar, mechanics, and punctuation. It reminds them—or it allows us as instructors to remind them—that the educated writer has command of much more than the correct use of the comma.

Connecting Concepts and Writing Practice. To emphasize further the connection between the writing assignments and the grammar exercises, the writing assignment in each chapter is modeled by three thematic exercises within the grammar sections of the chapter. For instance, in Chapter 3, Exercises 1C, 2C, and 3C are paragraphs that use examples to support a statement made in a topic sentence. The writing practice section then extends this groundwork by presenting instruction in the writing of a similar expository paragraph or essay.

In each writing assignment, the students are introduced gradually to the writing process and encouraged to improve their writing through prewriting and careful revision. They are also introduced to the basic concepts of academic writing—thesis statements, topic sentences, unity, specificity, completeness, order, and coherence. However, the main purpose of the writing instruction is to give the students an opportunity to use their new knowledge of grammar and sentence structure to communicate their own thoughts and ideas.

Changes to This Edition

We have improved the Seventh Edition of *Inside Writing* in several areas:

- Fifty percent of nearly all practices and exercises are new.

- Each chapter contains a new thematic exercise that functions not only as a way to test the students' comprehension of grammar, punctuation, or usage principles but also as an example of the writing assignment introduced in the chapter.

- As with all previous editions, we have included allusions designed to interest both the instructor and the student. For example, in just the first two sections of Chapter 1 are allusions to Pandora, Benjamin Franklin, Hafiz, P. T. Barnum, John Donne, Emily Dickinson, Persephone, Madonna, the *Hindenburg*, Steve Jobs, Thor, Ichabod Crane, Elmo, and Dido.

  Many instructors use these allusions as part of their classes, asking students if they know what they refer to, or, if a joke is involved, whether or not they get the joke. Here's an example from page 3: "Pandora stared curiously at the box in her hand." Instructors can use this sentence as they would any other sentence in the practice (underlining nouns), or they can stop for a moment and ask if anyone knows whether Pandora opened that box—or if she should open the box. A few students at this level will have heard of Pandora, but not many. Those who can answer the question teach the other students a little about mythology. Not all the allusions are serious. Some are just fun: "Dr. Frankenstein proudly told his neighbors about the success of his latest experiment" or "Neptune was looking forward to a hefty fillet-of-fish sandwich." The point is that such allusions provide a depth of content and a light-hearted tone that go beyond the rote recitation of practices and exercises.

An Exceptional Support Package

The Instructor's Manual provides suggestions for how to use the text, answers to the exercises, diagnostic and achievement tests, a series of six chapter tests and six alternate chapter tests, a final examination, answers to the tests and final examination, additional writing assignments, and model paragraphs. With this material, the instructor can use a traditional lecture approach, working through each chapter and then testing the students together, or the instructor can allow the students to work through the book at their own pace, dealing with the students' questions individually and giving students tests as they complete each chapter.

This text is available in an alternate version, "Form B," for added teaching flexibility in the second semester.

Acknowledgments

We thank our friends and colleagues in the English Department at Palomar College, particularly Jack Quintero, who has consistently and generously given his encouragement and advice. We wish him the best in his retirement. We also thank Brent Gowen and Bruce Orton, whose valuable comments and suggestions have contributed to this text.

We extend our thanks to Annie Todd at Cengage Learning, to Kirsten Stoller, Marketing Manager, Janine Tangney, Associate Editor, Melanie Opacki, Editorial Assistant and Margaret Bridges, Senior Content Project Manager at Cengage Learning, and to Cate Richard Dodson, who has kept us on track and moving forward as we prepared this revision. We also gratefully acknowledge the following students, who graciously allowed us to use their writing assignments as models: Michael Heading, Kelli Newell, Lana Futch, Brian Yeskis, Cathy Martin, Laurence Suiaunoa, Patricia Muller, and Dora Cerda.

We are very grateful to the following professors who provided valuable input for this revision:

Hilary Wilson	*St. Louis Community College Forest Park,* St. Louis, MO
Sandia Tuttle	*Mesa College,* and *Grossmont College,* San Diego, CA
Brian Longacre	*Asheville Buncombe Technical Community College,* Asheville, NC
Esther Rosenstock	*Stevenson University,* Stevenson, MD
Chris Lint	*Pennsylvania Highlands Community College,* Johnstown, PA

Finally, of course, we thank our families and friends for their patience and support as we once again worked late into the night.

William Salomone
Stephen McDonald

Naming the Parts

Let's face it. Few people find grammar a fascinating subject, and few study it of their own free will. Most people study grammar only when they are absolutely required to do so. Many seem to feel that grammar is either endlessly complicated or not important to their daily lives.

The problem is not that people fail to appreciate the importance of writing. The ability to express oneself clearly on paper is generally recognized as an important advantage. Those who can communicate their ideas and feelings effectively have a much greater chance to develop themselves, not only professionally but personally as well.

Perhaps the negative attitude toward grammar is due in part to the suspicion that studying grammar has little to do with learning how to write. This suspicion is not at all unreasonable—a knowledge of grammar by itself will not make anyone a better writer. To become a better writer, a person should study *writing* and practice it frequently.

However, the study of writing is much easier if one understands grammar. Certainly a person can learn to write well without knowing exactly how sentences are put together or what the various parts are called. But most competent writers do know these things because such knowledge enables them not only to develop their skills more easily but also to analyze their writing and discuss it with others.

Doctors, for example, don't necessarily have to know the names of the tools they use (stethoscope, scalpel, sutures), nor do mechanics have to know the names of their tools (wrench, screwdriver, ratchet). But it would be hard to find competent doctors or mechanics who were not thoroughly familiar with the tools of their trades, for it is much more difficult to master any important skill and also more difficult to discuss that skill without such knowledge.

The terms and concepts you encounter in this chapter are familiar to most of you, but probably not familiar enough. It is not good enough to have a vague idea of what a linking verb is or a general notion of what a prepositional phrase is. You should know *precisely* what these terms mean. This chapter and subsequent chapters present only what is basic and necessary to the study of grammar, but it is essential that you learn *all* of what is presented.

A sound understanding of grammar, like a brick wall, must be built one level at a time. You cannot miss a level and go on to the next. If you master each level as it is presented, you will find that grammar is neither as difficult nor as complicated as you may have thought. You will also find, as you work through the writing sections of the text, that by applying your knowledge of grammar you can greatly improve your writing skills.

Subjects and Verbs

Of all the terms presented in this chapter, perhaps the most important are **SUBJECT** and **VERB**, for subjects and verbs are the foundation of every sentence. Sentences come in many forms, and the structures may become quite complex, but they all have one thing in common: Every sentence must contain a SUBJECT and a VERB. Like most grammatical rules, this one is based on simple logic. After all, without a subject you have nothing to write about, and without a verb you have nothing to say about your subject.

Subjects: Nouns and Pronouns

Before you can find the subject of a sentence, you need to be able to identify nouns and pronouns because the subjects of sentences will always be nouns or pronouns (or, occasionally, other words or groups of words that function as subjects). You probably know the definition of a noun: **A noun names a person, place, thing, or idea.**

> **noun**
> A noun names a person, place, thing, or idea.

This definition works perfectly well for most nouns, especially for those that name concrete things we can *see, hear, smell, taste,* or *touch.* Using this definition, most people can identify words such as *door, road,* or *tulip* as nouns.

EXAMPLES

       N   N   N
Paula reads her favorite **book** whenever she goes to the **beach.**

       N   N   N
My **brother** likes to watch **football** on **television.**

Unfortunately, when it comes to identifying ideas as nouns, many people have trouble. Part of this problem is that nouns name even more than ideas. They name **emotions, qualities, conditions,** and many other **abstractions.** Abstract nouns such as *fear, courage, happiness,* and *trouble* do not name persons, places, or things, but they are nouns.

Following are a few examples of nouns, arranged by category. Add nouns of your own to each category.

Persons	Places	Things	Ideas
Paula	New York	spaghetti	sincerity
engineer	beach	book	anger
woman	India	sun	democracy
artist	town	bicycle	intelligence
_____	_____	_____	_____
_____	_____	_____	_____
_____	_____	_____	_____

◎◎ PRACTICE   Place an "N" above all the nouns in the following sentences.

           N   N   N   N

1. Brad asked Jennifer to look in the mirror at her hair.

2. Harebrained is the name of a new salon in our city.

3. Pandora stared curiously at the box in her hand.

4. Humpty hoped the men near the wall would solve his problem.

5. Barack Obama gave a confident speech at his inauguration.

To help you identify <u>all</u> nouns, remember these points:

1. <u>Nouns can be classified as **proper nouns** and **common nouns.**</u> **Proper nouns** name specific persons, places, things, and ideas. The first letter in each of these nouns is capitalized (Manuelita, Missouri, Mazda, Marxism). **Common nouns** name more general categories. The first letter of a common noun is not capitalized (man, mansion, moss, marriage).

2. <u>**A, an,** and **the** are noun markers.</u> A noun will always follow one of these words.

◎◎ EXAMPLES

                   N   N
The young **policeman** was given **a** new **car.**

           N   N   N   N
The final **point** of **the lecture** concerned **an inconsistency** in **the** last **report.**

3. If you are unsure whether or not a word is a noun, ask yourself if it <u>**could be introduced with a, an,** or **the.**</u>

◎◎ EXAMPLE

           N   N   N
My **granddaughter** asked for my **opinion** of her new **outfit.**

4. Words that end in **-ment, -ism, -ness, -ence, -ance,** and **-tion** are usually nouns.

⊚ EXAMPLE

            N   N

Her **criticism** of my **performance** made me very unhappy.

⊚ PRACTICE   Place an "N" above all the nouns in the following sentences.

          N   *N*   *N*   *N*

1. Relationships between gods and goddesses can create many problems.

2. Hades and Persephone had a volatile marriage.

3. In spring Persephone surfaced on the coast of Greece.

4. Her husband missed her as she enjoyed the cool breezes of the Aegean Sea.

5. In autumn she packed her clothes and descended to her home in the

    underworld.

6. Alice stared in amazement at the cat with the enormous grin.

7. Love and tolerance are not usually characteristics of racism and prejudice.

8. The success of his experiment came as no shock to Benjamin Franklin.

9. The tiny votive candle cast a thin light that did little to improve the

    depressing condition of the room.

10. Hafiz was a poet of the fourteenth century who combined wit, humor,

     eroticism, and a deep reverence for the sacred.

A pronoun takes the place of a noun. The "pro" in *pronoun* comes from the Latin word meaning "for." Thus, a pronoun is a word that in some way stands "for a noun." Pronouns perform this task in a variety of ways. Often, a pronoun will allow you to refer to a noun without having to repeat the noun. For instance, notice how the word *John* is awkwardly repeated in the following sentence:

John put on John's coat before John left for John's job.

Pronouns allow you to avoid the repetition:

John put on his coat before he left for his job.

pronoun
A pronoun takes the place of a noun.

In later chapters we will discuss the use of pronouns and the differences among the various types. For now, you simply need to be able to recognize pronouns in a sentence. The following list includes the most common pronouns. Read over this list several times until you are familiar with these words.

Personal Pronouns

I	we	you	he	she	they	it
me	us	your	him	her	them	its
my	our	yours	his	hers	their	
mine	ours				theirs	

Indefinite Pronouns

some	everyone	anyone	someone	no one
all	everything	anything	something	nothing
many	everybody	anybody	somebody	nobody
each				
one				
none				

Reflexive/Intensive Pronouns

myself	ourselves
yourself	yourselves
himself	themselves
herself	
itself	

Relative Pronouns

who, whom, whose
which
that

Demonstrative Pronouns

that	this
those	these

Interrogative Pronouns

who, whom, whose
which
what

PRACTICE Place an "N" above all nouns and a "Pro" above all pronouns in the following sentences.

1. Erik noticed their boat was drifting toward the falls, so he dropped its anchor.

2. Each of us should know which little piggy went to market.

3. The *Minnow* left the harbor for a three-hour tour, but it never returned.

4. Do you know what P. T. Barnum said about suckers?

5. Bambi looked at his father with admiration when he saw the impressive antlers.

6. Does anyone understand her explanation of fractals?

7. The Super Bowl is well known for its unique advertisements, but my brother does not enjoy them.

8. Many of the veterans of Korea and Vietnam are assisting those who return from Iraq with injuries.

9. My collection of rare books does not include anything by Herman Melville or Nathaniel Hawthorne.

10. Almost anyone who reads the poetry of Emily Dickinson will admire her description of a hummingbird.

◎◎ PRACTICE In the following sentences, write nouns and pronouns of your own choice as indicated.

         N   N   Pro   N

1. The *sailor* on the *pier* stared at *his* *pipe* .

     N   Pro   N   Pro   N

2. _____ will share _____ _____ with _____ _____.

     N   Pro   N   Pro

3. _____ asked _____ to be quiet while _____ shot _____ free throw.

     N   N   Pro   N

4. _____ liked the _____ that _____ bought at the _____.

     N   Pro   N

5. _____ searched _____ backpack to find a _____ because

   Pro   N   Pro

_____ _____ had cut _____ foot.

Verbs

Once you can identify nouns and pronouns, the next step is to learn to identify verbs. Although some people have trouble recognizing these words, you should be able to identify them if you learn the following definition and the few points after it: **A verb either shows action or links the subject to another word.**

> ### verb
> A verb either shows action or links the subject to another word.

As you can see, this definition identifies two types of verbs. Some are "action" verbs (they tell what the subject is <u>doing</u>), and others are "linking" verbs (they tell what the subject is <u>being</u>). This distinction leads to the first point that will help you recognize verbs.

Action Verbs and Linking Verbs

<u>One way to recognize verbs is to know that some verbs can do more than simply express an action.</u> Some verbs are action verbs; others are linking verbs.

ACTION VERBS

Action verbs are usually easy to identify. Consider the following sentence:

> The deer leaped gracefully over the stone wall.

If you ask yourself what the **action** of the sentence is, the answer is obviously *leaped*. Therefore, *leaped* is the verb.

EXAMPLES OF ACTION VERBS *run, read, go, write, think, forgive, wait, laugh*

PRACTICE   Underline the action verbs in the following sentences.

    1. Madonna <u>leaned</u> on the drummer.

    2. The German blimp *Hindenburg* burned after its trip to the United States.

    3. Pirates and football players wear bandanna on their heads.

    4. The cat searched everywhere for a better hat.

    5. Mr. Lincoln talked to General Grant on his cell phone.

LINKING VERBS

Linking verbs are sometimes more difficult to recognize than action verbs. Look for the verb in the following sentence:

> Helen **is** a woman of integrity.

Notice that the sentence expresses no real action. The verb *is* simply links the word *woman* to the word *Helen*.

EXAMPLES OF LINKING VERBS forms of *be:* am, is, are, was, were, be, being, been

forms of *become, seem, look, appear, smell, taste, feel, sound, grow, remain*

Linking verbs can link three types of words to a subject.

1. They can link nouns to the subject:

    Hank <u>became</u> a hero to his team. (*Hero* is linked to *Hank*.)

2. They can link pronouns to the subject:

    Cheryl <u>was</u> someone from another planet. (*Someone* is linked to *Cheryl*.)

3. They can link adjectives (descriptive words) to the subject:

    The sky <u>was</u> cloudy all day. (*Cloudy* is linked to *sky*.)

PRACTICE Underline the linking verbs in the following sentences.

1. The author <u>was</u> sad about the lack of success of his novel.

2. Steve Jobs is the cofounder of a major American company.

3. Rip Van Winkle felt dizzy after his long nap.

4. Our new neighbors seem rather quiet and shy.

5. Andrew and his wife are angry about the results of the last election.

Verb Tense

Another way to identify verbs is to know that they appear in different forms to show the time when the action or linking takes place. These forms are called *tenses*. The simplest tenses are present, past, and future.

Present		*Past*	
I walk	we walk	I walked	we walked
you walk	you walk	you walked	you walked
he, she, it walks	they walk	he, she, it walked	they walked

Future	
I will walk	we will walk
you will walk	you will walk
he, she, it will walk	they will walk

Note that the verb *walk* can be written as *walked* to show past tense and as *will walk* to show future tense. When a verb adds "d" or "ed" to form the past tense, it is called a **regular verb.**

Other verbs change their forms more drastically to show past tense. For example, the verb *eat* becomes *ate*, and *fly* becomes *flew*. Verbs like these, which do not add "d" or "ed" to form the past tense, are called **irregular verbs**. Irregular verbs will be discussed in Chapter Six. For now, to help you identify verbs, remember this point: Verbs change their forms to show tense.

PRACTICE

In the following sentences, first underline the verb and then write the tense (present, past, or future) in the space provided.

present **1.** Aeneas praises Dido once a week.

_____ **2.** Odysseus wanted to go home.

_____ **3.** Mark's new papillon will sit for treats.

_____ **4.** The Johnstown Flood killed 2,200 people in 1889.

_____ **5.** Ian plays cello pieces by Jacqueline du Pré every Wednesday.

Helping Verbs and Main Verbs

A third way to identify verbs is to know that the verb of a sentence is often more than one word. The **MAIN VERB** of a sentence may be preceded by one or more **HELPING VERBS** to show time, condition, or circumstances. The helping verbs allow us the flexibility to communicate a wide variety of ideas and attitudes. For example, note how adding a helping verb changes the following sentences:

I run indicates that an action is happening or happens repeatedly.

I will run indicates that an action is not now occurring but will occur in the future.

I should run indicates an attitude toward the action.

The **COMPLETE VERB** of a sentence, then, includes a **MAIN VERB** and any **HELPING VERBS**. The complete verb can contain as many as three helping verbs.

EXAMPLES

　　　　　MV
He *writes*.

　　HV　MV
He *has written*.

　　HV　HV　　MV
He *has been writing*.

　　　HV　　HV　　HV　　MV
He *might have been writing*.

You can be sure that you have identified all of the helping verbs in a complete verb simply by learning the helping verbs. There are not very many of them.

These words are **always** helping verbs:

can	may	could
will	must	would
shall	might	should

These words are sometimes helping verbs and sometimes main verbs:

Forms of have	*Forms of* do	*Forms of* be		
have	do	am	was	be
has	does	is	were	being
had	did	are		been

In the following examples, note that the same word can be a helping verb in one sentence and a main verb in another:

EXAMPLES

        MV
Anna **had** thirty pairs of shoes.

        HV   MV
Thomas **had** thought about the problem for years.

      MV
She **did** well on her chemistry quiz.

      HV MV
Bob **did** go to the game after all.

        MV
The bus **was** never on time.

     HV   MV
He **was** planning to leave in the morning.

When you are trying to identify the complete verb of a sentence, remember that any helping verbs will always come before the main verb; however, other words may occur between the helping verb(s) and the main verb. For instance, you will often find words such as *not, never, ever, already,* or *just* between the helping verb and the main verb. Also, in questions you will often find the subject between the helping verb and the main verb.

EXAMPLES

HV   S   MV
Will the telephone company raise its prices?

     S   HV   MV
Nobody has **ever** proved the existence of the Loch Ness Monster.

🌀 PRACTICE   In the spaces provided, identify the underlined words as main verbs (MV) or helping verbs (HV).

_MV_ **1.** The cowboy <u>is</u> a popular figure in American folklore.

_____ **2.** Early cowboys in the Southwest <u>had</u> the Spanish title of *vaquero*.

_____ **3.** Soon American pronunciation <u>had</u> changed *vaquero* to *buckeroo*.

_____ **4.** Buckeroos <u>were</u> not called cowboys until the 1820s.

_____ **5.** Cowboys <u>were</u> mostly simple ranch hands.

_____ **6.** They <u>did</u> many physically demanding jobs on the ranch.

_____ **7.** However, they <u>did</u> not drive cattle across country until the late 1860s.

_____ **8.** Texans had <u>been</u> raising cattle for many years before that.

_____ **9.** But their problem had always <u>been</u> the distance between Texas and the markets to the north and east.

_____ **10.** In response, the cowboys <u>would</u> move hundreds of thousands of cattle across the country from Texas to the railheads in Kansas and Nebraska.

🌀 PRACTICE   **A.** In the following sentences, place "HV" over all helping verbs and "MV" over all main verbs.

                     HV MV
1. LaDainian Tomlinson is considering another knee operation.

2. The Sirens have caused many shipwrecks.

3. Thor was swinging his hammer in all directions.

4. Will Bill try a little harder during the next rehearsal?

5. The man with the take-out boxes should have offered his leftovers to that homeless person.

B. In the following sentences, write helping verbs and main verbs of your own choice as indicated.

                    MV
6. John Lee Hooker _played_ some blues for his friends.

                    MV   MV

7. Jesse James _____ the engraved revolver and _____ it to his brother.

            HV   MV

8. Penelope _____ _____ patiently for Odysseus for twenty years.

      HV   MV   MV

9. _____ Shakespeare _____ the tragedy that I _____ him for?

           HV   HV   MV

10. Lady Godiva _____ not _____ _____ her horse when

     HV   MV

she _____ not _____ any clothes.

Verbals

A fourth way to identify verbs is to recognize what they are not. Some verb forms do not actually function as verbs. These are called **VERBALS.** One of the most important verbals is the **INFINITIVE,** which usually begins with the word *to* (*to write, to be, to see*). The infinitive cannot serve as the verb of a sentence because it cannot express the time of the action or linking. *I wrote* communicates a clear idea, but *I to write* does not.

Another common verbal is the "-ing" form of the verb when it occurs without a helping verb (*running, flying, being*). When an "-ing" form without a helping verb is used as an adjective, it is called a **PRESENT PARTICIPLE.** When it is used as a noun, it is called a **GERUND.**

EXAMPLES

   MV   Verbal
I **hope to pass** this test.

   HV   MV
I **should pass** this test.

     Verbal   MV
The birds **flying** from tree to tree **chased** the cat from their nest.

     HV MV
The birds **were flying** from tree to tree.

  Verbal MV
Jogging is good cardiovascular exercise.

  MV
I **jog** for the cardiovascular benefits of the exercise.

PRACTICE   In the following sentences, write "HV" above all helping verbs, "MV" above all main verbs, and "Verbal" above all verbals.

              HV MV   *Verbal*

1. Paradise should be a good place to sleep late.

2. Playing on a sprained ankle, the tennis player could not defeat her opponent.

3. To illustrate Meryl Streep's talent, Penelope will describe her comedic, musical, and dramatic performances.

4. The photographer had taken a picture of Mother Teresa attending a sick man.

5. The old lady stirring the broth of bat wings and spider legs might agree to give you a taste.

PRACTICE   Place "HV" above all helping verbs and "MV" above all main verbs in the following sentences. Draw a line through any verbals.

              HV   MV

1. Paul had intended ~~to reach~~ Damascus before dark.

2. Brent and Bruce were discussing Bill Gates's attempts to alleviate world famine and disease.

3. Does Oedipus really want to marry Jocasta?

4. The Sphinx has a rather simple riddle for you.

5. The anthropologist must have seen the full moon rising exactly between the two Anasazi ruins.

6. To please the audience, Woody has agreed to play his most popular folk song.

7. To tell the truth, the Trojans should never have accepted that strange gift.

8. Impressing everyone, Heath Ledger was awarded an Oscar for his role as an evil clown.

9. Josita has been trying for years to find the long-lost city of *El Dorado*.

10. Does anyone recognize the man attacking that windmill with his lance?

Identifying Subjects and Verbs

Finding the Subject

Most sentences contain several nouns and pronouns used in a variety of ways. One of the most important ways is as the subject of a verb. In order to identify which of the nouns or pronouns in a sentence is the subject, you need to identify the complete verb first. After identifying the verb, it is easy to find the subject by asking yourself "Who or what __(verb)__ ?"

EXAMPLE

S   HV MV

The **man** in the green hat **was following** a suspicious-looking stranger.

The complete verb in this sentence is *was following*, and when you ask yourself "Who or what was following?" the answer is "the man." Therefore, *man* is the subject.

Remember, most sentences contain several nouns and pronouns, but not all nouns and pronouns are subjects.

EXAMPLE

S   MV

The **people** from the **house** down the **street** often borrow our **tools**.

This sentence contains four nouns, but only *people* is the subject. The other nouns in this sentence are different types of **objects**. The noun *tools* is called a **direct object** because it receives the action of the verb *borrow*. The nouns *house* and *street* are called **objects of prepositions**. Direct objects will be discussed in Chapter Four. Objects of prepositions will be discussed later in this chapter. For now, just remember that not all nouns and pronouns are subjects.

PRACTICE

In the following sentences, place an "HV" above any helping verbs, an "MV" above the main verbs, and an "S" above the subjects.

S   HV MV
1. Al Capone was sent to Alcatraz Federal Penitentiary in 1932.

2. The famous prison sits in the middle of San Francisco Bay.

3. Escaping prisoners would drown in the cold waters of the bay.

4. Over the years, several men were shot while trying to escape.

5. After only twenty-nine years as a prison, Alcatraz was closed in 1963.

Subject Modifiers

Words that modify or describe nouns or pronouns should not be included when you identify the subject.

EXAMPLE

S   MV
The red **wheelbarrow is** in the yard.

The subject is *wheelbarrow,* not *the red wheelbarrow.*

Remember that the possessive forms of nouns and pronouns are also used to describe or modify nouns, so do not include them in the subject either.

EXAMPLES

S   MV
My brother's **suitcase is** very worn.

S   MV
His **textbook was** expensive.

The subjects are simply *suitcase* and *textbook,* not *my brother's suitcase* or *his textbook.*

Verb Modifiers

Just as words that describe or modify the subject are not considered part of the subject, words that describe or modify the verb are not considered part of the verb. Watch for such modifiers because they will often occur between helping verbs and main verbs and may be easily mistaken for helping verbs. Notice that in the following sentence the words *not* and *unfairly* are modifiers and, therefore, not part of the complete verb.

EXAMPLE

S   HV   MV
Parents should not unfairly **criticize** their children.

Some common verb modifiers are *not, never, almost, just, completely, sometimes, always, often,* and *certainly.*

PRACTICE

Place "HV" over helping verbs, "MV" over main verbs, and "S" over the subjects of the following sentences.

        S   HV   MV
   1. The **fight** for Little Roundtop **has** not yet **begun.**

   2. Stewed prunes were always offered at the neighborhood coffee shop.

   3. Last night's championship football game did not attract a large crowd.

   4. Harry's grocery store was often praised for its low prices.

   5. Charging up the hill, Pickett's men bravely faced the rifles and cannons.

Multiple Subjects and Verbs

Sentences may contain more than one subject and more than one verb.

⊚⊚ **EXAMPLES**

    S   MV
Fred petted the dog.

    S   S   MV
Fred and Mary petted the dog.

    S   S   MV   MV
Fred and Mary petted the dog and scratched its ears.

    S   MV   S   MV
Fred petted the dog, and Mary scratched its ears.

    S   S   MV   S   MV
Fred and Mary petted the dog before they fed it.

⊚⊚ **PRACTICE**

Place "HV" over helping verbs, "MV" over main verbs, and "S" over subjects in the following sentences.

                          S   MV
1. For twenty years, Telemachus helped his mother.

2. The dish and the spoon ran away from the mad cow.

3. John Glenn and his assistants prepared for his historic flight and then ate a big dinner.

4. The Eighteenth Amendment was ratified in 1919, but it was repealed in 1933.

5. When Barack Obama was inaugurated on January 20, 2009, many people felt a new sense of hope.

Special Situations

SUBJECT UNDERSTOOD

When a sentence is a command (or a request worded as a polite command), the pronoun *you* is understood as the subject. *You* is the only understood subject.

⊚⊚ **EXAMPLES**

MV
Shut the door. (Subject is *you* understood.)

MV
Please **give** this book to your sister. (Subject is *you* understood.)

VERB BEFORE SUBJECT

In some sentences, such as in questions, the verb comes before the subject.

EXAMPLE

MV   S
Is your **mother** home?

The verb also comes before the subject in sentences beginning with *there* or *here*, as well as in some other constructions.

EXAMPLES

MV   S
There **is** a **bug** in my soup.

MV   S
Here **is** another **bowl** of soup.

MV   S
Over the hill **rode** the **cavalry**.

MV   S
On the front porch **was** a **basket** with a baby in it.

PRACTICE

Place "HV" over helping verbs, "MV" over main verbs, and "S" over subjects in the following sentences. Verbals and verb modifiers should not be included in the complete verb.

MV
1. Give the nose spray to Cyrano.

2. In the wheelchair was President Franklin D. Roosevelt.

3. Could Colonel Mustard have hidden the candlestick?

4. There is an elephant in the middle of their living room.

5. Forget their predictions of failure.

PRACTICE

Underline all subjects once and complete verbs twice in the following sentences. Remember that the complete verb contains the main verb and all helping verbs and that verbals and verb modifiers should not be included in the complete verb.

1. You certainly wear those baggy shorts with style.

2. Sonny could have treated the injured dog better.

3. Neil Armstrong might have hesitated before taking that first step.

4. The glue on postage stamps in Israel is certified to be kosher.

5. Will the person in the back row close his cell phone?

6. Godzilla was looking forward to his vacation in Jurassic Park.

7. Tell the marketing department to stop those disgusting duck ads.

8. My daughter loves her iPod Touch, but I would prefer to own an iPhone.

9. There must have been two thousand people at the concert.

10. The Little Mermaid looked at Aladdin and winked.

PRACTICE Write sentences of your own that follow the suggested patterns. Identify each subject (S), helping verb (HV), and main verb (MV).

1. A statement with one subject and two main verbs (S-MV-MV):

   A large black cat hopped off the fence
   and crept into our yard.

2. A statement with a subject and two main verbs (S-MV-MV):

   _____

   _____

3. A statement with one subject, one helping verb, and one main verb (S-HV-MV):

   _____

   _____

4. A question with one helping verb, one subject, and one main verb (HV-S-MV):

   _____

   _____

5. A command that begins with a main verb (MV):

_____

_____

6. A statement that starts with "Here" and is followed by a main verb and a subject ("Here" MV-S):

_____

_____

7. A statement with two subjects and one main verb (S-S-MV):

_____

_____

8. A statement with one subject, one helping verb, and one main verb followed by "until" and another subject and another main verb (S-HV-MV "until" S-MV):

_____

_____

9. A statement with a subject, a helping verb, a main verb followed by ", but" and another subject, helping verb, and main verb (S-HV-MV ", but" S-HV-MV):

_____

_____

10. A statement with a subject and a main verb followed by "although" and another subject and main verb (S-MV "although" S-MV):

_____

_____

Section One Review

1. A **noun** names a person, place, thing, or idea.

   a. **Proper nouns** name specific persons, places, things, or ideas. They begin with a capital letter. **Common nouns** name more general categories and are not capitalized.

   b. **A, an,** and **the** are noun markers. A noun always follows one of these words.

   c. If you are unsure whether or not a word is a noun, ask yourself if it could be introduced with **a, an,** or **the.**

   d. Words that end in -**ment**, -**ism**, -**ness**, -**ence**, -**ance**, and -**tion** are usually nouns.

2. A **pronoun** takes the place of a noun.

3. A **verb** either shows **action** or **links** the subject to another word.

4. Verbs appear in different **tenses** to show the time when the action or linking takes place.

5. The **complete verb** includes a **main verb** and any **helping verbs**.

6. **Verbals** are verb forms that do not function as verbs.

   a. The **infinitive** is a verbal that begins with the word *to*.

   b. The "-ing" form of the verb without a helping verb is called a **present participle** if it is used as an adjective.

   c. The "-ing" form of the verb without a helping verb is called a **gerund** if it is used as a noun.

7. To identify the **subject** of any sentence, first find the verb. Then ask, "Who or what <u>(verb)</u>?"

8. **Subject modifiers** describe or modify the subject. They should not be included when you identify the subject.

9. **Verb modifiers** describe or modify verbs. They are not considered part of the verb.

10. Sentences may contain **multiple subjects** and **multiple verbs**.

11. When a sentence is a command (or a request worded as a polite command), the pronoun *you* is understood as the subject. *You* is the only understood subject.

12. In some sentences the verb comes before the subject.

Exercise 1A

In the spaces provided, indicate whether the underlined word is a subject (write "S"), a helping verb (write "HV"), or a main verb (write "MV"). If it is none of these, leave the space blank.

_MV_ **1.** Homer <u>scorched</u> his armadillo-and-beet soup.

_____ **2.** The television series *Weeds* has startled many <u>people</u> because of its attitude toward drugs.

_____ **3.** <u>Ulysses</u> knew that it would be ten more years before he saw his wife, Penelope.

_____ **4.** After much soul searching, the big-game hunter <u>decided</u> to join PETA.

_____ **5.** The New York <u>firemen</u> gathered for a memorial at the church.

_____ **6.** <u>Should</u> we be surprised that most house dust is made up of dead skin cells?

_____ **7.** The film *Doubt* starred Philip Seymour Hoffman as a <u>priest</u> and Meryl Streep as a nun.

_____ **8.** Some of the olive trees in the Garden of Gethsemane <u>are</u> over two thousand years old.

_____ **9.** In 1872 Susan B. Anthony <u>was</u> arrested for voting in the presidential election.

_____ **10.** Once Huck got to know Jim, he <u>realized</u> that Jim was a person with feelings and values.

_____ **11.** Frustrated by the bad weather, <u>Icarus</u> canceled his flight.

_____ **12.** Hillary Clinton <u>has</u> a challenging task as Secretary of State.

_____ **13.** <u>Somebody</u> noticed that Santa had forgotten his suspenders.

_____ **14.** The Chernobyl nuclear power plant <u>suffered</u> a major meltdown in 1986.

_____ **15.** Anthropologists <u>have</u> always enjoyed digging among the Pre-Puebloan ruins in the Four Corners area.

Exercise 1B

A. Underline all subjects once and complete verbs twice in the following sentences. Remember that a sentence may have more than one subject and more than one verb.

1. Indiana Jones <u>was</u> not entirely a fictional character.

2. In fact, *Raiders of the Lost Ark* was written in part about a real person.

3. Vendyl Jones is the head of the Institute for Judaic-Christian studies.

4. The writer of the story had met Jones on an archeological dig.

5. Do you remember the gigantic rolling boulder in the movie?

6. The real-life Vendyl Jones and his assistants escaped from a booby-trap of four gigantic bouncing boulders.

7. One assistant was almost crushed by the boulders, but he survived by jumping off a cliff.

8. Before he finds the lost Ark, Jones wants to find the ashes of the Red Heifer.

9. According to one of the Dead Sea Scrolls, the Ark is buried near those ashes.

10. Jones is using the Dead Sea Scrolls and has already found twenty of the reference points leading to the Red Heifer.

B. Write sentences of your own that follow the suggested patterns. Identify each subject (S), helping verb (HV), and main verb (MV).

11. A statement with two subjects and one main verb (S-S-MV):

   The baseball player and his agent decided to

   meet for lunch.

12. A question that begins with "Where" followed by a helping verb, a subject, and a main verb ("Where" HV-S-MV):

   _____

   _____

13. A command that begins with a main verb (MV):

   _____

   _____

continued

14. A statement with two subjects, a helping verb, and a main verb (S and S-HV-MV):

_____

_____

15. A statement with a subject and main verb followed by ", for" and another subject and main verb (S-MV ", for" S-MV):

_____

_____

Exercise 1C

In the following paragraph, underline all subjects once and complete verbs twice.

1. An unfortunate <u>incident</u> in fifth grade <u><u>was</u></u> one of the most traumatic experiences of my life. **2.** It started when both Raymond and I wanted to pitch the ball in a game of kickball.

3. We started to argue about it, but recess ended in the middle of our argument. **4.** Ray was still angry, and he expressed his displeasure by striking me in the forehead. **5.** He had just hit me and turned to go back to our classroom when someone threw me the kickball. **6.** The large ball bounced twice before I caught it. **7.** In one motion, I gained control of the ball and lost control of myself. **8.** As if in slow motion, I drew back and then hurled the ball at Ray with the bitter words, "You can have the ball!" **9.** After leaving my hand and traveling through the air, the ball struck Ray in the back of the neck. **10.** He immediately collapsed, holding his neck with both hands. **11.** The teacher rushed to his side as Ray shouted, "I can't feel my legs!" **12.** I could not believe what I was seeing. **13.** As our teacher called for help, I found myself in line with my classmates watching as though a nightmare were unfolding before my eyes. **14.** I pressed my body against a pine tree and thought that I surely would go to jail. **15.** Then the sound of the sirens and the sight of the helicopter landing on the distant soccer field made my stomach twist, and a great feeling of sickness came over me.

Modifiers

Although subjects and verbs form the basis of any sentence, most sentences also contain many other words that serve a variety of purposes. One such group of words includes the modifiers, which limit, describe, intensify, or otherwise alter the meaning of other words. The word *modify* simply means "change." Notice how the modifiers change the meaning in each of the following sentences.

The dictator had **total** power.

The dictator had **great** power.

The dictator had **little** power.

The dictator had **no** power.

As you can see, the word *power* is significantly changed by the different modifiers in these sentences.

Although modifiers can change the meaning of words in many different ways, there are basically only two types of modifiers, **ADJECTIVES** and **ADVERBS.** You will be able to identify both types of modifiers more easily if you remember these three points:

1. Sentences often contain more than one modifier.

EXAMPLE The **new** moon rose **slowly** over the desert.

In this example, the word *new* modifies *moon*; it describes the specific phase of the moon. The word *slowly* modifies *rose*; it describes the speed with which the moon rose.

2. Two or more modifiers can be used to modify the same word.

EXAMPLE The moon rose **slowly** and **dramatically** over the desert.

In this example the words *slowly* and *dramatically* both modify *rose*. *Slowly* describes the speed, and *dramatically* describes the manner in which the moon rose.

3. All modifiers must modify *something*. You should be able to identify the specific word that is being modified as well as the modifier itself.

EXAMPLE **Slowly** the **new** moon rose over the desert.

In this example, notice that the word *slowly* still modifies *rose*, though the two words are not close to each other. The arrows point from the modifiers to the words being modified.

PRACTICE   Draw an arrow from the underlined modifier to the word it modifies.

1. Merchants <u>once</u> sold <u>pink</u> ducklings at Easter.

2. The fries were <u>hot</u> and <u>crispy</u>.

3. Craig <u>usually</u> has a <u>tuna</u> sandwich for lunch.

4. The <u>tedious</u> movie was <u>mercifully</u> <u>short</u>.

5. <u>Tiny</u> animals ran <u>continually</u> down the path.

Adjectives

An adjective modifies a noun or a pronoun. In English, most adjectives precede the noun they modify.

> ### adjective
> An adjective modifies a noun or a pronoun.

EXAMPLE

$\overset{\text{Adj}}{}$ $\overset{\text{Adj}}{}$
The **young** eagle perched on the **rocky** cliff.

In this example, the word *young* **modifies** *eagle*, and the word *rocky* **modifies** *cliff*.

Although most adjectives precede the noun or pronoun they modify, they may also follow the noun or pronoun and be connected to it by a linking verb.

EXAMPLE

Adj   Adj
Poisonous plants are **dangerous**.

In this example, the word *poisonous* describes the noun *plants*. Notice that it **precedes** the noun. However, the word *dangerous* also describes the noun *plants*. It is **linked** to the noun by the linking verb *are*. Both *poisonous* and *dangerous* are adjectives that modify the noun *plants*.

Many different types of words can be adjectives, as long as they **modify** a noun or pronoun. Most adjectives answer the questions **which? what kind?** or **how many?** Here are the most common types of adjectives.

1. Descriptive words

EXAMPLES

I own a **blue** suit.

That is an **ugly** wound.

2. Possessive nouns and pronouns

EXAMPLE   I parked **my** motorcycle next to **John's** car.

3. Limiting words and numbers

EXAMPLES   **Some** people see **every** movie that comes out.

Two accidents have happened on **this** street.

4. Nouns that modify other nouns

EXAMPLE   The **basketball** game was held in the **neighborhood** gym.

PRACTICE   **A.** In the following sentences, circle all adjectives and draw an arrow to the noun or pronoun each adjective modifies.

1. Strange cats have appeared on our front lawn recently.

2. Our team's orange uniforms are unique.

3. Our two turtledoves keep fighting with that stupid partridge in the pear tree.

4. My fancy new espresso maker has many buttons with unknown uses.

5. Emily Dickinson wrote many excellent poems, yet she asked her sister to burn them.

B. Add two adjectives of your own to each of the following sentences.

6. The garage was filled with *dusty* boxes and *broken* tools.

7. An aardvark wandered into our yard and looked for ants.

8. The hermit lived in a cabin in the woods.

9. The dog in the street avoided the car and the truck.

10. Officials tried to blame the mess on the birds that lived near the pond.

Adverbs

An adverb modifies a verb, adjective, or another adverb. Adverbs are sometimes more difficult to recognize than adjectives because they can be used to modify three different types of words—verbs, adjectives, and other adverbs. They can either precede or follow the words they modify and are sometimes placed farther away from the words they modify than are adjectives.

adverb
An adverb modifies a verb, adjective, or another adverb.

EXAMPLES

V   Adv
The president walked across the room **quickly**.
(adverb modifying a verb)

Adv   Adj
The president seemed **unusually** nervous.
(adverb modifying an adjective)

Adv   Adv
The president left **very** quickly after the press conference.
(adverb modifying an adverb)

Because adverbs are often formed by adding "ly" to adjectives such as *quick* or *usual*, many adverbs end in "ly" (*quickly* and *usually*). However, you cannot always use this ending as a way of identifying adverbs because some words that end in "ly" are *not* adverbs and because some adverbs do not end in "ly," as the following list of common adverbs illustrates:

already	never	often	soon	too
also	not	quite	still	very
always	now	seldom	then	well

Here are two ways to help you identify adverbs:

1. <u>Find the word that is being modified.</u> If it is a verb, adjective, or adverb, then the modifier is an adverb.

EXAMPLES

V
Thelma **seriously** injured her finger during the tennis match.

Adj
My brother and I have **completely** different attitudes toward Spam.

Adv
Tuan **almost** always arrives on time for work.

2. <u>Look for words that answer the questions **when? where? how?** or **to what extent?**</u>

◎◎ EXAMPLES   My grandparents **often** bring gifts when they visit. (**when?**)

The turnips were grown **locally**. (**where?**)

Rachel **carefully** removed the paint from the antique desk. (**how?**)

Homer is **widely** known as a trainer in a flea circus. (**to what extent?**)

NOTE: Adverbs are **not** considered part of the complete verb, even if they come between the helping verb and the main verb. (See page 28 for a list of common adverbs that come between the helping verb and the main verb.)

◎◎ EXAMPLE   HV Adv   MV
He has **not** failed to do his duty.

◎◎ PRACTICE   **A.** In the following sentences, circle all adverbs and draw an arrow to the word that each adverb modifies.

   1. The detective (quietly) stepped into the corridor and (slowly) raised his revolver.

   2. The happy couple always said that they were extremely lucky.

   3. The black widow sometimes gleefully destroys her mate.

   4. As Ichabod Crane rode swiftly down the lane, he was already beginning to worry about the headless horseman.

   5. Dido was excruciatingly sad as she stood on the rather sheer cliff.

   B. Add one adverb of your own to each of the following sentences.

   6. The full moon moved *slowly* across the sky.

   7. The frightened school children escaped from the Twin Towers.

   8. Elmo ran to the garbage can and looked for the puppet.

   9. The dune buggy missed the cactus but smashed into the tree.

   10. The ship escaped many perils, but it reached its destination.

Comparative and Superlative Forms

Adjectives and adverbs are often used to compare two or more people or things. **The comparative form is used to compare two people or things. The superlative form is used to compare three or more people or things.**

⟲⟲ EXAMPLES   (comparative)   He is **happier** than I am.

(superlative)   He is the **happiest** man in town.

Writing Comparatives

Use the following guidelines for most adjectives and adverbs.

- Add *-er* to adjectives and adverbs of one syllable.

green	greener
soon	sooner

- Use the word *more* before adjectives and adverbs of two or more syllables.

tedious	more tedious
swiftly	more swiftly

- If a two-syllable adjective ends in *-y*, change the *y* to *i* and add *-er*.

crispy	crispier
sunny	sunnier

Writing Superlatives

Use the following guidelines for most adjectives and adverbs.

- Add *-est* to adjectives and adverbs of one syllable.

green	greenest
soon	soonest

- Use the word *most* before adjectives and adverbs of two or more syllables.

tedious	most tedious
swiftly	most swiftly

- If a two-syllable adjective ends in *-y*, change the *y* to *i* and add *-est*.

crispy	crispiest
sunny	sunniest

👁 PRACTICE

Write the comparative and superlative form of each of the following words.

1. quiet   _____   _____

2. slow   _____   _____

3. pretty   _____   _____

4. deceitful   _____   _____

5. rapidly   _____   _____

6. easy   _____   _____

7. convenient   _____   _____

8. far   _____   _____

9. slowly   _____   _____

10. effective   _____   _____

Using Adjectives and Adverbs Correctly

1. <u>Do not use an adjective when you need an adverb.</u>

👁 EXAMPLES

(incorrect)   He does not speak very **clear.**

(correct)   He does not speak very **clearly.**

(incorrect)   He breathes **deep** whenever he is worried.

(correct)   He breathes **deeply** whenever he is worried.

2. <u>Distinguish between *good* and *well*, *bad* and *badly*, *real* and *really*.</u> The words *good*, *bad*, and *real* are always adjectives. The words *badly* and *really* are always adverbs. The word *well* is usually an adverb, although it is used as an adjective to describe someone's health.

👁 EXAMPLES

(incorrect)   He sells a lot of novels because he writes **good.**

(correct)   He sells a lot of novels because he writes **well.** (The adverb *well* modifies the verb *writes*.)

(incorrect) Joey says he feels fine, but he does not look **good** to me.

(correct) Joey says he feels fine, but he does not look **well** to me.
(The adjective *well* describes the health of *Joey*.)

(incorrect) April felt **badly** when she accidentally insulted her friend.

(correct) April felt **bad** when she accidentally insulted her friend.
(The adjective *bad* modifies the noun *April*.)

(incorrect) Slim says that it's **real** hot in Phoenix today.

(correct) Slim says that it's **really** hot in Phoenix today. (The adverb
really modifies the adjective *hot*.)

3. Avoid doubling the comparative or superlative form. Do not use *more* with
an *-er* form or *most* with an *-est* form.

EXAMPLES

(incorrect) Michael is **more taller** than Oscar.

(correct) Michael is **taller** than Oscar.

(incorrect) Sabrina is the **most smartest** student in the class.

(correct) Sabrina is the **smartest** person in the class.

4. Avoid using the superlative when you are comparing only two persons or
things.

EXAMPLES

(incorrect) His Toyota seems to be the **fastest** of the two cars.

(correct) His Toyota seems to be the **faster** of the two cars.

5. Use *than*, not *then*, in comparisons. This common spelling error is
discussed in more detail in Chapter.

EXAMPLES

(incorrect) Melissa is taller **then** her older sister.

(correct) Melissa is taller **than** her older sister.

PRACTICE Correct any errors in the use of adjectives and adverbs (or in the use of *then*
and *than*) in the following sentences.

1. My sister considers Will Smith a ~~more~~ better actor ~~then~~ *than* Sean Penn.

2. The worse mistake he made was deciding to buy the expensivest car on

the lot.

3. Although Abraham Lincoln was one of our greatest presidents, some say he was the most ugly one.

4. Karl Marx was real intelligent, although his theory of economics did not work very good.

5. Of the two, who is the most famous, Marie Antoinette or Anne Boleyn?

6. Russell Crowe, who is from Australia, is the most best actor on the screen today.

7. Marlon Brando felt badly when he forgot his lines during rehearsal.

8. The Trojans were more better prepared than the Greeks, but the Greeks were more trickier.

9. The eggplant frosting tasted worst to Bill then the Brussels sprouts pie.

10. Sofia always drives safe, even when she has to get somewhere as quick as possible.

Section Two Review

1. **Modifiers** limit, describe, intensify, or otherwise alter the meaning of other words.

    a. Sentences often contain more than one modifier.

    b. Two or more modifiers can be used to modify the same word.

    c. All modifiers must modify *something*.

2. An **adjective** modifies a noun or a pronoun.

3. Most adjectives answer the questions which? what kind? or how many?

4. Common types of adjectives are the following:

    a. Descriptive words

    b. Possessive nouns and pronouns

    c. Limiting words and numbers

    d. Nouns that modify other nouns

5. An **adverb** modifies a verb, adjective, or another adverb.

6. There are two ways to identify adverbs:

    a. Find the word that is being modified. If it is a verb, an adjective, or an adverb, then the modifier is an adverb.

    b. Look for words that answer the questions when? where? how? or to what extent?

7. The **comparative form** is used to compare two people or things.

8. The **superlative form** is used to compare three or more people or things.

9. Use adjectives and adverbs correctly.

    a. Do not use an adjective when you need an adverb.

    b. Distinguish between *good* and *well, bad* and *badly, real* and *really.*

    c. Avoid doubling the comparative or superlative form.

    d. Avoid using the superlative when you are comparing only two persons or things.

    e. Use *than,* not *then,* in comparisons.

Exercise 2A

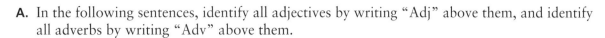

A. In the following sentences, identify all adjectives by writing "Adj" above them, and identify all adverbs by writing "Adv" above them.

1. The curtain *Adv* slowly rose, and the *Adj* grateful actress accepted the roses.

2. In his dreams Nathaniel Hawthorne often chased the first letter of the alphabet.

3. At the famous corral, Wyatt Earp carefully checked his revolver.

4. James Joyce knew without any doubt that he would always be misunderstood.

5. The Mad Hatter was angry because Alice stubbornly refused to share the mushrooms.

B. Add one adjective and one adverb to each of the following sentences. Do not use the same adjective or adverb more than once.

6. Geppetto worked *carefully* on the *wooden* shoes all night.

7. Many people volunteered to adopt the dogs that the football player had abused.

8. The poet recited poems, answered questions, and joined people in the audience for coffee.

9. Our parents asked us to meet the stranger in the kitchen and talk to him.

10. On the stage the actors whispered to each other and glanced into the auditorium.

C. Correct any errors in the use of adjectives and adverbs (or in the use of *then* and *than*) in the following sentences.

11. Christine was ~~real~~ *very* happy when she did ~~good~~ *well* on her test.

12. Mark Twain was more funnier then David Letterman.

13. The dog next door howls loud every night, louder than the dog across the street.

14. It was the worse dinner of my life because you treated the waiter so rude.

15. Of the two contestants, who threw her cow chip farthest?

Exercise 2B

In the following sentences, write "Adj" above all adjectives and "Adv" above all adverbs. Underline all subjects once and all verbs twice.

1. People *(Adv)* often ignore the information on a common *(Adj)* coin.

2. Our commonest coin, the lowly penny, is an especially good example.

3. The right profile of Abraham Lincoln appears on one side of the coin.

4. Above his head is the sometimes controversial sentence "IN GOD WE TRUST."

5. "LIBERTY" can easily be seen to the left of Lincoln.

6. Near Mr. Lincoln's bow tie is the coin's date.

7. A capital letter below the date precisely indicates which city minted the coin.

8. The famous Lincoln Memorial appears on the reverse side, and "E PLURIBUS UNUM" is minutely embossed above it.

9. This widely familiar phrase means "from many, one."

10. Interestingly, Benjamin Franklin strongly objected to the phrase.

11. He favored an alternate quotation: "Rebellion to Tyrants Is Obedience to God."

12. "UNITED STATES OF AMERICA" is clearly written in large letters across the top.

13. In even larger letters "ONE CENT" occurs under the memorial.

14. America was severely short of copper during World War II, so the penny of 1943 was made of zinc-coated steel.

15. Today's pennies are always made of copper-coated zinc.

Exercise 2C

In the following sentences, identify each of the underlined words as noun (N), pronoun (Pro), verb (V), adjective (Adj), or adverb (Adv).

1. In my youth, <u>parents</u> [N], teachers, and clergy would share advice with me like "Always tell the truth" or "Pride goes before the fall," and one incident when I was fourteen illustrates the wisdom of those <u>two</u> [Adj] principles. **2.** <u>I</u> <u>was</u> a first-year student at an all-male high school in Alabama. **3.** I was <u>very</u> "fresh" and inexperienced; in fact, I <u>had</u> never even danced with a girl. **4.** An all-girl Catholic academy was about a <u>mile</u> away, and after football games we <u>would</u> invite the girls to dances in the gym. **5.** <u>My</u> friends <u>always</u> gave vivid and alluring descriptions of the beauties at these dances. **6.** Finally, after the <u>third</u> football game, I very calmly <u>wandered</u> into the gym. **7.** After a while, I saw a <u>lovely</u> young woman, so I <u>nervously</u> took the long walk to the other side. **8.** When I <u>asked</u> her to dance, she politely accepted, and that is when my <u>problems</u> began. **9.** <u>It</u> was a <u>slow</u> dance, and I had noticed that couples just shuffled around slowly.

10. I <u>somewhat</u> <u>confidently</u> took one of her hands and put my other hand behind her back.

11. Unfortunately, I had placed my <u>hands</u> incorrectly, <u>which</u> she pointed out to me. **12.** Too proud to admit my mistake, I stammered, "No, I've always <u>done</u> it <u>this</u> way." **13.** Any <u>sympathetic</u> person can imagine my <u>embarrassment</u> as I danced that whole, endless dance "my own way."

14. Every time I looked over her wrong shoulder, I saw all of the other couples, <u>who</u> were <u>happily</u> dancing the right way, and my friends laughing and pointing at me. **15.** At the end of the dance, I <u>walked</u> my partner, who had politely danced the whole time with me the <u>wrong</u> way, back to her place on the gym wall. **16.** Then, with a very <u>red</u> face, I ran <u>quickly</u> back across the gym and out the exit as my friends continued to laugh.

Connectors

The final group of words consists of the connectors. These are signals that indicate the relationship of one part of a sentence to another. The two types of connectors are **conjunctions** and **prepositions.**

Conjunctions

A conjunction joins two parts of a sentence. The word *conjunction* is derived from two Latin words meaning "to join with." The definition is easy to remember if you know that the word *junction* in English refers to the place where two roads come together.

> conjunction
>
> A conjunction joins two parts of a sentence.

The two types of conjunctions are **coordinating** and **subordinating.** In Chapter Two we will discuss the subordinating conjunctions. You will find it much easier to distinguish between the two types if you memorize the coordinating conjunctions now.

The **coordinating conjunctions** are *and, but, or, nor, for, yet,* and *so.*

NOTE: An easy way to learn the coordinating conjunctions is to remember that their first letters can spell **BOYSFAN:** (<u>B</u>ut <u>O</u>r <u>Y</u>et <u>S</u>o <u>F</u>or <u>A</u>nd <u>N</u>or).

Coordinating conjunctions join elements of the sentence that are <u>equal</u> or <u>parallel</u>. For instance, they may join two subjects, two verbs, two adjectives, or two parallel groups of words.

◎◎ EXAMPLE

   S   Conj S   MV   Conj   MV
Ernie **and** Bert often disagree **but** never fight.

In this example, the first conjunction joins two subjects, and the second joins two verbs.

◎◎ EXAMPLE

   S   MV   Adj Conj   Adj   Conj   MV
Susan often felt awkward **or** uncomfortable **yet** never showed it.

In this example, the first conjunction joins two adjectives, and the second joins two verbs.

Coordinating conjunctions may even be used to join two entire sentences, each with its own subject and verb.

⟲⟲ EXAMPLE

            S   HV MV   S   MV

The rain had fallen steadily all week long. The river was close to overflowing.

            S   HV MV   Conj   S   MV

The rain had fallen steadily all week long, **so** the river was close to overflowing.

     Notice that the coordinating conjunctions have different meanings and that changing the conjunction can significantly change the meaning of a sentence. *A person should never drink **and** drive* communicates a very different idea from *A person should never drink **or** drive.*

■ The conjunction *and* indicates **addition.**

⟲⟲ EXAMPLE

Jules **and** Jim loved the same woman.

■ The conjunctions *but* and *yet* indicate **contrast.**

⟲⟲ EXAMPLES

She wanted to go **but** didn't have the money.

I liked Brian, **yet** I didn't really trust him.

■ The conjunctions *or* and *nor* indicate **alternatives.**

⟲⟲ EXAMPLES

You can borrow the record **or** the tape.

He felt that he could neither go **nor** stay.

■ The conjunction *for* indicates **cause.**

⟲⟲ EXAMPLE

The plants died, **for** they had not been watered.

■ The conjunction *so* indicates **result.**

⟲⟲ EXAMPLE

Her brother lost his job, **so** he had to find another.

⟲⟲ PRACTICE

A. In the following sentences, circle all coordinating conjunctions. Underline all subjects once and all complete verbs twice.

    1. The cook (or) the dishwasher will clear the tables.

    2. Kate Winslet won a Golden Globe Best Actress award in 2008 and an Oscar for Best Actress in 2009.

    3. Kate's fans were unhappy in 2008, for she did not receive an Oscar that year.

    4. Sam did not like Gollum, nor did he care much for Shelob.

    5. The sink in the kitchen would not drain, so we called the plumber.

B. In the following sentences, add coordinating conjunctions that show the relationship indicated in parentheses.

    6. We can go to the baseball game, ___*or*___ we can see a movie, but we can't do both. (alternatives)

7. Columbus was convinced he could reach the Orient, _____ very few

people agreed with him. (contrast)

8. President Franklin Delano Roosevelt had to face war _____ harsh

financial conditions. (addition)

9. President Obama faces similar circumstances, _____ he must deal with

the war in Iraq and serious economic issues. (cause)

10. Cesar Chavez was concerned about the conditions of Mexican-American

farm workers, _____ he organized the National Farm Workers

Association. (result)

Prepositions

> **preposition**
> A preposition relates a noun or pronoun to some other word in the sentence.

A preposition relates a noun or a pronoun to some other word in the sentence.
Prepositions usually indicate a relationship of **place** (*in, near*), **direction**
(*toward, from*), **time** (*after, until*), or **condition** (*of, without*).

EXAMPLE
          Prep
The boy ran **to** the store.

    Notice how the preposition *to* shows the relationship (direction) between
ran and *store*. If you change prepositions, you change the relationship.

EXAMPLES
          Prep
The boy ran **from** the store.

          Prep
The boy ran **into** the store.

          Prep
The boy ran **by** the store.

Here are some of the most common prepositions:

about	because of	during	near	to
above	before	except	of	toward
across	behind	for	on	under
after	below	from	onto	until
among	beneath	in	over	up
around	beside	in spite of	past	upon
as	between	into	through	with
at	by	like	till	without

NOTE: *For* can be used as a coordinating conjunction, but it is most commonly used as a preposition. *To* can also be used as part of an infinitive, in which case it is not a preposition.

🌀 PRACTICE

Write "Prep" above the prepositions in the following sentences.

1. Mr. Duong sat *in* the waiting room and thought *about* his wife.

2. Without hesitation, he lifted his new laptop from the box.

3. During the hotly contested election, the nominees remained friendly on the campaign trail.

4. When they were near La Mancha, Dulcinea and Sancho Panza called for Don Quixote.

5. The Trojans behind the walls looked at the huge wooden horse.

Prepositional Phrases

The word *preposition* is derived from two Latin words meaning "to put in front." The two parts of the word (pre + position) indicate how prepositions usually function. They are almost always used as the first words in **prepositional phrases.**

> **prepositional phrase**
> Preposition + Object (noun or pronoun) = Prepositional Phrase.

A prepositional phrase consists of a preposition plus a noun or a pronoun, called the object of the preposition. This object is almost always the last word of the prepositional phrase. Between the preposition and its object, the prepositional phrase may also contain adjectives, adverbs, or conjunctions. A preposition may have more than one object.

⊚⊚ **EXAMPLES**

Prep   Obj
after a short **lunch**

Prep   Obj   Obj
with his very good **friend** and his **brother**

Prep Obj   Obj
to you and **her**

Prep   Obj
through the long and dismal **night**

Although prepositions themselves are considered connectors, prepositional <u>phrases</u> actually act as modifiers. They may function as adjectives, modifying a noun or pronoun, or they may function as adverbs, modifying a verb.

⊚⊚ **EXAMPLES**

The cat (**from next door**) caught a gopher.

The burglar jumped (**from the window**).

In the first example, the prepositional phrase functions as an adjective, modifying the noun *cat,* and in the second example, the prepositional phrase functions as an adverb, modifying the verb *jumped*.

NOTE: If you can recognize prepositional phrases, you will be able to identify subjects and verbs more easily **because neither the subject nor the verb of a sentence can be part of a prepositional phrase.**

In the following sentence it is difficult at first glance to determine which of the many nouns is the subject.

⊚⊚ **EXAMPLES**

In a cave near the village, a member of the archaeological team found a stone ax from an ancient civilization.

If you first eliminate the prepositional phrases, however, the true subject becomes apparent.

⊚⊚ **EXAMPLES**

                                             S
(In a cave) (near the village), a member (of the archaeological team)

     MV
found a stone ax (from an ancient civilization).

⊚⊚ **PRACTICE**

Place parentheses around the prepositional phrases and write "Prep" above all prepositions and "Obj" above the objects of the prepositions.

                             Prep   *Obj Prep Obj*
1. Francis Scott Key wrote the words (to the national anthem) (of our country.)

2. However, the music itself came from a popular drinking song.

3. Francis Scott Key witnessed the British bombardment of Fort McHenry in 1814.

4. He was inspired by the sight of the American flag flying over the fort.

5. During the attack, he composed the first stanza of "The Star-Spangled Banner" on the back of an envelope.

6. The next day Key was told that his poem would go well with a tune that was popular in many taverns.

7. The original tune, called "Anacreon in Heaven," was probably written by John Stafford Smith in 1780.

8. Anacreon was a Greek poet who wrote about wine, song, love, and revelry.

9. "The Star-Spangled Banner" was sung at official ceremonies for many years.

10. In spite of its popularity, it was not declared the official national anthem until March 3, 1931.

Section Three Review

1. A **conjunction** joins two parts of a sentence.

2. The **coordinating conjunctions** are *and, but, or, nor, for, yet,* and *so.*

3. A **preposition** relates a noun or pronoun to some other word in the sentence.

4. A **prepositional phrase** consists of a **preposition** plus a noun or a pronoun, called the **object of the preposition.**

5. Neither the subject nor the verb of a sentence can be part of a prepositional phrase.

Exercise 3A

A. Combine each pair of sentences into one sentence. Use the coordinating conjunction indicated in the parenthesis.

1. (addition)
Alice Walker is a well-known African-American novelist.
Amy Tan is a respected Asian-American writer.

Alice Walker is a well-known African-American novelist, and Amy Tan

is a respected Asian-American writer.

2. (contrast)
Carla liked *Alchemy*, her new computer game.
She could not get beyond Level One.

3. (cause)
Donald Trump missed the *Trivial Pursuit* question.
He could not recall why Abraham Lincoln was called "Honest Abe."

4. (alternative)
The Steelers could fumble.
They could throw an interception.

5. (alternative)
Mrs. Peacock had not committed the murder.
She did not know what weapon was used.

Exercise 3A

continued

6. (result)
It was the seventh year of the drought.
We were ordered to use less water.

_____

_____

B. In each of the following sentences, change the underlined *and* to a coordinating conjunction that expresses the relationship between the ideas in the sentence. If the *and* does not need to be changed, do nothing to it.

7. Ellen loves Kentucky Fried Chicken, <u>and</u> she ordered a barrel of it for her wedding party.

Ellen loves Kentucky Fried Chicken, so she ordered a barrel of it for her

wedding party.

8. The Greeks tried to convince Achilles to fight, <u>and</u> he refused to leave his tent.

_____

_____

9. Achilles could stay in his tent, <u>and</u> he could get off his cot and be a hero.

_____

_____

10. Achilles was quite proud, <u>and</u> he decided to fight the Trojans.

_____

_____

11. Secretly, Achilles was worried, <u>and</u> his ankle was irritating him.

_____

_____

continued

12. To make him invulnerable, Achilles's mother had dipped him in the River Styx, <u>and</u> she missed his ankle.

_____

_____

13. Achilles killed many Trojans, <u>and</u> then he killed the Trojan hero Hector.

_____

_____

14. Paris, the brother of Hector, wanted revenge, <u>and</u> he shot Achilles in the heel.

_____

_____

15. With Achilles dead, the Greeks seemed defeated, <u>and</u> then they came upon the idea of a large wooden horse.

_____

_____

Exercise 3B

Place all prepositional phrases in parentheses and circle all conjunctions. For additional practice, underline all subjects once and all complete verbs twice.

1. Clarise (and) three teammates drove (to the orphanage)

2. Sully had been trying to hit a homerun for three seasons.

3. Michelangelo stared at the ceiling and started to paint.

4. In his nose, ears, and tongue were gold and silver rings.

5. Snow White and one of her favorite dwarfs have eloped to Magic Mountain.

6. The symbol of the caduceus is often associated with the medical profession.

7. The caduceus was a staff with two entwined serpents, and it was carried by Mercury.

8. A total of thirty thousand people saw that play, but not one of them liked it.

9. Michelle's great-grandfather served as an officer during World War I.

10. He saw battle at the Somme Offensive, one of the bloodiest battles of the war.

11. In World War II, her grandfather was stationed at a remote airfield in Burma.

12. His living conditions were rather crude, for there was no indoor plumbing.

13. He shared a thatched hut with another pilot, and he flew fuel and other supplies over the Himalayas.

14. The Himalayas are the world's highest mountain range and dangerous to fly over.

15. The pilots called the Himalayan range "The Hump," so the pilots were called "Hump pilots."

Exercise 3C

In the following sentences, identify each of the underlined words as noun (N), pronoun (Pro), verb (V), adjective (Adj), adverb (Adv), conjunction (Conj), or preposition (Prep).

1. According to many Native American legends, the *Adj* <u>animal</u> character Woodpecker was instrumental *Prep* <u>in</u> bringing fire to earth. **2.** Long ago, when there was no fire, the chief of the animal people <u>devised</u> a plan to enter the sky country and bring back some <u>fire</u>. **3.** <u>He</u> told the animal people to make bows <u>and</u> arrows to shoot at the sky. **4.** When they hit the sky, they <u>would</u> make a chain <u>of</u> arrows down to the earth. **5.** They would <u>then</u> climb the chain to the sky and steal <u>some</u> fire. **6.** Unfortunately, <u>none</u> of <u>them</u> succeeded in hitting the sky with their arrows.

7. Then <u>Woodpecker</u> <u>began</u> to work. **8.** He made a bow <u>from</u> the rib of Elk and arrows from the <u>serviceberry</u> bush. **9.** He <u>used</u> feathers from Golden Eagle and Bald Eagle and <u>arrowheads</u> from Flint Rock. **10.** When the animal people met <u>again</u>, they all laughed at Woodpecker, saying he could <u>not</u> hit the sky with his arrows. **11.** However, <u>their</u> own arrows fell short of the sky, <u>so</u> the chief asked Woodpecker to try. **12.** When Woodpecker shot his <u>first</u> arrow, <u>it</u> hit the sky. **13.** Then <u>each</u> following arrow stuck in the neck of the preceding arrow until there was a chain of arrows down <u>to</u> the earth. **14.** One by one, <u>they</u> all ran <u>swiftly</u> up the chain of arrows to the sky. **15.** After each one <u>had</u> stolen some fire, they raced to the arrow chain, chased by the sky people, <u>but</u> the chain had broken. **16.** To escape, each bird took an animal to earth on <u>its</u> <u>back</u>. **17.** When they reached the earth, their chief told them to divide the fire <u>among</u> all people, so Horsefly and Hummingbird carried the fire to all <u>parts</u> of the country.

Sentence Practice: Embedding Adjectives, Adverbs, and Prepositional Phrases

You have now learned to identify the basic parts of a sentence, but this skill in itself is not very helpful unless you can use it to compose clear and effective sentences. Obviously, you have some flexibility when you compose sentences, but that flexibility is far from unlimited. The following sentence has a subject, a verb, five modifiers, one conjunction, and two prepositional phrases, but it makes no sense at all.

> Architect the quickly president for the drew up building new and plans the them to showed company.

With the parts arranged in a more effective order, the sentence, of course, makes sense.

> The architect quickly drew up plans for the new building and showed them to the company president.

There is no single correct pattern for the English sentence. The patterns you choose will be determined by the facts and ideas you wish to convey. For any given set of facts and ideas, there will be a relatively limited number of effective sentence patterns and an enormous number of ineffective ones. Knowing the parts of the sentence and how they function will help you choose the most effective patterns to communicate your thoughts.

Assume, for example, that you have four facts to communicate:

1. *Moby Dick* was written by Herman Melville.

2. *Moby Dick* is a famous novel.

3. *Moby Dick* is about a whale.

4. The whale is white.

You could combine all these facts into a single sentence:

> *Moby Dick* was written by Herman Melville, and *Moby Dick* is a famous novel, and *Moby Dick* is about a whale, and the whale is white.

Although this sentence is grammatically correct, it is repetitious and sounds foolish.

If you choose the key fact from each sentence and combine the facts in the order in which they are presented, the result is not much better:

> *Moby Dick* was written by Herman Melville, a famous novel about a whale white.

A much more effective approach is to choose the sentence that expresses the fact or idea you think is most important and to use that as your **base sentence.** Of course, the sentence you choose as the base sentence may vary depending upon the fact or idea you think is most important, but, whichever sentence you choose, it should contain the essential fact or idea that the other sentences somehow modify or explain. Once you have found the base sentence, you can **embed** the other facts or ideas into it as **adjectives, adverbs,** and **prepositional phrases.**

For example, let's use "*Moby Dick* is a famous novel" as the base sentence since it states an essential fact about *Moby Dick*—that it is a famous novel. The idea in sentence number 1 can be embedded into the base sentence as a **prepositional phrase:**

by Herman Melville
Moby Dick ⌃ is a famous novel.

The idea in sentence 3 can now be embedded into the expanded base sentence as another **prepositional phrase:**

about a whale
Moby Dick, by Herman Melville, is a famous novel ⌃ .

Sentence 4 contains an **adjective** that modifies the noun *whale,* so it can be embedded into the sentence by placing it before *whale:*

Moby Dick, by Herman Melville, is a famous novel

white
about a ⌃ whale.

Thus, your final sentence will read:

Moby Dick, by Herman Melville, is a famous novel about a white whale.

The same facts could be embedded in a number of other ways. Two of them are:

Moby Dick, a famous novel by Herman Melville, is about a white whale.

Herman Melville's *Moby Dick* is a famous novel about a white whale.

This process of embedding is called **sentence combining.** The purpose of practicing sentence combining is to give you an opportunity to apply the grammatical concepts you have learned in the chapter. For instance, in the above example the base sentence was expanded into a more interesting sentence by means of prepositional phrases and an adjective. Practicing this process will also help you develop greater flexibility in your sentence structure and will show you how to enrich your sentences through the addition of significant details. After all, the use of specific details is one of the most important ways of making writing interesting and effective.

PRACTICE   a. The farmer was old.
b. The farmer waited in front of the bank.
c. The farmer was in overalls.
d. The overalls were faded.
e. The farmer was patient.

1. In the space below, write the base sentence, the one with the main idea.

_____

_____

2. Embed the **adjective** from sentence a into the base sentence by placing it before the noun that it modifies.

_____

_____

3. Embed the **prepositional phrase** from sentence c into the sentence by placing it after the word that it modifies.

_____

_____

4. Embed the **adjective** from sentence d into the sentence by placing it before the noun that it modifies.

_____

_____

5. Change the **adjective** in sentence e into an **adverb** (add "ly") and embed it into the sentence by placing it after the verb that it modifies.

_____

_____

Sentence Combining: Exercise A

In each of the following sets of sentences, use the first sentence as the base sentence. Embed into the base sentence the adjectives, adverbs, and prepositional phrases underlined in the sentences below it.

◎◎ EXAMPLE
    a. A man strode into the nightclub.
    b. The man was <u>young</u>.
    c. He was <u>in a bright orange bathrobe</u>.
    d. He strode <u>confidently</u>.
    e. The nightclub was <u>fashionable</u>.

A young man in a bright orange bathrobe strode

confidently into the fashionable nightclub.

1. a. The editor fired the reporter.
    b. The editor was <u>enraged</u>.
    c. The reporter was <u>incompetent</u>.

2. a. The cab driver honked his horn.
    b. The cab driver was <u>angry</u>.
    c. He honked <u>at the pedestrian</u>.
    d. The pedestrian was <u>confused</u>.

3. a. A duck was watching a movie.
    b. The duck was <u>strange</u>.
    c. It was <u>in a sailor suit</u>.
    d. The movie was <u>about two chipmunks</u>.
    e. The chipmunks were <u>fat</u>.

continued

4. a. The bullfighter waved his cape.
   b. The bullfighter was waving <u>at the bull</u>.
   c. The bullfighter was <u>young</u>.
   d. The bullfighter was <u>in the arena</u>.
   e. The bull was <u>angry</u>.

   _____

   _____

5. a. The guard handed the list.
   b. The guard was <u>nervous</u>.
   c. The guard handed the list <u>quietly</u>.
   d. The list was <u>of missing items</u>.
   e. The guard handed the list <u>to the detective</u>.
   f. The detective was <u>frowning</u>.

   _____

   _____

Sentence Combining: Exercise B

First, choose a base sentence and circle the letter next to it. Then, using adjectives, adverbs, and prepositional phrases, embed the other facts and ideas into the base sentence.

⟲⟲ EXAMPLE

a. The mountains were tall.
b. The mountains were snow-covered.
ⓒ. The mountains towered over the hikers.
d. There were three hikers.
e. The hikers were from France.
f. The hikers were lost.
g. The mountains towered menacingly.

The tall, snow-covered mountains towered menacingly

over the three lost hikers from France.

1.
a. The poet was frustrated.
b. The poet threw the letter.
c. The letter was a rejection.
d. He threw it into the trashcan.
e. The trashcan was next to his desk.

_____

_____

2.
a. The dancer was lonely.
b. The dancer walked.
c. She walked silently.
d. She walked across the stage.
e. The stage was empty.

_____

_____

3.
a. The girl was frightened.
b. The dog was tiny.
c. The scarecrow was in the field.
d. The girl and her dog stared.
e. They stared at the scarecrow.

_____

_____

Sentence Combining: Exercise B

continued

4. a. The flames were red.
   b. The flames were fierce.
   c. They were the flames of a forest fire.
   d. The flames destroyed the village.
   e. The village was ancient.

_____

_____

5. a. The children were excited.
   b. The children placed their hands on the fur.
   c. They placed their hands carefully.
   d. The tiger was sleeping.
   e. Its fur was rough.

_____

_____

6. a. A person has invented a talking tombstone.
   b. The person is imaginative.
   c. It was invented recently.
   d. The talking tombstone is solar powered.

_____

_____

7. a. A statement is tape-recorded.
   b. The case is Plexiglas.
   c. A statement is placed in a case.
   d. It is a case that sits in an area of the tombstone.
   e. The area is hollowed out.

_____

_____

continued

8. a. A speaker is small.
   b. A speaker and a panel are installed.
   c. It is a solar panel.
   d. A speaker and panel are on the tombstone.
   e. It is a three-inch panel.

   _____

   _____

9. a. The recording can be activated with the correct key.
   b. You can activate the recording and listen to a statement.
   c. The recording is in the case.
   d. The statement is from the grave's occupant.

   _____

   _____

10. a. The sunlight must be enough.
    b. With sunlight, the recording will run.
    c. The recording will run for as long as two hours.
    d. The recording is in the tombstone.
    e. The tombstone costs $10,000.

    _____

    _____

Paragraph Practice: Narrating an Event

If you have ever sat for hours before a blank sheet of paper or stared for what seemed like forever at a blank computer screen, you know how difficult and frustrating it can be to write a paper. In fact, some people have such trouble simply <u>starting</u> their papers that, for them, writing becomes a truly agonizing experience.

Fortunately, writing does not have to be so difficult. If you learn how to use the steps involved in the process of writing, you can avoid much of the frustration and enjoy more of the satisfaction that comes from writing a successful paper. In this section, you will practice using the three general activities that make up the writing process—**prewriting, writing,** and **rewriting**—to produce a paragraph based on the following assignment.

Assignment

Exercises 1C (page 24), 2C (page 37), and 3C (page 49) in this chapter are about three events: an unfortunate incident on a playground, an embarrassing experience at a high school dance, and the bringing of fire to earth by Woodpecker and the other animal people. Although few of us have had experiences as unusual as these, we all have experienced events that were important to us for one reason or another.

For this writing assignment, use the writing process explained below to describe an event that has happened to you. You do not need to have lost your temper or to have been kidnapped. Ask yourself, "What events—either from the distant past or from more recent times—have happened to me that I remember well?" Perhaps you remember your first date, your first traffic ticket, or even your first child. Or perhaps you remember the day you won a race in a track meet, performed alone on a stage, or attended your first college class. Often the <u>best</u> event to write about will not be the first one you think of.

Prewriting to Generate Ideas

Prewriting is the part of the writing process that will help you get past "writer's block" and into writing. It consists of <u>anything</u> you do to generate ideas and get started, but three of the most successful prewriting techniques are **freewriting, brainstorming,** and **clustering.**

Freewriting

Freewriting is based on one simple but essential idea: When you sit down to write, you write. You don't stare at your paper or look out the window, wondering what in the world you could write about. Instead, you <u>write down</u> your thoughts and questions even if you have no idea what topic you should focus on. In addition, as you freewrite, you do not stop to correct spelling, grammar, or punctuation errors. After all, the purpose of freewriting is to generate ideas, not to write the final draft of your paper.

Here is how some freewriting might look for the assignment described above.

> To describe an event? What could I write about that? I don't have a lot of "events" that I can think of—but I suppose I must have some. What do I remember? How about recently? Have I gone anywhere or has anything happened to me? I went skiing last month and took a bad fall—but so what? That wouldn't be very interesting. How about something I remember that I didn't like—like what? Death? Too depressing. Besides, I have never been closely involved in death. I was in a car accident once, but that was too long ago, and it doesn't really interest me. How about—what? I'm stuck. How about events I have good memories about—wait—I remember almost drowning when I was practicing for water polo in high school. <u>That</u> was a wild event. I could do it. Any other possibilities? How about good memories—like the time I made that lucky catch in Little League. That would be good. Or the fish I caught with my dad when I was a kid. Lots of good memories there. Any others? Yeah—I joined a softball league recently—that was a real experience, especially because it'd been so long since I'd played baseball. But I can't think of any particular thing I'd write about it.—Of all these, I think I like the drowning one best. I <u>really</u> remember that one and all the feelings that went with it.

You can tell that the above writer was not trying to produce a clean, well-written copy of his paper. Instead, he wrote down his thoughts as they occurred to him, and the result was a very informal rush of ideas that eventually led him to a topic, a near-drowning that occurred when he was in high school. Now that he has his topic, he can continue to freewrite to generate details about the event that he can use in his paper.

Prewriting Application: Freewriting

1. Freewrite for ten minutes about any memories you have of events that were important to you. Don't stop to correct any errors. Just write about as many events as you can remember. If you skip from one event to another, that's fine. If you get stuck, just write "I'm stuck" or something like that over and over—but keep writing for ten minutes.

2. Now reread your initial freewriting. Is there some event in there that interests you more than the others? Choose one event and freewrite only on it. Describe everything you can remember about the event, but don't stop to correct errors—just write.

Brainstorming

Brainstorming is another prewriting technique that you can use to generate ideas. Brainstorming is similar to freewriting in that you write down your thoughts without censoring or editing them, but it differs in that the thoughts usually appear as a list of ideas rather than as separate sentences. Here is an example of how the above freewriting might have looked as brainstorming.

An event I remember well—what could I use?

recently?

    fall while skiing—no

things I didn't like

    death? too depressing

    car accident I was in? too long ago

    almost drowned at practice—<u>good one</u>

good memories?

    lucky catch in Little League

    fishing with Dad

<u>Use the one about almost drowning.</u>

Prewriting Application: Brainstorming

1. Make a brainstorming list of events from your life that were important to you. Include events from as far back as your early childhood to as recently as yesterday.

2. Choose the event that interests you the most. Make a brainstorming list of everything you can remember about it.

Clustering

Clustering is a third prewriting technique that many people find helpful. It differs from brainstorming and freewriting in that it is written almost like an informal map. To "cluster" your ideas, start out with an idea or question and draw a circle around it. Then connect related ideas to the circle and continue in that way. Here is how you might use clustering to find a memorable event to write about.

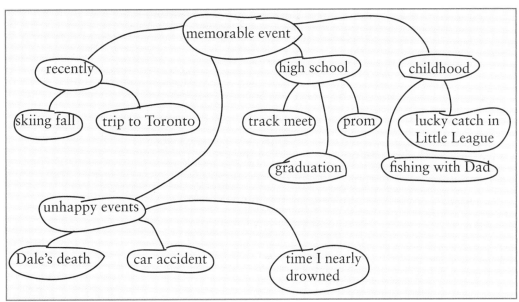

As you can see, clustering provides a mental picture of the ideas you generate. As such, it can help you organize your material <u>as</u> you think of it.

Prewriting Application: Clustering

1. Develop a "memorable events" cluster of your own. Include as many associations as you can to find the one event that interests you the most.

2. Now choose the event that interests you the most and use it as the center of a new cluster. Write in as many memories of the event as you can.

   Freewriting, brainstorming, and clustering are only three of many techniques to help you get started writing. When you use them, you should feel free to move from one to the other at any time. And, of course, your instructor may suggest other ways to help you get started. Whatever technique you use, the point is to <u>start writing</u>. Do your thinking on paper (or at a computer), not while you are staring out a window. Here's a good motto that you should try to follow whenever you have a writing assignment due: **Think in ink.**

Choosing and Narrowing the Topic

Choosing the Topic

Perhaps you have already found the event that most interests you. If you have, continue to prewrite to develop as many details as you can. If you are still undecided about a topic, use the following suggestions to think of possibilities.

1. What experiences of yours have been particularly exciting, happy, or pleasant?

2. What experiences are you most proud of?

3. What events bring you disappointing, unpleasant, or fearful memories?

4. What are your most embarrassing memories?

5. What strange or unusual things have happened to you?

6. What dangerous or frightening experiences have you had?

7. What are the "firsts" in your life? Consider your first day in high school, your first day on a team or as part of a group, your first performance, your first date, your first camping trip, your first traffic ticket.

8. What experiences have inspired you, changed the way you think about life, or made you into a different person?

9. What events do you remember from your early childhood?

10. What events do you remember from elementary school or high school, from vacations or trips?

Narrowing the Topic

Many topics that interest you might be too broad—that is, explaining them might require a much longer paper than has been assigned. And sometimes instructors provide only broad topic ideas when they assign a paper, expecting you to narrow the topic to something appropriate for the length of the assignment. In such cases you need to *narrow* your topic, discussing, perhaps, only part of the event rather than the entire thing. Learning to narrow a topic is an important step in the writing process because broad topics usually lead to general, unconvincing papers.

For example, let's say you have chosen as your topic a high school football game—the championship game in which you scored the winning touchdown. It would be natural to want to cover the entire game because all of it was important to you, but the topic is much too large to be covered in one paragraph. So you must narrow the topic. A successful single paragraph might describe only one play, the one in which you scored the winning touchdown. It would describe everything about the play, from the noise in the stands to the looks on your teammates' faces in the huddle to the smell of the grass to the sound of the quarterback's voice—everything you can think of to provide detail and add excitement to the event.

Prewriting Application: Narrowing the Topic

Consider the following events as possible topics for a paragraph. Write "OK" next to any that you think would work. If any seem too broad, explain why and discuss how you might narrow them.

_____ **1.** Giving birth to my first child

_____ **2.** My vacation to Atlanta

_____ **3.** The car accident that changed my life

_____ **4.** The last time I saw my father

_____ **5.** A day at Disneyland

_____ **6.** Prom night dinner

_____ **7.** Skiing in Aspen

_____ **8.** My first date

_____ **9.** Getting lost in Tijuana

_____ **10.** Moving to Texas

Prewriting Application: Talking to Others

Once you have chosen and narrowed your topic, form groups of two, three, or four and tell your experiences to each other. Telling others about an event is a good way to decide what details to include and how much to say. And listening to someone else's story will help you learn what will keep an audience interested in your own story.

As you describe your event to others, make it as interesting as you can by describing what happened, how you felt, and what you thought. As you listen to the stories of others and as you describe your own experience, consider these questions:

1. What are the time and place of the event? How old were you? What time of day did it occur? What time of year? What was the weather like?

2. Can you visualize the scene? What is the name of the place where the event occurred? What physical features are in the area—trees? buildings? furniture? cars? other people?

3. How did you feel as the event progressed? What were you thinking each step of the way?

4. Did your thoughts and feelings change as the event occurred?

5. What parts of the event would be clearer if they were explained more?

Writing a Topic Sentence

The topic sentence is the one sentence in your paragraph that states both your **narrowed topic** and the **central point** you intend to make about the topic. To find your central point, reread your prewriting. Look for related details that seem to focus on *one particular reaction* to the event. That reaction is your central point.

College texts and your own college papers describe events in order to make a point. In a psychology text, for example, an airplane crash might be described in detail to help the reader understand how such an event can affect the relatives of those involved. And a history text might describe what happened at the Battle of Gettysburg to help the reader understand why it was a major turning point in the Civil War. Certainly in your own college papers, you will be expected to describe events to illustrate the points you are trying to make.

Although the topic sentence can appear in a variety of places, in college paragraphs you should usually write it as the first sentence so that your central point is clear from the very start. Here are some examples of topic sentences drawn from the exercises in this chapter. Note that each topic sentence contains a topic and a central point and that each one is the first sentence of its paragraph.

◎◎ EXAMPLES

         topic   central point

An unfortunate incident in fifth grade was <u>one of the most traumatic</u>

<u>experiences of my life</u>.

In my youth, parents, teachers, and clergy would share advice with me like

                      topic

"Always tell the truth" or "Pride goes before the fall," and **one incident**

         central point

when I was fourteen <u>illustrates the wisdom of these two principles.</u>

                topic

According to many North American Indian stories, the **animal character**

        central point

Woodpecker was <u>instrumental in bringing fire to earth</u>.

The **central point** of your topic sentence needs to be *limited* and *precise* so that it is not too broad, general, or vague. For example, in the topic sentence *My first date was an interesting experience,* the central idea that the date was *interesting* is much too vague. It could mean the date was the best experience of your life or that it was absolutely horrible. As a general rule, the more precise the topic sentence, the more effective your paragraph will be. Consider the following characteristics of a well-written topic sentence.

1. <u>A topic sentence must include a central point.</u>

◎◎ EXAMPLE   (weak)   My paragraph is about my youngest sister's wedding.

         In this sentence the topic (my youngest sister's wedding) is clear, but no central point about that wedding is expressed. An improved topic sentence might be:

◎◎ EXAMPLE   (improved) My youngest sister's wedding last year was one of the most hilarious events I have ever experienced.

In this sentence, a central point—that the wedding was hilarious—has been clearly expressed.

2. A topic sentence does not merely state a fact.

ⓢ EXAMPLE   (weak)   A few months ago I saw a car accident.

This sentence simply states a fact. There is no central point to be explained after the fact is stated. An improved topic sentence might be:

ⓢ EXAMPLE   (improved)   I will never forget how horrified I was a few months ago
                               when I was an unwilling witness to a major car accident.

This sentence now makes a statement about the accident that causes the reader to want more explanation.

3. A topic sentence must include a narrowed topic and central point.

ⓢ EXAMPLE   (weak)   My spring break this year was really something.

Both the topic (spring break) and the central point (it was "something") are far too general to describe in detail in one paragraph. Here is a more focused topic sentence:

ⓢ EXAMPLE   (improved)   On the last day of spring break this year, my vacation in
                               Palm Springs, California, turned from wonderful to
                               absolutely miserable in just one hour.

This sentence now focuses on a specific event (the last day of spring break in Palm Springs) and on a precise central point (it changed from wonderful to miserable).

Prewriting Application: Working with Topic Sentences

In each sentence below, underline the topic once and the central point twice.

1. While driving to Arrowhead Stadium last night, I had a terrifying experience.

2. I don't think I have ever been as embarrassed as I was on the night that I first met my future husband.

3. When I stepped out on the stage at Rancho Buena Vista High School, I had no idea that what was about to happen would change my life.

4. My first scuba diving experience was as exhilarating as it was nerve-racking.

5. I feel a great sense of pride and satisfaction whenever I think of the day

I decided to take the biggest risk of my life.

Prewriting Application: Evaluating Topic Sentences

Write "No" before each sentence that would not make a good topic sentence and "Yes" before each sentence that would make a good one. Using ideas of your own, rewrite the unacceptable topic sentences into effective ones.

_____   **1.** Last August I visited Lake Ponsett, South Dakota.

_____

_____

_____   **2.** Giving birth to my first child made me wonder if I would ever want to have children again.

_____

_____

_____   **3.** My heart nearly broke the day that I decided it was time to take my dog Jasper on his last ride to the veterinarian's office.

_____

_____

_____   **4.** My first year in college was definitely interesting.

_____

_____

_____   **5.** One of my earliest memories of my father and me spending time together is also one of my most disappointing ones.

_____

_____

_____ **6.** It all happened when I decided to go skiing in Aspen, Colorado.

_____

_____

_____ **7.** My paragraph will be about the time I was in the Rose Parade.

_____

_____

_____ **8.** I was amazed at everything that happened to us while driving from Amarillo, Texas, to Atlanta, Georgia.

_____

_____

_____

_____ **9.** Spooky, strange, weird—these words don't even begin to describe what happened to me that night in the abandoned house on Elm Street.

_____

_____

_____ **10.** A simple ride on the roller coaster in Belmont Park turned out to be one of the most thrilling experiences of my life.

_____

_____

Organizing Details

When describing an event, you will usually present the details in **chronological order.** That is, you will organize them according to how they occurred in time. However, other assignments might require different organizations to present your supporting details effectively. (Other organizational patterns are discussed in future chapters.)

Prewriting Application: Organizing Supporting Details

The following details describe a time a person almost drowned at a water polo practice. Number the details so that they appear in their probable chronological order.

_____ joined water polo

_____ volunteered to try the challenge set

_____ two laps underwater

_____ felt okay during the first lap

_____ woke up in coach's arms

_____ choking under water

_____ second lap seemed okay at first

_____ determined to make it

_____ everyone around me when I woke up

_____ everything went black

_____ lungs gave out

_____ saw lane markers just before passed out

Writing the Paragraph

Writing a full draft of your paper is the next step in the writing process. The trick to writing your first draft without getting stuck is to remember that what you write now is not your final copy, so you can allow yourself to make mistakes and to write awkward sentences. Don't worry about how "correct" your writing is. Instead, just write your preliminary topic sentence and then describe your experience as thoroughly as you can.

Here is a sample first draft of the paper on drowning. As you read it, notice that the writer has not yet corrected any errors it may contain.

The Challenge Set (First Draft)

An unusual experience happened to me when I was sixteen. It all happened one day at practice for water polo. I was a sophomore on the Kearney High School water polo team. One day I volunteered for the dreaded "Challenge Set." I had just finished the first lap underwater. I still felt good. As I come to the wall, I make the decision to go for another lap, I keep swimming, but my lungs collapse. I took a few more strokes, and then it happened. I blacked out. All I remember was seeing black. I felt completely relaxed. Then I remember hearing voices. Suddenly, starting to cough violently. When I opened my eyes, the first person I saw was my coach. He told me what had happened, I was a little shaken. I couldn't believe that I almost died. This was really a frightening experience that I remember whenever I go for a swim.

The above first draft is far from perfect. It contains writing errors and could use more descriptive details. However, it has accomplished its purpose: *It has given the writer a draft to work with and to improve.*

Writing Application: Producing Your First Draft

Now write the first draft of your paragraph. Remember that your goal is *not* to write an error-free draft. Instead, it is to write a *first* draft that opens with a preliminary topic sentence, a draft that you can then continue to work on and improve.

Rewriting and Improving the Paragraph

Rewriting consists of two stages: **revising** and **proofreading.** In the **revising** stage of the writing process, you improve the "larger" areas of your paper—its content, organization, and sentence structure. Here are some suggestions.

■ Improve your preliminary topic sentence.

You can often improve your topic sentence *after* you have written your first draft because now you really have something to introduce. In fact, if you look at the *concluding* sentences of your first draft, you may find a clearer statement of the central point of your paragraph than the one you have in your preliminary topic sentence. If that is the case, rewrite your topic sentence to include that statement.

- <u>Add more details.</u>

  After you have written the first draft, add any further details that might improve your paper. Look especially for those that will emphasize the central point of your topic sentence.

- <u>Reorganize the details in the first draft.</u>

  There are many ways to organize a paper, but one of the most common ones is to save the most important details for last. Another way to organize details, especially if you are describing an event, is to list the details in chronological order. Whichever way you choose, now is the time to make any changes in the order of your material.

- <u>Combine related sentences and ideas.</u>

  Combine sentences that are obviously related. Where possible, use sentence-combining techniques to embed material from one sentence into another. (Sentence-combining techniques are discussed in Section 4 of each chapter.)

Improving Supporting Details

The supporting details in many first drafts tend to be vague, colorless, and mediocre. But with just a little work they can be transformed into strong, dramatic sentences. Consider adding details that emphasize specific sights and sounds. Wherever you can, use the precise names of people, places, and things. Look especially for new details and words that will emphasize the central point of your paragraph. Note how the colorless example below is transformed with precise, descriptive details.

EXAMPLE   (weak)   My father went in one direction while I went in another. I saw a fence covered with all sorts of decorations from local Indians. Inside the fence on the ground was the medicine wheel. I stared at it silently.

EXAMPLE   (improved)   My father veered off to the west as I continued straight ahead, toward what I perceived to be the main attraction. On this fist of land was a protective, circular chain link fence sixty feet in diameter, festooned with ribbons, scraps of paper, little totem bags made by the local Indian women and girls, eagle feathers and strings of beads: simple poetic offerings and prayers. Inside the fence was the medicine wheel, a fifty-foot spoked wheel etched into the dust of centuries. It was a moment of pause. I stopped and felt the wind and the still sacredness of the view.

Rewriting Application: Improving Supporting Details

Read the following brief paragraphs and identify places where the support could be more descriptive and precise. Then rewrite the paragraphs, adding stronger, more dramatic details.

A. My trip to the grocery store turned into a complete nightmare. When I walked down one of the aisles, I saw a person shoplifting, so I told the manager. She stopped the shoplifter, and they argued. Then the manager said I had to stay to talk to the police. I had some important things to do, so I said I had to leave. As I walked to my car, the manager became really mad at me too.

B. One of the highlights of my short career playing Little League baseball happened when my best friend was at bat. He and I played on opposing teams. I was in the outfield when he hit the ball toward me. It was going to go over my head, so I backed up. When I reached the fence, I stuck up my glove and caught the ball. I looked at the stands and saw people standing and cheering for me. It was a great experience.

Proofreading

Proofreading is the final step in the writing process. It consists of correcting spelling, grammar, and punctuation errors. **Do not skip this step.** A paper focused on an excellent topic and developed with striking details will almost always still receive a poor grade if it is full of distracting writing errors. Here are some suggestions to help you proofread successfully.

- If you use a computer, run the spelling-checker program. (But don't rely only on that program. Read each word carefully yourself.)

- Use a dictionary to check the spelling of any words you are unsure of.

- Watch for incomplete sentences and run-on sentences. (These errors will be discussed in Chapter Two.)

- Look closely at your verbs and pronouns. If you are describing an event from the past, use past-tense verbs. (Verb and pronoun errors will be discussed in Chapter Four.)

- Ask someone you trust to read your paper. If your school has tutors available, use them. They can help you find many writing errors that you might have overlooked. **However, please note:** If a friend reads your paper, do not allow him or her to rewrite sentences for you. Most instructors consider that kind of help to be plagiarism.

- When you are satisfied with your paper, print a final copy, and then *read that copy one more time.* You will be surprised how often more errors seem to appear out of nowhere. If you find more errors, fix them and print another copy.

Rewriting Application: Responding to Writing

Reread the first draft of "The Challenge Set" on page 69. Then respond to the following questions:

1. What is the writer's central feeling about his experience? Where is it stated? How would you reword the opening sentence to express that central feeling?

2. Where should the writer add more details? What kind of details would make his paragraph more colorful and descriptive?

3. Should any of the details be reorganized or presented in a different order?

4. What sentences would you combine because they contain related ideas?

5. What changes should the writer make in spelling, grammar, or punctuation?

Here is how the student who nearly drowned revised his first draft. Compare it to his first draft.

The Challenge Set

Revised opening sentence includes reaction to the event.

When I was sixteen, I had a frightening experience that I still remember whenever I go for a swim. This took place when I was a sophomore on the Kearney High School water polo team. One day at practice, I volunteered to try the dreaded "Challenge Set." **It consisted of three to four players attempting to swim fifty yards, two laps of the pool, on a single breath. I dove into the cool, clear water full of confidence, but I had no idea what was about to happen.** When I came to the wall at the end of the first lap, I was well ahead of my teammate, Bryan, who was in the lane to my right.

Added details

I felt great, as if I could hold my breath forever, so I decided to go for the second lap. I made the flip turn and pushed off the blue tiles. I still felt okay, but without my knowing it, my lungs had started to collapse.

Added details

I remember beginning to feel pressure in my chest when I saw the blue hash marks, the halfway markers. I had just a little way to go, but my head was whirling, and my chest felt like it was about to explode. Suddenly everything slowed down. I knew I should stop and take a breath, but I refused to do it. I took a few more strokes, and then it happened. I started to black out.

Combined sentences

All I remember is seeing black and feeling completely relaxed. The next thing I knew, it seemed like someone was shaking me. As I began to hear voices, I started to cough violently. Every time I tried to take a breath, a searing pain shot through me. I was terrified. When I opened my eyes, the

Added details

first person I saw was **Coach Leonard, a state beach lifeguard. I was lying in his arms, not knowing where I was or what had happened to me.** When he told me that I had passed out in the pool and that Bryan had pulled me

Added details

out, I was really shaken. I couldn't believe I had almost drowned. **I got out of the pool, got dressed, and sat in the stands waiting for practice to end.** I don't think I'll ever forget that day.

Rewriting Application: Revising and Proofreading Your Own Draft

Now revise and proofread your first draft.

1. Improve your topic sentence.

2. Add more details, especially those that emphasize the central point.

3. Reorganize the details.

4. Combine related sentences and ideas.

5. Once you have revised, <u>proofread</u> for spelling, grammar, and punctuation errors.

As you can tell, thorough revising and editing will involve several new drafts, not just one. Once you have a draft with which you are satisfied, prepare a clean final draft, following the format your instructor has requested.

Chapter 1 Practice Test

A. Identify the underlined words by writing "S" over subjects, "HV" over helping verbs, and "MV" over main verbs. If the underlined word is none of these, leave it blank.

1. The quartz <u>crystal</u> in my watch <u>will</u> vibrate 32,768 times per second.

2. The vampire <u>staring</u> into my window <u>looked</u> very thirsty.

3. Here <u>are</u> three <u>people</u>, so here must be a crowd.

4. <u>Siddhartha</u> taught his followers to <u>live</u> what he called "The Middle Way."

5. <u>Ask</u> Zeus if he <u>has</u> ever heard of Jupiter.

B. Underline all subjects once and all complete verbs twice in the following sentences.

6. Steve Martin and Robin Williams cause many people to laugh.

7. There is a rhinoceros beetle on the floor of my living room.

8. Some of the people in the audience did not enjoy Beyoncé's singing.

9. Don Quixote would just ignore all of the insults and smiles.

10. The tarantula crawled onto her arm, but Deborah did not seem to mind.

11. A Greek won the Nobel Prize for literature, and an American was awarded the Pulitzer Prize for editorial writing.

12. No falling raindrop can exceed the speed of eighteen miles per hour.

13. Does the Nobel Peace Prize medal show the head of a single man, or are there three men with their hands on each other's shoulders?

14. Gawain was afraid that he would not survive his meeting with the Green Knight.

15. Although some Brits will deny it, England has always been smaller than the state of Georgia.

continued

C. Write sentences of your own that follow the suggested patterns.

16. A statement with one subject and two main verbs joined by "and" (S-MV "and" MV).

_____

_____

17. A question with one helping verb, one subject, and one main verb (HV-S-MV):

_____

_____

18. A statement with two subjects joined by "or" and two main verbs joined by "and" (S "or" S-MV "and" MV).

_____

_____

19. A statement with one subject, two helping verbs, and a main verb (S-HV-HV-MV):

_____

_____

20. A statement with a subject and a main verb followed by "after" and another subject and main verb (S-MV "after" S-MV):

_____

_____

D. In the following sentences, identify all adjectives by writing "Adj" above them, and identify all adverbs by writing "Adv" above them.

21. During the walk with an angry Elmo, Ernie suddenly started to sing.

22. Merle did not know the name of the third planet from the sun.

23. Peter Parker was suddenly bitten by a radioactive spider.

24. Tommy, the main character in *Rescue Me*, usually broods about the past.

25. Sean Astin once played Rudy in the film of the same name.

Chapter 1 Practice Test

continued

E. In the following sentences, correct any errors in the use of adjectives and adverbs (or in the use of *then* and *than*) by crossing out any incorrect words and writing the correct words above them.

26. It was real hot at the beach yesterday, but it was even more hotter today.

27. I would rather visit Monterey then Los Angeles because it has the cleanest air of the two.

28. Homer ate his Spam sundae quick because it tasted so well.

29. The people in *Lost* felt badly because their worse expectation had come true.

30. Would you say Abraham Lincoln was more wiser then Franklin Delano Roosevelt?

F. In the following sentences, place all prepositional phrases in parentheses.

31. Could a better thing have happened to a better person at a better time?

32. Charon refused to ferry us across the river Styx because of our healthy glow.

33. Brad got into his Chevy, and Angelina followed with her Harley.

34. Igor opened the door and stared at the package of spiders that had just arrived from Transylvania.

35. Between the two, Barack Obama looks more like a president than Warren G. Harding did.

G. In the following sentences, add coordinating conjunctions that show the relationship indicated in the parentheses.

36. Bill is taking care of the dog, _____ Hillary is traveling around the world. (addition)

37. Willy could not face the truth, _____ he asked Biff to lie to him. (result)

38. Little Toot did the best he could, _____ the ship seemed too large. (contrast)

39. Cole could be playing with his Elmo doll, _____ he could be with one of his grandfathers. (alternative)

40. Ulysses was feeling lonesome, _____ he had not been home for almost twenty years. (cause)

Chapter 1 Practice Test

continued

H. Identify the underlined words in these sentences by writing one of the following abbreviations above each word: noun (N), pronoun (Pro), verb (V), adjective (Adj), adverb (Adv), conjunction (Conj), or preposition (Prep).

41. After the <u>angry</u> chimpanzee had collected the stones, it threw <u>them</u> at the people in the zoo.

42. The school <u>changed</u> its <u>name</u> to September Eleventh Memorial High School.

43. An ancient mariner watched the <u>albatross</u> drift lazily <u>toward</u> his ship.

44. Katie <u>quietly</u> arose, went into the nursery, and picked up the <u>hungry</u> baby.

45. Putting on his special hog-hide glove, Homer <u>heaved</u> the cow chip <u>over</u> the goal line.

46. Pam had <u>not</u> finished her novel, <u>but</u> Deborah told her the ending anyway.

47. Last night, <u>someone</u> broke into Jessica's house and stole her entire <u>collection</u> of Elvis Presley records.

48. Mick seemed <u>happy</u>, <u>so</u> Keith kept playing left-handed.

49. The poet smiled to <u>himself</u> as he stood on the stage in New York and recited his poem "Where There Was No Pattern" <u>before</u> a crowded auditorium.

50. Stanley stumbled <u>drunkenly</u> into the street, where he <u>screamed</u>, "Stella!"

Understanding Sentence Patterns

In Chapter One you learned the terms that describe how words function in a sentence. These terms will help you understand how the various word groups operate in a sentence. Understanding these word groups will help you see not only how sentences are put together but also how to revise your writing effectively and systematically. Without some knowledge of these word groups, you really can't even define what a sentence is.

Consider, for example, two common definitions of a sentence:

1. A sentence is a group of words that expresses a complete thought.

2. A sentence is a group of words that contains a subject and a verb.

These definitions may seem adequate, but, if you consider them carefully, you will see that neither of them is really accurate. For example, some sentences do not seem to express "a complete thought." Consider the sentence "*It fell.*" Do these two words really convey a complete thought? In one sense they do: A specific action is communicated, and a subject, though an indefinite one, is identified. However, the sentence raises more questions than it answers. What fell? Why did it fall? Where did it fall to? The sentence could refer to an apple, a star, the sky, or the Roman Empire. If someone walked up to you in the street and said, "*It fell,*" you certainly would not feel that a complete thought had been communicated to you, and yet the two words do form a sentence.

The second definition is no more satisfactory. The words "*Because his father was sleeping*" do <u>not</u> make up a sentence even though they contain both a subject (*father*) and a verb (*was sleeping*). Although it is true that all sentences must contain a subject and a verb, it does not necessarily follow that every group of words with a subject and a verb is a sentence.

The only definition of a sentence that is <u>always</u> correct is the following one: A sentence is a group of words that contains at least one main clause.

---

sentence

A sentence is a group of words that contains at least one main clause.

You will understand this definition easily if you know what a **main clause** is, but it will be incomprehensible if you do not. Thus, it is critical that you be able to identify this word group, for, if you cannot identify a main clause, you cannot be certain that you are using complete sentences in your writing.

Clauses

Main Clauses and Subordinate Clauses

A clause is a group of words that contains at least one subject and at least one verb.

> **clause**
> A clause is a group of words that contains at least one subject and at least one verb.

The two types of clauses are **main clause** and **subordinate clause.**

1. A **main clause** is a group of words that contains at least one subject and one verb and that <u>expresses a complete idea</u>.

2. A **subordinate clause** is a group of words that contains at least one subject and one verb but that <u>does not express a complete idea</u>. All subordinate clauses begin with **subordinators.**

⊚⊚ EXAMPLE

                sub. clause   main clause
[Although he seldom plays,] [Raymond is an excellent golfer.]

This example contains two clauses, each with a subject and a verb. As you can see, the clause *Raymond is an excellent golfer* could stand by itself as a sentence. But the clause *Although he seldom plays* cannot stand by itself (even though it has a subject and a verb) because it needs the main clause to complete its thought and because it begins with the subordinator *although*.

Subordinators

Subordinators indicate the relationship between the subordinate clause and the main clause. Learning to recognize the two types of subordinators—subordinating conjunctions and relative pronouns—will help you identify subordinate clauses.

Subordinating Conjunctions		Relative Pronouns	
after	so that	that	who(ever)
although	than	which	whom(ever)
as	though		whose
as if	unless		
as long as	until		
because	when		
before	whenever		
even though	where		
if	wherever		
since	while		

NOTE: Some of the words in the above list of subordinators are underlined (*after, as, before, since, until*). These words are used as prepositions when they do not introduce a subordinate clause.

◎◎ EXAMPLES   prepositional phrase: *after dinner*

subordinate clause: *after I eat dinner*

The following are examples of sentences containing subordinate clauses. (Note that each subordinate clause begins with a subordinator.)

◎◎ EXAMPLES

sub. clause   main clause
[**Before** his horse had crossed the finish line,] [the jockey suddenly stood up in his saddle.]

main clause   sub. clause
[Fried Spam is a dish] [**that** few people love.]

main clause   sub. clause
[Antonio won the spelling bee] [**because** he spelled *penicillin* correctly.]

◎◎ PRACTICE   Identify the following word groups as main clauses (MC) or subordinate clauses (SC) or neither (N).

1. When the moon shone on the river.   *SC*

2. The baseball season had finally started.   _____

3. Then the sun twirled like a windmill.   _____

4. Below the clouds in the sky.   _____

5. When Beyoncé started to sing.   _____

6. The statue of the woman had no head.   _____

7. Which Abbie found hard to believe.   _____

8. Finally, we could get some sleep.   _____

9. That Karl Marx had written.   _____

10. Once upon a time.   _____

PRACTICE   Identify the following word groups as subordinate clauses (SC) or prepositional phrases (PP).

1. Since the dampness was harmful.   *SC*

2. Since the last triceratops disappeared.   _____

3. Since the Battle of Bull Run.   _____

4. As a successful rodeo clown.   _____

5. As Homer was stirring the black-eyed peas.   _____

6. After the Flat Earth Society opened its doors.   _____

7. After yesterday's heavy storm.   _____

8. After the President's inaugural address.   _____

9. Until Vincent saw the sky.   _____

10. Until the Sean Penn's last movie.   _____

PRACTICE   Underline the subordinate clauses in the following sentences and circle the subordinators. Not all sentences contain subordinate clauses.

1. A misanthrope is a sperson (who) does not like people.

2. Lewis Carroll created the word *chortle*, which is a combination of two

    other words.

3. After the battle in the lake, Beowulf returned to the hall.

4. Puck gave the potion to Titania, who was sleeping.

5. If you really loved me, you would give your chocolate to me.

6. A reformed slave trader wrote "Amazing Grace," which is played at police officers' funerals.

7. He retook the oath of office because the Chief Justice had misplaced one of the words.

8. Sylvia, whose clothes were totally inappropriate, was embarrassed.

9. Fergal was all smiles after he read *Ulysses* for the third time.

10. Gettysburg was the place where the most important battle was fought.

Adverb and Adjective Subordinate Clauses

Subordinate clauses may function as adverbs, adjectives, or nouns in their sentences. Therefore, they are called **adverb clauses, adjective clauses,** or **noun clauses.** We will be discussing adverb and adjective clauses, but not noun clauses. Although we frequently use noun clauses in our writing, they seldom present problems in punctuation or clarity.

Adverb Clauses

Like single-word adverbs, adverb subordinate clauses can modify verbs. For example, in the sentence *Clare ate a big breakfast because she had a busy day ahead of her,* the adverb clause *because she had a busy day ahead of her* modifies the verb *ate*. It explains <u>why</u> Clare ate a big breakfast.

Another characteristic of adverb clauses is that they begin with a **subordinating conjunction,** not a relative pronoun. In addition, in most cases an adverb clause can be moved around in its sentence, and the sentence will still make sense.

EXAMPLES [**When** she ate the mushroom,] Alice grew taller.

Alice grew taller [**when** she ate the mushroom.]

Alice, [**when** she ate the mushroom,] grew taller.

NOTE: When the adverb clause begins the sentence, it is followed by a comma, as in the first example. When the adverb clause ends a sentence, no comma is needed. When the adverb clause interrupts the main clause, it is enclosed by commas.

PRACTICE   Underline the adverb clauses in the following sentences. Circle the subordinating conjunctions.

1. (If)you leave now, you will miss the eruption of Vesuvius.

2. Whenever Homer wants a snack, he fries a thick slab of Spam.

3. Narcissus stared into the stream because he was in love.

4. Although the old man's wings were dirty and broken, everyone believed he was an angel.

5. James Barrie was inspired to write *Peter Pan* by a family after he told stories of Peter to the children of a friend.

PRACTICE   Add adverb clauses of your own to the following main clauses in the spaces indicated. Use commas where they are needed.

1. He laid his daughter Regan down for a nap *because she had been acting tired all morning.*

2. _____ , Robert E. Lee was appointed president of a college.

3. Cyrus eats twice a week at a Thai restaurant _____

_____ .

4. Homer asked for a bag for his black-eyed peas _____

_____

5. _____ , the emperor walked naked into the village.

Adjective Clauses

Adjective subordinate clauses modify nouns or pronouns just as single-word adjectives do. Adjective clauses follow the nouns or pronouns they modify, and they usually begin with a **relative pronoun**—*who, whom, whose, which, that* (and sometimes *when* or *where*). As you can see in the examples below, relative pronouns sometimes serve as subjects of their clauses. We will discuss the rules for punctuating adjective clauses in Chapter Three.

EXAMPLES   The horse [that Mr. Lee liked best] was named Traveller. (The adjective clause modifies *horse*.)

On the top shelf was the trophy [**that** Irma had won for her model of the Battle of Shiloh]. (The adjective clause modifies *trophy*.)

Hampton, [**which** is Michelle's hooded rat,] resides at the foot of her bed. (The adjective clause modifies *Hampton*, and the relative pronoun *which* is the subject of the clause.)

NOTE: As you can see in the example above, the adjective clause often appears between the subject and the verb of the main clause. In addition, as you can see in the following example, sometimes the relative pronoun is left out.

EXAMPLE   The man [I met yesterday] works for the CIA. (Here the adjective clause modifies the noun *man*, but the relative pronoun *whom* is left out.)

A note about relative pronouns:

1. Use *who* or *whom* to refer to people only.

2. Use *which* to refer to nonhuman things only, such as animals or objects.

3. Use *that* to refer to either people or nonhuman things.

PRACTICE   Underline the adjective clauses in the following sentences and circle the relative pronouns.

1. Beethoven's Fifth is the new bar that opened on Verde Avenue.

2. A cello player whom the owner knew led the house band.

3. The next player hired was a pianist who was the wife of the cellist.

4. Rum Adagio, which is my favorite drink, is always served in a bright red glass.

5. A Persian cat that everyone calls Ludwig begs for treats on the bar.

PRACTICE   Add adjective clauses of your own to the following main clauses.

1. Ludwig has her own special dish by the back door.

Ludwig, who is picky, has her own special dish by the back door.

2. The eagle flew into the trees.

3. No one at the Monterey Bay Aquarium had ever met Poseidon.

4. The Belly Up is a popular music venue in San Diego County.

5. Many people make resolutions for the next year on New Year's Eve.

PRACTICE   In the following sentences, underline the subordinate clauses and identify them as adverb clauses (Adv) or adjective clauses (Adj).

1. <u>After the club closes</u>, the musicians play their own compositions.   *Adv*

2. Because the new President values good music, Yo-Yo Ma played at his inauguration.   _____

3. Enrique often dreamed about his grandparents, who lived in Chihuahua, Mexico.   _____

4. When the double rainbow appeared in the sky, Finnegan grabbed

my mother and kissed her.   _____

5. A dog that had long ears and a goofy laugh kept following me

around the amusement park.   _____

⊚⊚ PRACTICE　　Add subordinate clauses of your own to the following main clauses and indicate whether you have added an adverb clause (Adv) or an adjective clause (Adj).

1. Rupert decided to sell his stamp collection.

   Rupert, who was desperate for extra money, decided

   to sell his stamp collection. (Adj)

2. The building burst into flames and burned to the ground.

   _____

   _____

3. The monk sat in a lotus position and took three deep breaths.

   _____

   _____

4. Prometheus warmed his hands by the fire.

   _____

   _____

5. Bill Gates and Steve Jobs began to argue.

   _____

   _____

Section One Review

1. A **clause** is a group of words <u>that contains at least one subject and at least one verb</u>.

2. A **main clause** is a group of words that contains at least one subject and one verb and that <u>expresses a complete idea</u>.

3. A **subordinate clause** is a group of words that contains at least one subject and one verb but that <u>does not express a complete idea</u>.

4. **Subordinate clauses** begin with <u>subordinators</u>.

5. **Adverb subordinate clauses** usually modify verbs and begin with <u>subordinating conjunctions</u>.

6. **Adjective subordinate clauses** modify nouns or pronouns and begin with <u>relative pronouns</u>.

Exercise 1A

Underline all subordinate clauses and circle the subordinators. In the spaces provided, indicate whether the subordinate clause is an adverb clause (Adv) or an adjective clause (Adj). If a sentence contains no subordinate clause, do nothing to it.

1. The chairman suggested a solution (that) he thought would help the homeless people in his town.   _Adj_

2. As Mr. Hyde made his appearance, Dr. Jekyll disappeared.   _____

3. After the poetry reading, we stopped by some snowy woods.   _____

4. Homer's plate of spaghetti, which he had covered with Spam meatballs, fell to the floor.   _____

5. If you text me again, I'll break your cell phone.   _____

6. Laura forgave her guest for breaking her glass unicorn even though it was her most prized possession.   _____

7. The man who was floating on a coffin said his name was Ishmael.   _____

8. When Oedipus realized the truth, he was somewhat upset.   _____

9. Wherever she looked, Dorothy saw lions and tigers and bears.   _____

10. Before leaving for China, we played a game of Marco Polo in the swimming pool. _____

11. _House,_ which features a drug-addicted, cynical doctor, was one of the most popular television shows in 2008.   _____

12. Hortense found a Spam recipe that she had not tried.   _____

13. Because Bill had graduated _summa cum laude_, he looked down on us little people.   _____

14. You will see the Nike in the Louvre if you look closely.   _____

15. Everyone still loved Steve even though he had moved into administration.   _____

Exercise 1B

A. Join the pairs of sentences below by making one of them either an adverb or an adjective subordinate clause. You may need to delete or change some words.

1. The zookeeper comforted the frightened king cobra.
   The cobra had been attacked by a mongoose.

   The zookeeper comforted the frightened king cobra that had been attacked by a mongoose.

2. Mick Jagger draws huge crowds.
   He is over sixty-five years old.

3. The two of them looked for the feathers.
   The feathers had fallen into the maze.

4. Nike agreed to sponsor the golfer.
   The golfer wore the Nike "swoosh" in every tournament.

5. *Dia de los Muertos* had arrived.
   Josefina and her sisters visited her mother's grave.

B. Write subordinate clauses (adjective or adverb) in the blanks as indicated in parentheses at the beginning of the sentence. Make sure your clauses have subjects and verbs.

6. (Adv) *Because he was absolutely famished,*

   Homer added some pigs' feet to his casserole.

7. (Adj or Adv) Homer and Hortense visited the Grand Ole Opry _____ _____

8. (Adj) Adrian Monk, _____ , washes his hands at least ten times
   each day.

continued

   9. (Adv) _____ , Ahmed slept like a baby.

   10. (Adv or Adj) Fumiko missed her brothers and sisters _____

_____

C. To the main clauses below, add the types of subordinate clauses indicated in parentheses. Add your clause at any place in the sentence that you feel is appropriate. For instance, you may add an adjective clause to any noun in a sentence.

   11. (Adv) Driving your car along the Northwest Coast is a beautiful trip.

      If you take the time to enjoy the view, driving your car along

      the Northwest Coast is a beautiful trip.

   12. (Adj) Andrea took off her hat in the museum.

_____

_____

   13. (Adj) Brutus looked for the Ides of March on the calendar.

_____

_____

   14. (Adv or Adj) Jackson Pollock was once called "Jack the Dripper."

_____

_____

   15. (Adv) The sun rises in the east and sets in the west.

_____

_____

Exercise 1C

Underline all subordinate clauses and identify the type of clause (adjective or adverb) in the spaces provided.

1. One of my favorite places is San Francisco's Pier 39, <u>which I will always remember for its wonderful blend of unique sights, sounds, and smells.</u> _Adj_ **2.** As I walked down the pier one weekend last summer, I noticed a cook dressed all in white tossing pizza dough to lure hungry customers. _____ **3.** Near him I saw cooks who were roasting and baking all kinds of seafood. _____ **4.** Among the foods that caught my attention were lobster, shark, and clam chowder on sourdough bread. _____ **5.** I soon encountered some people being entertained by hundreds of sea lions making a tremendous racket as they played on the rocks and sunbathed by the pier. _____ **6.** When I turned away from the sea lions, my nose followed an aroma coming from a waffle ice cream stand. _____ **7.** Because I could not resist, I ordered vanilla ice cream with M & Ms mixed in. _____ **8.** The hot waffle cone warmed my hand while the cold ice cream refreshed my throat. _____ **9.** Next I came across a delightful shop, where I found all sorts of posters for children's books like _James and the Giant Peach_. _____ **10.** After I left the poster place, I spotted a chocolate shop and almost swooned in anticipation. _____ **11.** Although I was tempted, I declined the chocolate models of Alacatraz and the Golden Gate Bridge. _____ **12.** Across from the chocolate shop, I saw a restaurant that was built to look like Alcatraz Prison. _____ **13.** People could have their pictures taken in a prison cell while they were waiting to eat. _____ **14.** Close by I saw the tour boat that was taking tourists to Alcatraz Island. _____ **15.** As night fell across San Francisco Bay, I could admire the beauty of the Golden Gate Bridge from the tip of Pier 39. _____ **16.** Before I left, I felt the salty mist of the bay on my skin, a final remembrance of Pier 39. _____

Simple, Compound, Complex, and Compound-Complex Sentences

Sentences are categorized according to the number and types of clauses they contain. The names of the four types of sentences are **simple, compound, complex,** and **compound-complex.** You need to be familiar with these sentence patterns for a number of reasons:

1. **Variety.** Varying your sentence patterns creates interest and avoids monotony. Repeating a sentence pattern endlessly will bore even your most interested reader.

2. **Emphasis.** You can use these sentence patterns to emphasize the ideas that you think are more important than others.

3. **Grammar.** A knowledge of the basic sentence patterns of English will help you avoid the major sentence structure errors discussed in Section Three.

Being able to recognize and use these sentence patterns will help you control your writing and thus express your ideas more effectively.

The Simple Sentence

The introduction to this chapter points out that a sentence must contain at least one main clause. A sentence that contains only one main clause and no other clauses is called a **simple sentence.** However, a simple sentence is not necessarily an uncomplicated or short sentence because, in addition to its one main clause, it may contain a variety of phrases and modifiers.

The basic pattern for the simple sentence is subject–verb (SV). This pattern may vary in several ways:

EXAMPLES

                                   S   V
subject–verb (SV): The plane flew over the stadium.

                                     V   S
verb–subject (VS): Over the stadium flew the plane.

                                S   S   V
subject–subject–verb (SSV): The plane and the helicopter flew over the stadium.

                                S   V   V
subject–verb–verb (SVV): The plane flew over the stadium and turned north.

                                                                        S   S   V
subject–subject–verb–verb (SSVV): The plane and the helicopter flew

                                           V
over the stadium and turned north.

                                                        S   V
A simple sentence can be brief: It rained.

                                                                                                S
Or it can be rather long: Enraged by the taunting of the boys, the huge gorilla

     V   V
leaped from his enclosure and chased them up a hill and down a pathway to
the exit gates.

The important thing to remember about the simple sentence is that it has
only one main clause and no other clauses.

PRACTICE

Write your own simple sentences according to the instructions.

1. A simple sentence with the pattern subject–subject–verb:

   Two supermarkets and a department store collapsed in the

   recent earthquake.

2. A simple sentence that contains a prepositional phrase.

   _____

   _____

3. A simple sentence that begins with *there* and has the pattern verb–subject.

   _____

   _____

4. A simple sentence that expresses a command:

   _____

   _____

5. A simple sentence that has the pattern subject–subject–verb–verb:

_____

_____

_____

The Compound Sentence

Simply put, a **compound sentence** contains two or more main clauses but no subordinate clauses. The basic pattern of the clauses may be expressed as subject–verb/subject–verb (SV/SV). The main clauses are always joined in one of three ways:

1. Two main clauses may be joined by a comma and one of the seven coordinating conjunctions (*and, or, nor, but, for, so, yet*).

EXAMPLE

       S   V   S   V
Maria registered for all of her classes by mail, **but** Brad was not able to do so.

Remember, the two main clauses must be joined by **both a comma and a coordinating conjunction,** and the comma always comes before the coordinating conjunction.

2. Two main clauses may be joined by a semicolon (;).

EXAMPLE

       S   V   S   V
Maria registered for all of her classes by mail; Brad was not able to do so.

3. Two main clauses may be joined by a semicolon and a transitional word or phrase. Such transitional words or phrases are followed by a comma.

EXAMPLE

       S   V   S
Maria registered for all of her classes by mail; **however,** Brad

       V
was not able to do so.

Below is a list of the most commonly used transitional words and phrases. Do not confuse these words or phrases with coordinating conjunctions or subordinating conjunctions.

accordingly	hence	next	thus
also	however	nonetheless	undoubtedly
besides	instead	otherwise	for instance
consequently	meanwhile	similarly	for example
finally	moreover	still	on the other hand
further	namely	then	that is
furthermore	nevertheless	therefore	

PRACTICE   Write compound sentences of your own according to the instructions.

1. A compound sentence that uses a comma and *but* to join two main clauses:

I was very hungry after the game, but I decided not

to eat anything.

2. A compound sentence that joins two main clauses with a semicolon:

_____

_____

3. A compound sentence that joins two main clauses with a semicolon and an appropriate transitional word or phrase followed by a comma:

_____

_____

4. A compound sentence that joins two main clauses with a comma and *yet*.

_____

_____

5. A compound sentence that joins two main clauses with a semicolon followed by the transitional word *however* or *therefore*:

_____

_____

PRACTICE   In the following sentences, write S above each subject and V above each verb. Then, in the spaces provided, identify each sentence as either **simple** or **compound**.

1. Some of the earliest forms of writing appeared around

   3500 B.C.E.   *simple*

2. The Sumerians needed to keep track of food, grain, and other

   materials used in trade, so they made pictures of the items

   on clay tablets.   _____

3. These pictures were the first form of writing.   _____

4. The clay tablets were baked in a kiln; as a result, thousands

   of them have lasted throughout the centuries.   _____

5. The pictures were created with a wedge-shaped instrument;

   this type of writing is called *cuneiform*.   _____

6. Gradually, these pictures came to represent the syllables

   of the Sumerian language.   _____

7. Rather than clay, ancient Egyptians recorded their writing

   on leather or on a more fragile material.   _____

8. This fragile material was papyrus, and it later came

   to be called paper.   _____

9. About eighteen hundred years ago, a Chinese inventor made

   paper from bark and rags.   _____

10. Chinese books were soon written on paper, but the knowledge

    of paper-making did not reach Europe for a thousand years.   _____

The Complex Sentence

The **complex sentence** has the same subject–verb pattern (SV/SV) as the compound sentence. However, the complex sentence features only one main clause and always contains at least one subordinate clause and sometimes more than one. The subordinate clauses in a complex sentence may occur at any place in the sentence.

EXAMPLES

                                              S   V   S   V
Before a main clause: <u>After he retired from the Army,</u> Eisenhower ran for president.

                              S   V   S   V
After a main clause: Rugby is a sport <u>that I have played only once</u>.

                                       S   S   V
Interrupting a main clause: Emilio's grandfather<u>, who fought in World</u>

     V
<u>War II,</u> told him about his experiences during the war.

                                      S   V
Before and after a main clause: <u>When the pianist sat down at the piano,</u>

S   V   S   V
she played a melody <u>that she had written recently</u>.

PRACTICE

Write complex sentences of your own according to the instructions.

1. A complex sentence that includes an adjective clause using the relative pronoun *who:*

   Zelda searched for three days to find the

   person who had lost the German shepherd.

2. A complex sentence that ends with an adverb clause:

   _____

   _____

3. A complex sentence that contains an adjective clause using the relative pronoun *which*:

_____

_____

4. A complex sentence that begins with an adverb clause:

_____

_____

5. A complex sentence that contains an adjective clause that uses the word *where*:

_____

_____

The Compound-Complex Sentence

The **compound-complex sentence** is a combination of the compound and the complex sentence patterns. It is made up of two or more main clauses and one or more subordinate clauses. Therefore, it must contain a minimum of three sets of subjects and verbs (<u>at least</u> two main clauses and <u>at least</u> one subordinate clause).

EXAMPLES

main clause   sub. clause
[On the day-long bicycle trip, Ophelia ate the food] [that she had packed,]

main clause
[but Henry had forgotten to bring anything to eat.]

sub. clause   main clause
[Although he was exhausted,] [Ernesto cooked dinner for his mother,]

main clause
[and after dinner he cleaned the kitchen.]

main clause   sub. clause
[The travelers were excited] [when they arrived in Paris;]

main clause
[they wanted to go sightseeing immediately.]

PRACTICE   Write compound-complex sentences of your own according to the instructions.

1. A compound-complex sentence that contains two main clauses joined by *and* and one adjective clause beginning with *who:*

   Murphy, who works at the Mazda dealership, sold ten Miatas

   last month, and this month he plans to sell even more.

2. A compound-complex sentence that contains two main clauses and an adverb clause. Use *or* to join the two main clauses.

   _____

   _____

3. A compound-complex sentence that contains two main clauses and an adjective clause. Use a semicolon and a transitional word or phrase to join the two main clauses.

   _____

   _____

4. A compound-complex sentence that contains two main clauses and two adverb clauses:

   _____

   _____

5. A compound-complex sentence with a pattern of your own choice:

   _____

   _____

○○ PRACTICE   In the following sentences, write S above each subject and V above each verb. Then, in the spaces provided, identify the sentences as simple, compound, complex, or compound-complex.

               S   V

1. *Cinderella* is a European fairy tale with over five hundred versions.   *simple*

2. The oldest versions are from the ninth century; those early stories do not give Cinderella glass slippers.   _____

3. The glass slippers appeared when a French version of the story was translated incorrectly.   _____

4. In older versions, Cinderella's shoes were made of a rare metal or some other valuable covering.   _____

5. The French story used white squirrel fur for the slippers, but the French word that meant *fur* was similar to the word that meant *glass*.   _____

6. Charles Perrault, who translated the story in 1697, was the first person to describe the slippers as glass.   _____

7. Almost all later versions of the story depict Cinderella as wearing glass slippers.   _____

8. In most of the stories, Cinderella is helped by her fairy godmother; however, some versions use other characters.   _____

9. Although Cinderella's mother is dead, she magically appears in one story, and she takes the place of the fairy godmother.   _____

10. Sometimes cows or goats assist Cinderella, but in the Disney version mice come to her aid.   _____

Section Two Review

1. A **simple sentence** contains only one main clause and no other clauses.

2. A **compound sentence** contains two or more main clauses that are joined by a comma and a coordinating conjunction <u>or</u> a semicolon <u>or</u> a semicolon and a transitional word or phrase.

3. A **complex sentence** contains only one main clause and one or more subordinate clauses.

4. A **compound-complex sentence** contains two or more main clauses and one or more subordinate clauses.

Exercise 2A

In the spaces provided, identify the following sentences as simple, compound, complex, or compound-complex.

1. Alex was the name of a famous African gray parrot.   *simple*

2. Irene Pepperberg, who is a comparative psychologist, bought Alex from
   a pet shop in 1977.   _____

3. For twenty-two years, Dr. Pepperberg taught Alex to do tasks that only a few
   nonhuman species can do.   _____

4. Alex seemed to use words creatively.   _____

5. Alex's speech was not just imitation; instead, it suggested reasoning and choice.   _____

6. Dr. Pepperberg used a novel approach to teach Alex.   _____

7. Another trainer competed with Alex for a reward, and Alex would learn by
   watching the other trainer.   _____

8. When Alex was shown a blue paper triangle, he could identify the color,
   the shape, and the material.   _____

9. He had not simply memorized the colors that go with objects; he also identified
   the correct colors of new objects.   _____

10. Alex could identify fifty different objects, recognize quantities up to six,
    distinguish seven colors and five shapes, understand "bigger," "smaller,"
    "same," and "different," and was learning the concepts of "over"
    and "under."   _____

11. If Dr. Pepperberg asked Alex to identify the object that was orange and
    three-cornered, he would choose the right one.   _____

Exercise 2A

continued

12. Sometimes Alex would grow tired of the questions, so he would ask to

    go back to his cage.   _____

13. Although many researchers dispute Dr. Pepperberg's claims, others believe

    Alex demonstrated the intelligence of a five-year-old human.   _____

14. According to some scientists, Alex expressed conscious thoughts and feelings. _____

15. African gray parrots often live for fifty years, but Alex died unexpectedly

    during the night in 2009 when he was less than thirty years old.   _____

A. Combine each set of sentences to create the sentence type asked for. You may need to delete or change some words.

1. A simple sentence with the pattern verb–subject:
   a. The ship was in the harbor.
   b. The ship was a nineteenth-century three-masted schooner.

   In the harbor was a nineteenth-century three-masted schooner.

2. A compound sentence:
   a. Lance Armstrong had retired from racing.
   b. He decided to return for one more Tour de France.

3. A complex sentence:
   a. Hogart would not go to the dance.
   b. Sheba changed her dress.

4. A simple sentence:
   a. I plan to mow my lawn this morning.
   b. I also plan to take a nap this afternoon.

5. A complex sentence:
   a. Josh had not done his homework.
   b. He could not go to the movie with his friends.

Exercise 2B

continued

6. A simple sentence:
   a. The spider saw the little girl.
   b. The spider sat down beside her.

   _____

   _____

7. A compound sentence:
   a. The drought had lasted for three years.
   b. No one was allowed to water lawns or wash cars.

   _____

   _____

8. A compound-complex sentence:
   a. The Subreality Cafe is a dark and gloomy place.
   b. It appeals to people who wear black clothing and dark makeup.
   c. It is one of the most popular cafes in the city.

   _____

   _____

   _____

9. A compound-complex sentence:
   a. "Richard Cory" is a song composed by Paul Simon.
   b. It is included in Simon and Garfunkel's album *Sounds of Silence*.
   c. It is originally a poem composed by Edwin Arlington Robinson.

   _____

   _____

B. Following the instructions, construct sentences of your own.

   10. A compound-complex sentence that uses a semicolon:

   _____

   _____

continued

11. A complex sentence that includes an adjective clause:

_____

_____

12. A compound sentence that uses a semicolon and a transitional word:

_____

_____

13. A simple sentence:

_____

_____

14. A complex sentence that includes an adverb clause at the beginning of the sentence:

_____

_____

15. A compound-complex sentence that does not use a semicolon:

_____

_____

Identify the sentences as simple, compound, complex, or compound-complex.

1. After dark, the shore near my cabin is a mysterious place where the absence of light creates a new reality. ___*complex*___ **2.** As I was walking along the beach one night recently, I surprised a snow crab in the beam of my flashlight. _____ **3.** He lay in a pit just above the surface as if he were watching the sea and waiting. _____ **4.** When I turned off the flashlight, I could feel the darkness around me, and I felt alone with the snow crab. _____ **5.** I could hear nothing but the elemental sounds of wind blowing over sand and water and waves crashing on the beach. _____ **6.** When I am on that beach at night, time seems suspended, and I feel alone with the creatures of the shore. _____ **7.** Those creatures, like the sea anemones and the shore birds, have been there since the dawn of time. _____ **8.** As my eyes accustom themselves to the dark, the gulls and sanderlings become shadows. _____ **9.** When I am surrounded by those sights, sounds, and smells, I feel transported into another, older world before humankind. _____ **10.** The rhythm of the sea becomes the rhythm of the whole world, and the smell becomes a fundamental smell. _____ **11.** On that recent night, I sat near that snow crab and watched the sea with him. _____ **12.** Hidden beneath the water before me were patches of bright coral that were the home for blood-red starfish and green sea cucumbers. _____ **13.** All seemed peaceful then, but on the shore the battle for survival rages incessantly. _____ **14.** The largest shark and the smallest plankton must search constantly for the food that sustains them. _____ **15.** In the dim light I saw several hermit crabs scurrying across the sand, and I turned from the dark shore toward the lights of my home. _____

Fragments, Fused Sentences, and Comma Splices

Now that you are combining main and subordinate clauses to write different types of sentences, we need to talk about a few of the writing problems you might encounter. Fortunately, the most serious of these problems—the **fragment**, the **fused sentence**, and the **comma splice**—are also the easiest to identify and correct.

Fragments

The easiest way to identify a **sentence fragment** is to remember that <u>every sentence must contain a main clause</u>. If you do not have a main clause, you do <u>not</u> have a sentence. You can define a fragment, then, like this: A sentence fragment occurs when a group of words that lacks a main clause is punctuated as a sentence.

---

sentence fragment

A sentence fragment occurs when a group of words that lacks a main clause is punctuated as a sentence.

Using this definition, you can identify almost any sentence fragment. However, you will find it easier to locate fragments in your own writing if you know that fragments can be divided into three basic types.

Three Types of Sentence Fragments

1. <u>Some fragments contain no clause at all.</u> This type of fragment is simple to spot. It usually does not even sound like a sentence because it lacks a subject or verb or both.

🌀 **EXAMPLE**   The snow in the street.

2. <u>Some fragments contain a verbal but still no clause.</u> This fragment is a bit less obvious because a verbal can be mistaken for a verb. But remember, neither a participle nor an infinitive is a verb. (See Chapter One if you need to review this point.)

🌀 **EXAMPLES**   The snow **falling** on the street. (participle)

To **slip** on the snow in the street. (infinitive)

3. Some fragments contain a **subordinate clause** but no **main clause.** This type of fragment is perhaps the most common because it does contain a subject and a verb. But remember, <u>a group of words without a main clause is not a sentence</u>.

EXAMPLES

After the snow had fallen on the street.

Because I had slipped on the snow in the street.

Repairing Sentence Fragments

Once you have identified a fragment, you can correct it in one of two ways.

1. Add words to give it a main clause.

EXAMPLES

(fragment)	The snow in the street.
(sentence)	**I gazed** at the snow in the street.
(sentence)	The snow **was** in the street.
(fragment)	The snow falling in the street.
(sentence)	The snow falling in the street **covered my car.**
(sentence)	The snow **was** falling in the street.
(fragment)	After the snow had fallen in the street.
(sentence)	**I looked for a shovel** after the snow had fallen in the street.

2. Join the fragment to a main clause written before or after it.

EXAMPLES

(incorrect)	I love to see the ice on the lake. And the snow in the street.
(correct)	I love to see the ice on the lake and the snow in the street.
(incorrect)	My back was so sore that I could not stand straight. Because I had slipped on the snow in the street.
(correct)	My back was so sore that I could not stand straight because I had slipped on the snow in the street.

One final point might help you identify and correct sentence fragments. Remember that we all speak in fragments every day. (If a friend asks you how you are, you might respond with the fragment "Fine.") Because we speak in fragments, you may find that your writing seems acceptable even though it contains fragments. When you work on the exercises in this unit, do not rely on your "ear" alone. Look at the sentences. **If they do not contain main clauses, they are fragments, no matter how correct they may sound.**

☾☽ PRACTICE

Underline any fragment you find. Then correct it either by adding new words to give it a main clause or by joining it to a main clause next to it.

1. The small boy wandered slowly down the street. <u>Stopping sometimes to look into the store windows.</u>

   The small boy wandered slowly down the street, stopping

   sometimes to look into the store windows.

2. The vampire who had fallen in love with a mortal.

   _____

   _____

3. No one was smiling. Even though the state budget was finally approved.

   _____

   _____

4. Hansel and Gretel dropped bread crumbs. To mark the way out of the forest.

   _____

   _____

5. After they had given up almost all hope of rescue.

   _____

   _____

6. Davy tried to stop his canoe. Because the rapids and waterfall were

approaching.

_____

_____

7. Ricardo was winning the contest. Until he failed to define _Quetzalcoatl._

Thinking it was some kind of snake.

_____

_____

8. The trickster is an important figure. That appears in the myths of many

cultures.

_____

_____

9. To see the stars that were hidden by the city lights.

_____

_____

10. When you come to a fork in the road. Yogi said to take it.

_____

_____

Fused Sentences and Comma Splices

The **fused sentence** and **comma splice** are serious writing errors that you can correct with little effort. Either error can occur when you write a compound or compound-complex sentence. The fused sentence occurs when two or more main clauses are joined without a coordinating conjunction and without punctuation.

> ### fused sentence
> The fused sentence occurs when two or more main clauses are joined without a coordinating conjunction and without punctuation.

EXAMPLE   (fused)   Raoul drove by his uncle's house he waved at his cousins.

As you can see, the two main clauses in the above example (*Raoul drove by his uncle's house* and *he waved at his cousins*) have been joined without a coordinating conjunction and without punctuation of any kind.

The comma splice is a similar error: The comma splice occurs when two or more main clauses are joined with a comma but without a coordinating conjunction.

> ### comma splice
> The comma splice occurs when two or more main clauses are joined with a comma but without a coordinating conjunction.

EXAMPLE   (comma splice)   The hot sun beat down on the construction workers, they looked forward to the end of the day.

In this example, the two main clauses (*The hot sun beat down on the construction workers* and *they looked forward to the end of the day*) are joined by a comma, but a comma alone is not enough to join main clauses.

NOTE: One of the most frequent comma splices occurs when a writer joins two main clauses with a comma and a transitional word rather than with a semicolon and a transitional word.

EXAMPLE   (comma splice)   I wanted a dog for Christmas, however, my parents gave me a cat.

Repairing Fused Sentences and Comma Splices

Because both fused sentences and comma splices occur when two main clauses are joined, you can correct either error using one of five methods. Consider these two errors:

EXAMPLES   (fused)   Jack left for work early he arrived late.

(comma splice)   Jack left for work early, he arrived late.

Both of these errors can be corrected in one of five ways:

1. Use a comma and a coordinating conjunction.
   Jack left for work early, **but** he arrived late.

2. Use a semicolon.
   Jack left for work early; he arrived late.

3. Use a semicolon and a transitional word or phrase.
   Jack left for work early; **however,** he arrived late.

   NOTE: Do <u>not</u> use a semicolon before a transitional word that does <u>not</u> begin a main clause. For example, in the following sentence, *however* does not need a semicolon.

EXAMPLE   I have not seen my father, **however,** for ten years.

4. Change one of the clauses to a subordinate clause by beginning it with a subordinator.
   Although Jack left for work early, he arrived late.

5. Punctuate the clauses as two separate sentences.
   Jack left for work early. He arrived late.

NOTE: Sometimes the two main clauses in a fused sentence or comma splice are interrupted by a subordinate clause. When this sentence pattern occurs, the two main clauses must still be connected in one of the five ways.

EXAMPLES   (fused)   Alma bought a new Mercedes even though she could not afford one she fell behind in her monthly payments.

(comma splice)   Alma bought a new Mercedes even though she could not afford one, she fell behind in her monthly payments.

These errors can be corrected in any of the five ways mentioned above.

EXAMPLE   Alma bought a new Mercedes even though she could not afford one; consequently, she fell behind in her monthly payments.

⊚⊚ PRACTICE

Identify the following sentences as fused (F), comma splice (CS), or correct (C). Then correct the incorrect sentences. Use a different method of correction each time.

_____CS_____ **1.** Butler had wanted to join his brother in New York, his business was going too well for him to leave.

Butler had wanted to join his brother in New York,

but his business was going too well for him to leave.

_____ **2.** The huge blimp was attempting to dock in New Jersey suddenly it burst into flames.

_____

_____

_____ **3.** When the Ancient Mariner shot the albatross, he knew he was heading for trouble.

_____

_____

_____ **4.** Chuck Berry was playing "Hail, Hail, Rock and Roll" on the radio, meanwhile, Gomer and Homer finished the catfish and hushpuppies.

_____

_____

_____ **5.** Dia de los Santos Inocentes is similar to April Fool's Day it is celebrated on December 28.

_____

_____

_____ **6.** Hue had not heard of the Trung sisters, as a result, her grandmother was deeply embarrassed.

_____

_____

_____ **7.** Pluto kept feeding Cerberus chocolate turtles even though Cerberus knew they were not good for him he ate them anyway.

_____

_____

_____

_____ **8.** Jack was sure, however, that Bill had taken the chocolate cake.

_____

_____

_____ **9.** Andrea's memoir was a national success in fact it won two major literary awards.

_____

_____

_____ **10.** Mr. Nosferatu came over for dinner last night, he kept staring at my fiancee's neck.

_____

_____

Section Three Review

1. A **sentence fragment** occurs when a group of words that lacks a main clause is punctuated as a sentence.

2. There are three types of sentence fragments.

    a. Some contain no clause at all.

    b. Some contain a verbal but still no clause.

    c. Some contain a subordinate clause but no main clause.

3. You can correct a sentence fragment in one of two ways.

    a. Add words to give it a main clause.

    b. Join it to an already existing main clause.

4. The **fused sentence** occurs when two or more main clauses are joined without a coordinating conjunction and without punctuation.

5. The **comma splice** occurs when two or more main clauses are joined with a comma but without a coordinating conjunction.

6. You can correct fused sentences and comma splices in one of five ways.

    a. Use a comma and a coordinating conjunction.

    b. Use a semicolon.

    c. Use a semicolon and a transitional word or phrase.

    d. Change one of the clauses to a subordinate clause by adding a subordinator at the beginning of it.

    e. Punctuate the clauses as two separate sentences.

Exercise 3A

Identify each of the following as correct (C), fused (F), comma splice (CS), or sentence fragment (Frag). Then correct each error using any of the methods discussed in this unit.

Frag **1.** Because it was so cold and slimy and ugly that Carl was becoming nauseated just looking at it.

It was so cold and slimy and ugly that Carl was becoming

nauseated just looking at it.

_____ **2.** Aphrodite loved gyros, on the other hand, she disliked hummus.

_____ **3.** Please remind me to watch next year's Doo Dah Parade.

_____ **4.** Vincent was driving back to Arles suddenly he realized he had forgotten to buy canvas.

_____ **5.** The new President wondering what to do about the state of the economy.

_____ **6.** Meriwether Lewis began his journey home in 1806, William Clark accompanied him.

Exercise 3A

continued

_____ **7.** Homer brought a delicious salad of Spam and collard greens to the pot luck, yet no one would eat it.

_____

_____

_____ **8.** Chelsea enjoyed her job as a flight attendant however she was not paid very well.

_____

_____

_____ **9.** Julio knew that the name of the mythological river started with *L* he couldn't remember its exact name.

_____

_____

_____ **10.** The weather was so cold that Garrison's tongue stuck to the pump handle.

_____

_____

_____ **11.** The senator from New York could not believe that she had lost the nomination, her husband was even more surprised.

_____

_____

_____ **12.** The computer crashed, all his work was lost.

_____

_____

Exercise 3A

continued

_____ **13.** The student from Hawaii knew the history of his state, however, he did not know where the Sandwich Islands were.

_____ _____

_____

_____ **14.** Before Cyrano agreed to an operation on his nose.

_____

_____

_____ **15.** The elephant was chained to a stake, although it looked healthy, the protestors said it was underweight and poorly fed.

_____

_____

A. Correct the following sentence fragments by adding words to them to make them complete sentences.

   1. Shannon, who had been standing in the rain for two hours.

   Shannon, who had been standing in the rain for two hours,

   finally decided to give up and go home.

   2. If he had locked all the doors before he left.

   3. Rip Van Winkle, snoring into his beard.

   4. The asteroid that crashed into the Caribbean Sea.

   5. To the first person who walks through the door.

B. Join the following main clauses by using a comma and a coordinating conjunction, a semicolon, and a transitional word or phrase, or by making one of the clauses a subordinate clause. Use each of these four methods at least once.

   6. Regan asked Cordelia for her third of the kingdom. Eventually, Cordelia gave it to her and left for France.

   Regan asked Cordelia for her third of the kingdom;

   eventually, Cordelia gave it to her and left for France.

Exercise 3B

continued

7. Hester told their secret to everyone. Dimmesdale would not tell anyone.

_____

_____

8. Helena visited the Badlands in South Dakota last summer. She understood why they had received their name.

_____

_____

9. Leonardo looked at the new Picasso. The Picasso had just been purchased by the museum.

_____

_____

10. The music was unoriginal, and the lyrics were overly sentimental. The CD sold over one million copies.

_____

_____

C. Expand each of the following sentences by adding a **clause** to it. Identify the subject and verb of each clause you use and vary the placement of the clauses. (Don't place every clause at the end of its sentence.) When you add the clauses, use each of the following methods at least once: (a) use a comma and a coordinating conjunction; (b) use a semicolon; (c) use a semicolon and a transitional word or phrase; (d) make one clause a subordinate clause.

11. Sitting in their patrol car, the police officers tried to comfort the lost child.

Sitting in their patrol car, the police officers tried to comfort the lost child; however, the child would not stop crying.

12. Savion Glover is a contemporary tap dancer.

_____

_____

Exercise 3B

continued

13. The lake was full of toxins and dead fish.

_____

_____

14. Sydney tried to flirt with Ambrosia.

_____

_____

15. The tornado touched down near Crater Lake.

_____

_____

Exercise 3C

In the following paragraph, correct any fragments, fused sentences, or comma splices.

    1. *La Tzararacua* is an awe-inspiring cascade. **2.** ~~L~~ocated near my hometown in Mexico.

, located [handwritten correction above]

3. The last time I visited it, I walked for two hours through the wet, slippery forest. **4.** As I approached the cascade, I could hear the falling water, red and yellow birds were screeching and singing all around us. **5.** I enjoyed the fresh air and the gentle breeze on my skin. **6.** As well as the fresh, relaxing smell of the many tropical bushes and trees. **7.** I walked forward and sat down on a huge boulder right by the river it was so smooth and warm that I could not resist lying down on it. **8.** Later I walked to the main waterfall, it is over one-hundred meters high. **9.** And is surrounded by thousands of little cascades. **10.** I could hear water running underneath the rocks that I was walking on. **11.** The water of *La Tzararacua* seems to spring from the rocks, the waterfall is amazingly clear. **12.** Behind the huge waterfall, green moss covering huge boulders. **13.** The water originates in the middle of the forest it is fresh, pure, and satisfying. **14.** I did not worry about contamination. **15.** As I cupped it in my hands and took a deep drink.

Sentence Practice:
Combining Main and Subordinate Clauses

In this chapter you have learned the basic sentence patterns of English, and you have seen that you can combine the major word groups of a sentence—the clauses—in various ways. Of course, how you present your ideas in your sentences can affect the way a reader perceives your ideas. Take, for instance, the following sentences.

1. Sub-compact cars are economical.

2. Sub-compact cars are easy to handle.

3. Sub-compact cars are simple to park.

4. Full-size sedans are roomier.

5. Full-size sedans are safer.

6. Full-size sedans are quieter.

You can present these ideas in six simple sentences like those above, but doing so makes the writing choppy and simplistic. On the other hand, you can use the sentence patterns discussed in this chapter to combine these six ideas in several ways.

1. You can present these ideas as two simple sentences.

EXAMPLE
Sub-compact cars are economical, easy to handle, and simple to park. Full-size sedans are roomier, safer, and quieter.

2. Or you can group the ideas into one compound sentence by using a comma and a coordinating conjunction.

EXAMPLE
Sub-compact cars are economical, easy to handle, and simple to park, but full-size sedans are roomier, safer, and quieter.

Note that the coordinating conjunction *but* allows you to emphasize the contrast between the ideas in the two main clauses.

3. You can also group these ideas into a compound sentence by using a semicolon as a connector.

EXAMPLE
Sub-compact cars are economical, easy to handle, and simple to park; full-size sedans are roomier, safer, and quieter.

In this sentence the contrast in the ideas is implied rather than directly stated.

4. Of course, you can add a transitional word after the semicolon.

EXAMPLE

Sub-compact cars are economical, easy to handle, and simple to park; however, full-size sedans are roomier, safer, and quieter.

Note that *however* now signals the contrast between the ideas in the two clauses.

5. Finally, you can group the ideas into a main clause and a subordinate clause by adding a subordinator. Now you have a complex sentence.

EXAMPLE

Although sub-compact cars are economical, easy to handle, and simple to park, full-size sedans are roomier, safer, and quieter.

Like the other sentences, this sentence shows the reader the contrast between the ideas in the two clauses. However, it also shows the ideas the writer thinks are most important—the ones in the main clause.

Sentence Combining Exercises

Using the knowledge of sentence patterns that you have gained from this chapter, combine the following lists of sentences into longer sentences according to the directions. Be sure to punctuate carefully to avoid comma splices or fused sentences. Remember to look for a base sentence or a main idea to build upon. The most important idea should be in a main clause.

⊚⊚ EXAMPLE   First, combine these ideas into a compound sentence, using one of the three methods presented in Section Two of this chapter. Then form a complex sentence, using a subordinator to make one clause subordinate.

1. New York City often seems dirty.
2. New York City often seems overcrowded.
3. New York City often seems full of crime.
4. New York City has excitement.
5. New York City has charming ethnic communities.
6. New York City has a great variety of cultural attractions.

A. Compound sentence:

_____

_____

_____

_____

B. Complex sentence:

_____

_____

_____

_____

Sentence Combining Exercises

continued

1. Combine the following sentences into one complex sentence. Form sentences b and c into one adjective clause that begins with *who*.

   a. Samuel Wilson was the original "Uncle Sam."
   b. He lived during the Revolutionary War.
   c. He also lived during the War of 1812.

   _____

   _____

   _____

   _____

2. Combine these sentences into one complex sentence. Begin the sentence with a prepositional phrase. Form sentence c into an adjective clause that begins with *who*.

   a. It was the day of Paul Revere's historic ride.
   b. Samuel Wilson alerted the townspeople.
   c. He was the drummer boy for Menotomy, Massachusetts.
   d. He saw the British coming.

   _____

   _____

   _____

   _____

Sentence Combining Exercises

continued

3. Combine these sentences into one complex sentence. Form sentences b and c into one main clause.

    a. He was fourteen.
    b. Sam Wilson joined the army.
    c. He fought against the British.

    _____

    _____

    _____

    _____

4. Combine these sentences into one complex sentence by using sentence d as a subordinate clause starting with *where*.

    a. It was after Sam had served in the Revolutionary War.
    b. He opened a meat-packing company.
    c. It was in Troy, New York.
    d. People soon started to call him "Uncle Sam."
    e. He was like a friendly uncle.

    _____

    _____

    _____

    _____

Sentence Combining Exercises

continued

5. Combine these sentences into one compound-complex sentence. Start the sentence with a prepositional phrase. Form sentence c into an adjective clause that starts with *that*.

   a. It was during the War of 1812.
   b. Sam began to stamp "U.S." on crates of beef and pork.
   c. The crates were to be sold to the United States government.
   d. Those initials were not in common use for "United States."

_____

_____

_____

_____

6. Combine these sentences into one complex sentence.

   a. Government inspectors asked what the initials meant.
   b. The employees joked that they probably referred to their employer.
   c. The employees were at the meat plant.
   d. Their employer was called "Uncle Sam."

_____

_____

_____

_____

Sentence Combining Exercises

continued

7. Combine these sentences into one sentence. Use the most effective pattern you can find. At the end of your new sentence, indicate which type of sentence you have written.

   a. The story of "Uncle Sam" spread.
   b. Soldiers started calling all supplies the property of Uncle Sam.
   c. They began to call themselves Uncle Sam's men.

   _____

   _____

   _____

   _____

8. Combine these sentences into one sentence. At the end of your new sentence, indicate which type of sentence you have written.

   a. The first illustrations showed a man in a coat and hat.
   b. The illustrations were of Uncle Sam.
   c. The man was friendly.
   d. The man was clean-shaven.
   e. The coat and hat were black.

   _____

   _____

   _____

   _____

Sentence Combining Exercises

continued

9. Combine these sentences into one sentence. At the end of your new sentence, indicate which type of sentence you have written.

   a. Time passed.
   b. Uncle Sam came to be portrayed as a tall figure.
   c. He was white-whiskered.
   d. He wore a jacket.
   e. The jacket was decorated with stars.
   f. He wore pants.
   g. The pants had red and white stripes.
   h. He wore a top hat.
   i. The top hat was covered with stars and stripes.

   _____

   _____

   _____

   _____

   _____

10. Combine these sentences into one sentence. At the end of your new sentence, indicate which type of sentence you have written.

    a. The best-known portrait is probably the figure above the caption.
    b. The portrait is of Uncle Sam.
    c. The figure is severe.
    d. The figure is finger-pointing.
    e. The figure appeared on World War I posters.
    f. The caption reads, "I Want You for U.S. Army."

    _____

    _____

    _____

    _____

Paragraph Practice:
Describing a Place

Assignment

In Chapter Two you have read paragraphs that describe a variety of places. Exercise 1C (page 92) describes San Francisco's Pier 39, Exercise 2C (page 108) describes a shore scene at night, and Exercise 3C (page 124) describes the falls called *La Tzararacua*. Your assignment in this writing section is to describe a place that you remember for one particular reason. As you do so, you will practice limiting your paragraph to one idea that is expressed in a topic sentence and developing your paragraph with details that are both specific and concrete.

Prewriting to Generate Ideas

To find a topic, use freewriting, brainstorming, or clustering (or all three) to generate ideas about places that you remember well. Try to develop a list of as many places as you can. Sometimes the most interesting place to describe will be buried deep in your memory, so give prewriting a chance to uncover that memory before you decide on a topic.

Choosing and Narrowing the Topic

As you prewrite, avoid topics that are too broad to cover in one paragraph. For example, a city or an amusement park would be too large of a topic to cover in detail in a brief piece of writing. However, one particular part of a small town or one particular section of an amusement park might work very well.

Prewriting Application: Finding Your Topic

Consider the following questions as you prewrite:

1. What places have you visited in the past several years? Think about vacations you have taken or places you have traveled to.

2. Where have you been in the past two weeks? Make a list of everywhere you have gone.

3. What places from your childhood give you the most pleasant memories?

4. Where do you go to relax, to meditate, or to find peace of mind?

5. Have you ever been somewhere when you felt frightened or concerned for your safety?

6. What are the most beautiful places you have ever seen?

7. What are the most unpleasant ones? What are the strangest ones?

8. Have any places ever made you feel confused or lost?

9. Do you know any places that are particularly chaotic and noisy?

10. Where have you been today? Can you describe an ordinary, everyday place so that a reader sees it in a new way?

Once you have chosen the one place that is most interesting to you, keep prewriting about it. Try to remember as many details as you can about the place. Don't worry about writing well at this point—just brainstorm (make lists) or freewrite to get down as many of the details as you can remember.

Writing a Topic Sentence

After you have written for a while, read over what you have. Look for related details that focus on *one particular impression* of the place. These details and others that give that same impression are the ones you should emphasize in your paragraph. Once you have identified that particular impression, you are ready to write a preliminary **topic sentence.**

Remember, a topic sentence contains both a **topic** and a **central point.** In this writing assignment, your topic will be the place you are describing, and your central point will be the particular impression about the place that your details emphasize and illustrate.

Prewriting Application: Working with Topic Sentences

In each sentence below, underline the topic once and the central point twice.

1. Mammoth Cave, in southwestern Kentucky, is full of eerie, unearthly sights.

2. One of the most confusing places I have ever visited was the Los Angeles International Airport.

3. Snow Summit, in Big Bear, California, is a popular ski resort because it has such a variety of ski runs to choose from.

4. My grandmother's kitchen was one of the few places where I always felt safe and welcome.

5. The artificial decorations and dreary atmosphere were not at all what I had expected when I decided to visit the Excalibur casino in Las Vegas.

Prewriting Application: Evaluating Topic Sentences

Write "No" before each sentence that would not make a good topic sentence and "Yes" before each sentence that would make a good one. Using ideas of your own, rewrite the unacceptable topic sentences into topic sentences that might work.

_____ 1. Last year I spent three days hiking through Yellowstone National Park.

_____

_____

_____ 2. Balboa Island, near Newport Beach, California, is clearly a place designed for the rich and famous.

_____

_____

_____ 3. Whenever I look around at my bedroom, I become thoroughly depressed.

_____

_____

_____ 4. One of my favorite places to visit is the beach.

_____

_____

_____ 5. The waiting area in Dr. Larson's dentist's office is one of the most welcoming, relaxing places that I have ever seen.

_____

_____

_____ 6. Last December 30, we had the opportunity to visit Stone Mountain in Atlanta, Georgia.

_____

_____

_____ 7. My paragraph will describe the Hearst Castle in San Simeon, California.

_____

_____

_____ 8. The undeveloped canyon behind my house is one place where I can feel free and unrestricted.

_____

_____

_____ 9. The most unusual restroom that I have ever seen was the one at the Bahia de Los Angeles Research Station in Baja California, Mexico.

_____

_____

_____ 10. The deep South is one of the most memorable places that I have ever seen.

_____

_____

Prewriting Application: Talking to Others

Before you write your first draft, form groups of two, three, or four people and describe the place that you have decided to write about. Tell the members of your group what central point you are trying to emphasize, and then describe as many details as you can to make that point. As you tell others about the place you have chosen, describe all of the sights, sounds, and smells that contributed to your overall impression of the place. As you listen to the places described by others and as you describe your own place, consider these questions:

1. Where exactly is this place? Has its location been clearly identified? What time of year is it? What time of day? What is the weather like?

2. Can you visualize the place? What physical features are in the area—trees? buildings? furniture? cars? other people? What colors should be included?

3. How did you feel about this place? Is the central point or impression of the place clear?

4. Were there sounds, smells, or physical sensations that should be included in the description of the place?

5. What parts of the scene should be described in more detail?

Organizing Descriptive Details

Writers of descriptive papers use **spatial order** to organize supporting details. Unlike **chronological order,** which describes events as they occur in time, **spatial order** presents details according to their physical placement or characteristics. For example, you might describe the larger, more obvious details of a scene first and then move to the smaller, less obvious details. Or you might mention the details closer to you first and then move to those farther away. Other spatial organizations might involve describing details from left to right or top to bottom or describing the most dominant sense impression first, such as a strong smell, and then moving to other sense impressions.

Descriptions of places often combine spatial and chronological order, especially if you are moving as you describe the place. In such a situation, you might describe what you encounter first in time, then what you encounter second, and so on. If you take such an approach, remember that the purpose of this assignment is to describe the place itself, not to describe what you are doing there.

Prewriting Application: Organizing Supporting Details

Read Exercises 1C (page 92); 2C (page 108); and 3C (page 124). Examine the details in each paragraph and explain why they are organized as they are.

Writing the Paragraph

Once you have a preliminary topic sentence and a list of related details, it is time to write the first draft of your paragraph. Open your paragraph with your topic sentence and then write out the details that illustrate the central point of your topic sentence. Do <u>not</u> worry about writing a "perfect" first draft. You will have the chance to improve the draft when you revise it.

Rewriting and Improving the Paragraph

1. When you have completed the first draft, read it over to see if your preliminary topic sentence accurately states the central point of your paper. If you can improve the topic sentence, do so now.

2. As you read over your draft, see if you can add still more descriptive details that relate to your central point. Add those that come to mind.

3. Check the words and phrases you have used in your first draft. You will find that many of them can be more descriptive if you make them more **specific** and **concrete**.

Adding Specific and Concrete Details

A **specific** detail is limited in the number of things to which it can refer. For example, the word *poodle* is more specific than the word *dog*, and the word *elm* is more specific than *tree*. A **concrete** detail appeals to one of the five senses. It helps a reader to **see, hear, smell, taste,** or **feel** what you describe. For instance, rather than writing that your grandmother's kitchen smelled "wonderful," you might write that it was always "filled with the aromas of freshly baked bread and my grandfather's cigar smoke."

Unfortunately, most writers—even most professional writers—do not write specific and concrete details naturally. You need to *add* these details to your draft. You do so by reading back through what you have written and changing words from general to specific and from abstract to concrete. As you read, consider these areas.

- Specificity: Which words could be made more specific? Use precise names of people, places, things, emotions, and actions wherever you can.

- Sight: What sights can be included? Consider color, shapes, and sizes.

- Sound: What sounds should be added? Were there loud noises; subtle background sounds; peaceful, relaxing sounds; piercing, metallic, or unpleasant sounds?

- Smell: Were any smells present? Were you in a kitchen, near the ocean, passing by a newly oiled street? Were you at a produce stand or in a gymnasium? Many places have distinctive smells that you should include.

- Taste: Taste might be involved even if you did not eat or drink anything. A strong smell often evokes a taste sensation too. A dusty field as well as dry desert might also elicit a taste reaction.

- Touch: Consider the less obvious touch sensations as well as obvious ones involving pain or pleasure. Were you standing in sand or on hot pavement? Did you touch anything with your hands? Was there a breeze? Was it raining? Did your collar blow up against your face? All of these might involve touch sensations.

Not all senses need to be included, especially if they don't emphasize your central point, but most first drafts have too few specific and concrete details rather than too many.

Rewriting Application: Adding Specific and Concrete Details

In each of the following sentences, identify which words could be made more specific or concrete. Then rewrite the sentence to replace and improve the general, abstract words.

EXAMPLE   The house was run down.

The three-bedroom tract house on the corner of Elm and Vine had deteriorated into a ruin of broken windows, peeling paint, and splintered, termite-infested walls.

   1. The woman walked through the entrance.

_____

_____

_____

_____

2. The food tasted terrible.

_____

_____

_____

_____

3. The man looked angry.

_____

_____

_____

_____

4. Her bedroom walls were colorful.

_____

_____

_____

_____

5. The trees along the driveway smelled wonderful.

_____

_____

_____

Rewriting Application: Responding to Writing

Read the following description of Breaks Interstate Park. Then respond to the questions following it.

Breaks Interstate Park

There is no more beautiful place in the spring than the Breaks Interstate Park. Last year I spent part of the spring with my father and my grandmother in the Smoky Mountains of Virginia. Because the Smoky Mountains are a very remote area, there was not much to do during my vacation until some of my cousins wanted to go to a place called "The Breaks." We drove into the mountains for about an hour. When we got to the entrance, the first thing I noticed was the incredible number of flowers. There were flowers on the ground, flowers in the trees and on the rocks, and there were some on the log cabins and picnic tables. We pulled off the road to one of the campsites and got out of the car. The smell of spring was everywhere. We could smell honeysuckle, strawberry, and the heady scent of wildflowers. All we could hear were bees working the blossoms and birds bathing in the springs trickling out of the mountainside. My cousin Charon came up to me and told me to follow her. We went across the road and down a winding dirt path, past a sign that said "Twin Towers Overlook." I then beheld one of the most striking and magnificent views I have ever seen in my life. I was on an overlook, looking down at a gorge where the river flowing through it makes a horseshoe-shaped bend and the mountains on the other side look like twin towers. I ran back to the car to get my camera. While on my way back, I slipped on a moss-covered rock and skinned my knee. When I got back to the overlook, I sat down on some strawberry vines, ate wild strawberries, and took pictures. I finally ran out of film and deliciously sweet strawberries, not to mention daylight. We packed it up and went back home; however, I will never forget about the Breaks Interstate Park in the springtime.

---

1. Identify the topic sentence. State its topic and central idea. Is it an effective topic sentence? Why or why not?

2. Identify specific and concrete details. What words do you find particularly effective?

3. Which of the five senses does the writer employ in her description? Identify each of them in the paragraph.

4. What details would you make still more specific or concrete? Would you omit any details because they do not support the central point of the paragraph?

5. What sentences would you combine because they contain related ideas?

Adding Subordinate Clauses

In this chapter you have studied main and subordinate clauses and the four sentence types: simple, compound, complex, and compound-complex. As you rewrite papers, look for opportunities to change main clauses to subordinate clauses.

Rewriting Application: Adding Subordinate Clauses

A. Combine the following sentences by changing some of them to subordinate clauses.

1. a. We pulled off the road to one of the campsites and got out of the car.
   b. The smell of spring was everywhere.

2. a. My cousin Charon came up to me and told me to follow her.
   b. We went across the road and down a winding dirt path, past a sign that said "Twin Towers Overlook."
   c. I then beheld one of the most striking and magnificent views I have ever seen in my life.

3. a. Bright, warm sunlight filters through eucalyptus trees and presses against my shoulders.
   b. An old man greets me with a warm smile.
   c. The old man is raking leaves in the middle of the yard.

4. a. My grandfather sits on an old rust-covered metal stool.
   b. The stool used to be painted yellow.
   c. He tells me stories about my father's boyhood.

5. a. I have visited my grandparents' house many times during my childhood.
   b. I have not fully appreciated it until recently.

B. Revise each of the following sentences by changing one of the main clauses to a subordinate clause.

1. I looked to the right, and I could see an astonishingly high water slide.

2. I visited the cemetery in Escondido, California, to attend the funeral of my friend Jake McDonnell, for he had died in a head-on motorcyle accident.

3. The brevity of life was impressed on me, and I read the short accounts of unknown people's lives on the hundreds of tombstones.

4. Each weekend our family visited the Waimanalo Beach Park, and it is surrounded by the evergreen mountain range that towers over the valley below.

5. We took off our jackets and sweaters, but we still felt uncomfortably warm.

C. Now examine your own draft. Identify any main clauses that would work better as subordinate clauses. Consider changing some of your compound sentences to complex sentences. If you have a series of short sentences, combine them by changing some of the short main clauses to subordinate clauses.

Proofreading

When you are finished, proofread your paper. Check the spelling of words you are uncertain about. Examine each sentence closely to be sure it is not a **fragment, comma splice,** or **fused sentence.** If it is, repair the error using the techniques you have studied in this chapter. Once you have a draft you are satisfied with, prepare a clean final draft, following the format your instructor has asked for.

I. Review of Chapter One

A. In the following sentences, identify the underlined words by writing one of the following abbreviations above the words: noun (N), pronoun (Pro), verb (V), adjective (Adj), adverb (Adv), conjunction (Conj), or preposition (Prep).

1. The Rolling Stones concert <u>attracted</u> thousands to the <u>outdoor</u> arena.

2. The man <u>behind</u> the curtain did not <u>really</u> look like a wizard.

3. Hortense showed Gomer the black-eyed <u>peas</u> and hog jowls that she <u>was</u> cooking.

4. The <u>concept</u> of Pangea was dismissed at first, <u>but</u> now it is widely accepted.

5. Persephone ran <u>onto</u> the magic stairs because <u>she</u> was in a hurry.

6. <u>Everyone</u> groaned when Rodney offered to read another one <u>of</u> his poems.

7. Dante could <u>not</u> believe Virgil was down there, <u>nor</u> did he believe Virgil could never leave.

8. If people were <u>dolphins</u>, what would they <u>call</u> the planet Earth?

9. Irene had <u>always</u> thought *carpe diem* was an <u>orange</u> fish.

10. Herman Munster was disappointed to hear that his <u>only</u> son had called <u>him</u> a "bolthead."

B. For the following sentences, underline all subjects once and all complete verbs twice. Place parentheses around all prepositional phrases.

11. Will someone tell Morton about the interesting features of the wombat?

12. Behind the wall Stephen Crane listened to the battle and wrote in his journal.

13. Jack did not worry about earthquakes, but he stocked his emergency pantry just in case.

14. Chelsea's candy from Halloween has disappeared because her father ate it.

15. The Supreme Court justice who administered the oath of office misplaced the word *faithfully*.

continued

C. In the following sentences, correct any errors in the use of adjectives and adverbs (or in the use of *then* or *than*) by crossing out any incorrect words and writing the correct words above them.

16. We had a real nice picnic at the park, but it was more cloudier than I had expected it to be.

17. Arbuelita's chicken tamales tasted badly, but she is a much better cook then anyone else I know.

18. The worse day of my life also turned out to be the most funniest day.

19. The Bard of Avon laughed loud at the comedy because the actors performed their parts so good.

20. Of the two characters, the Mad Hatter seemed to be the craziest; however, the Queen of Hearts also seemed real crazy.

II. Chapter Two

A. Underline the subordinate clauses and identify the type of clause (adjective or adverb) in the space provided.

21. The sculpture that you see above the steps is the Nike of Samothrace. _____

22. Because he wanted a heart so badly, the Tin Woodman was willing to compromise. _____

23. After Nashville, we visited Tupelo, Mississippi, where Homer's favorite singer was born. _____

24. Anne would lose her head if she did not have a good excuse for the king. _____

25. Unless you wear that bolo tie, you will look out of place at the party. _____

B. To the main clauses below, add the types of subordinate clauses indicated in parentheses. Add your clause at any place in the sentence that is appropriate.

26. (adverb clause) The Wicked Witch of the West always carried an umbrella.

_____

_____

27. (adjective clause) Dark storm clouds filled the sky above San Francisco.

_____

_____

28. (adjective clause) Brent crossed the street and headed for the basketball court.

_____

_____

29. (adverb clause) Carlton enjoys riding his mountain bike.

_____

_____

30. (adverb clause) Charlie Brown tried to kick the football one more time.

_____

_____

continued

C. In the spaces provided, identify the following sentences as simple, compound, complex, or compound-complex.

    31. If Rocco finds an unusual comic book, he will buy it.   _____

    32. Piles of books filled the office; however, Barb knew her computer was in there somewhere.   _____

    33. Before the ice cream store with the crazy picture of an angel talking to Humphrey Bogart stood Steve with just enough money for a triple decker.   _____

    34. Anne was fond of Santa Cruz, where she had lived for many years, but she also enjoyed San Diego.   _____

    35. Charlie read his copy of *Weekly World News* before he left for class.   _____

D. Compose sentences of your own according to the instructions.

    36. Write a simple sentence that contains two prepositional phrases.

    _____

    _____

    37. Write a compound sentence. Use a coordinating conjunction and appropriate punctuation to join the clauses.

    _____

    _____

    38. Write a compound sentence. Use a transitional word or phrase and appropriate punctuation to join the clauses.

    _____

    _____

    39. Write a complex sentence. Use *if* as the subordinator.

    _____

    _____

Chapter 2 Practice Test

continued

40. Write a compound-complex sentence. Use the subordinator *unless*.

_____

_____

E. Identify each of the following sentences as correct (C), fused (F), comma splice (CS), or fragment (Frag). Then correct any errors by using the methods discussed in Chapter Two.

_____**41.** Before Miles Davis stepped onto the stage.

_____

_____

_____**42.** The snake rubbed its nose against the tree, then it began to shed its skin.

_____

_____

_____**43.** Stop the aardvark from crossing the road.

_____

_____

_____**44.** Patti, wondering how she would finish the scheduling on time.

_____

_____

_____**45.** Barry Bonds denied using steroids he set a new home-run record.

_____

_____

continued

_____**46.** After the meeting was over, Charlie treated us to kidney pie, it was delicious.

_____

_____

_____**47.** Because the printer in the hallway had broken.

_____

_____

_____**48.** Ptolemy was certain the sun circled the earth, however, Copernicus was not
so sure.

_____

_____

_____**49.** By wearing a hat with candles on it, Goya was able to paint at night.

_____

_____

_____**50.** Frodo entered the dark cave he did not know Shelob was waiting.

_____

_____

Improving Sentence Patterns

Now you have a fundamental knowledge of the sentence patterns of English. Although sentences may fall into four broad categories according to the number and types of clauses, the ways to express any thought in a sentence are almost infinitely variable.

You may make a sentence short and to the point:

> Eniko sold her netsuke collection.

Or, through the addition of modifying words, phrases, and additional clauses, you can expand it.

> After much soul searching and after seeking the advice of her mother, her brother, and her best friend, Eniko, a person who always carefully considered important decisions, sold her netsuke collection, which was worth several thousand dollars, but she kept one special carving of a frog and a sacred bird.

The essential idea—*Eniko sold her netsuke collection*—is the same for both sentences. Sometimes you will want to be short and to the point, and a five-word sentence will serve your purpose best. But sometimes you will want to be more explanatory, and then you may need more words.

The difference between the five words of the first sentence and the fifty words of the second one is the addition of modifying words, phrases, and clauses. These modifiers can help you write more clearly and vividly. The second sentence, though admittedly a bit overdone, tells a story, paints a picture. Modifying words, phrases, and clauses can be overused and should never be substituted for strong verbs and nouns, but most writers err in the opposite direction, leaving their writing limp and colorless.

You need to follow certain guidelines when you use the various modifying phrases and clauses. First we will discuss the most effective ways to use phrases and clauses in your sentences, and then we will discuss how to avoid the typical errors that writers make in using these devices. We hope that by the end you will have gained an appreciation of the wonderful flexibility of the English sentence and that you will have acquired more tools for making your own writing more interesting and effective.

Modifying with Participial and Infinitive Phrases

You can use **participial and infinitive phrases** as modifiers in your sentences. These phrases can help you streamline your sentences and achieve sentence variety. In most cases, participial and infinitive phrases take the place of subordinate clauses.

EXAMPLES

(subordinate clause)   **As he drove to work,** Harry saw a black cat run in front of his car.

(participial phrase)   **Driving to work,** Harry saw a black cat run in front of his car.

As you already know, **a clause is a word group that contains a subject and a verb. A phrase,** on the other hand, **is a word group that does not contain a subject and a verb.** You are already aware of prepositional phrases. Other phrases, generally called verbal phrases, include **present participial phrases, past participial phrases,** and **infinitive phrases.**

Present Participial Phrases

As we mentioned in Chapter One, the present participle is a verbal. It is the form of the verb that ends in "ing" (*running, typing, looking*). Without a helping verb it cannot be used as the verb of a sentence. Instead, it is used as an adjective. For example, you can use it as a one-word adjective.

EXAMPLE   The **running** man stumbled as he rounded the corner.

In this sentence, the present participle *running* modifies the noun *man*.

You can also use the present participle as part of a phrase that functions as an adjective. Such a phrase is called a **participial phrase,** and it is often used to begin sentences.

EXAMPLE   Rounding the corner, the running man stumbled.

In this sentence, the present participial phrase *Rounding the corner* is an adjective phrase modifying the noun *man*. The present participle is *Rounding*.

The present participial phrase, then, is an adjective phrase consisting of the present participle plus any other words attached to it. When a present participial phrase introduces a sentence, it is always followed by a comma.

Past Participial Phrases

The past participle is the form of the verb that you use with the helping verbs *have, has,* or *had* (*have eaten, has defeated, had bought*). Like the present participle, the past participle is a verbal when used without a helping verb. And, like the present participle, it is used as an adjective.

You can use a past participle as a single-word adjective.

EXAMPLE   The **defeated** army retreated into the mountains.

In this sentence, the past participle *defeated* modifies the noun *army.*

Or you can use the past participle as part of a past participial phrase.

EXAMPLE   **Pursued by the enemy,** the army retreated into the mountains.

In this sentence, the past participial phrase *Pursued by the enemy* modifies the noun *army.* Notice that it is followed by a comma. As with the present participial phrase, when the past participial phrase introduces a sentence, you should place a comma after it.

Participial phrases make good introductions to sentences, but you can use them anywhere. To avoid confusion, though, you should place them as closely as possible to the words they modify.

EXAMPLES   All of the students **submitting essays for the contest** used word processors.

The man **bitten by the rattlesnake** walked ten miles to the hospital.

The present participial phrase *submitting essays for the contest* modifies the noun *students.* The past participial phrase *bitten by the rattlesnake* modifies the noun *man.*

PRACTICE   Underline the participial phrases in the following sentences and circle the words they modify.

1. Put into the game in the last ten minutes, Zoila scored twelve points for her team.

2. Using questionable statistics, he claimed that half of all bank robberies happened on Friday.

3. Swimming silently under the ship, Nessie avoided the monster hunters.

4. We listened to "American Pie," the Don McLean song written after the death of Buddy Holly.

5. Robinson, standing alone on the beach, stared at the footprint in the sand.

6. The pink Cadillac parked by the curb in New York intrigued Andy.

7. Stunned by Mr. Spock's phaser, the Klingon fell to the deck of the ship.

8. Colonel Chamberlain's troops repulsed the rebels trying to outflank the Yankees at the Battle of Gettysburg.

9. Staring at the Grecian urn, Keats considered the nature of truth and beauty.

10. Comets, named after the Greek word for "long hair," are always exciting sights.

Infinitive Phrases

The infinitive is a verbal that you can use as a noun, an adjective, or an adverb. You form the infinitive by adding *to* to the present tense form of the verb (*to write, to run, to listen*).

You can use the infinitive by itself.

EXAMPLE To fly, you must first take lessons and get a license.

Or you can use the infinitive to form an infinitive phrase.

EXAMPLE To play the saxophone well, you must practice often.

Notice that the infinitive phrase consists of the infinitive plus any words attached to it. Like the two participial phrases, it is followed by a comma when it introduces a sentence. However, when you use the infinitive as a noun, it can act as the subject of a sentence. In this case, you do not use a comma.

EXAMPLE To be a good husband was Clint's ambition.

The infinitive phrase *To be a good husband* is the subject of the verb *was*.

Generally, like the two participial phrases, the infinitive phrase can appear in a variety of places in a sentence.

EXAMPLE Carla's motives were hard to understand at first.

Here the infinitive phrase *to understand at first* acts as an adverb to modify the adjective *hard*.

EXAMPLE Eduardo liked having a sister to talk to even though she teased him constantly.

Here, the infinitive phrase *to talk to* acts as an adjective to modify the noun *sister*.

⟲⟲ PRACTICE   Underline the modifying participial and infinitive phrases in the following sentences and circle the words they modify.

1. Mahdieh finally found a (pot) <u>to hold her geraniums.</u>

2. Placing the letter in an obvious spot, Mr. Poe knew that no one would find it.

3. Luckily, William Tell knew the correct way to aim a crossbow.

4. Bitten by a radioactive spider, Peter Parker dreamed about houseflies.

5. The wretched man looked at the only sentence to contain 823 words without a period.

6. *Les Miserables,* written by Victor Hugo, is the only French book with such an extended sentence.

7. Yelling loudly, the Rebels charged up the hill toward the Yankees.

8. Frightened by the bright light, Gollum returned to the darkness of the cave.

9. Goya picked up his candle hat and wondered which candle to light first.

10. The Black Knight stood on the tall building and pondered his promise to save the city.

Section One Review

1. The **present participle** is a verbal that ends in "ing" and that is used as an adjective. (When the "ing" form is used as a noun, it is called a **gerund.**)

2. A **present participial phrase** consists of the present participle plus any words attached to it.

3. A comma follows a **present participial phrase** that introduces a sentence.

4. The **past participle** is the form of the verb used with the helping verbs *have, has,* and *had.*

5. The **past participle** is a verbal used as an adjective.

6. A **past participial phrase** consists of the past participle plus any words attached to it.

7. A comma follows a **past participial phrase** that introduces a sentence.

8. An **infinitive** is formed by adding *to* to the present tense of a verb.

9. The **infinitive** is a verbal that can be used as a noun, an adjective, or an adverb.

10. An **infinitive phrase** consists of the infinitive plus any words attached to it.

11. A comma follows an **infinitive phrase** that introduces a sentence and acts as a modifier.

Exercise 1A

Underline all participial and infinitive phrases. Circle the words that they modify. In the spaces, identify the phrase as present participle (Pres P), past participle (Past P), or infinitive (Inf).

Inf   **1.** In Roman times, the intersection of three roads was used as a (place) <u>to stop</u>

<u>and talk.</u>

_____   **2.** Sharing the events of the day, Roman travelers would rest for a few minutes.

_____   **3.** Farmers, concerned about their crops, would discuss the weather or the land.

_____   **4.** This kind of place was called a *trivium*, meaning a "three-road intersection."

_____   **5.** Found in words like *triple, trinity*, and *tricycle, tri* means "three."

_____   **6.** A common Spanish word to refer to a street or road is *via* (from the Latin *vium*).

_____   **7.** "Trivial" conversation, referring to discussions of unimportant matters, really

means "three-road" conversation.

_____   **8.** In 1906, a catastrophic fire caused by a major earthquake destroyed San Francisco.

_____   **9.** Ignited by broken gas and electrical lines, fires started throughout the city.

_____ **10.** Collapsing from the earthquake, many buildings became vulnerable to the fires.

_____ **11.** Gaps in roofs became chimneys to help fuel the fires.

_____ **12.** This ferocious fire, lasting for four days and nights, destroyed 28,000 buildings.

_____ **13.** Leaving 250,000 people homeless and well over 500 dead, the earthquake lasted

only forty-five or sixty seconds.

continued

_____**14.** The earthquake shock, covering an area of over 375 square miles, damaged an area of 400 miles up and down the coast and 30 miles out to sea.

_____**15.** The 135 aftershocks occurring after the great quake and fires destroyed many more buildings.

Exercise 1B

In the places indicated by ^, add your own participial or infinitive phrases to the following sentences. Use the verbs in parentheses. Be sure to place a comma after any phrase that introduces a sentence.

1. ^ Jalayne checked the tires, the oil level, the coolant, and the amount of gas in her car. (prepare)

    To prepare for her trip across the country, Jalayne checked the tires,

    the oil level, the coolant, and the amount of gas in her car.

2. Steve was pleasantly surprised when he discovered he had enough money ^ . (pay)

    _____

    _____

3. The house ^ was where the second little pig lived. (make)

    _____

    _____

4. ^ Sisyphus decided to try one more time. (frustrate)

    _____

    _____

5. At the poetry reading, we were surprised to see Billy Collins and Steve McDonald ^. (fight)

    _____

    _____

6. A secondhand store is an excellent place ^. (find)

    _____

    _____

7. ^ Galileo wondered if the sun really did circle the earth. (stare)

    _____

    _____

Exercise 1B

continued

8. ^ Prufrock kept the bottoms of his trousers rolled. (walk)

    _____

    _____

9. The people ^ caused the doors to become blocked. (push)

    _____

    _____

10. ^ The Clown knew that Batman was unaware of him. (creep)

    _____

    _____

11. No one could find the secret message ^ in the Prado museum in Madrid. (conceal)

    _____

    _____

12. ^ The dwarfs headed down the hall toward Jack's office. (whistle)

    _____

    _____

13. The circus audience stared in disbelief at the baby elephant ^ . (fly)

    _____

    _____

Exercise 1B

continued

14. The firemen were always willing ^. (help)

_____

_____

15. Wonder Woman and The Silver Surfer, the super heroes ^, were able to save the trapped children. (call)

_____

_____

Exercise 1C

Underline all infinitive and participial phrases and circle the words that they modify.

1. Jackie Robinson, the first (African-American) to play baseball in the major leagues, has been honored in many cities across the United States and Canada. **2.** For instance, a statue honoring Jackie stands outside Olympic Stadium in Montreal, Quebec, where Jackie played for a Dodger farm club. **3.** In addition, Daytona, Florida, is home to Robinson Stadium, named after this great player. **4.** Jersey City, New Jersey, dedicating a bronze plaque to Jackie at Society Hill, has also honored Robinson. **5.** Of course, New York, home of the Brooklyn Dodgers, showed its appreciation to Jackie when it made the decision to change the name of Interboro Parkway to Jackie Robinson Parkway. **6.** In Los Angeles, UCLA has honored Jackie, who was the first UCLA athlete to star in four sports. **7.** UCLA baseball teams now play at Jackie Robinson Stadium, named after the legendary player. **8.** Erected at the stadium in 1985, a statue of Robinson was generously paid for by Jackie's brother, Mack Robinson. **9.** Pasadena, California, is another city showing its appreciation for Jackie's accomplishments. **10.** Moving to the city when they were young, Jackie and Mack grew up in Pasadena. **11.** On New Year's Day, 1997, the grateful city honored Robinson with a beautiful Rose Parade float donated by the Simon Wiesenthal Center. **12.** Naming a youth center, a post office, a park, and a baseball field after Jackie, Pasadena further showed its respect for the famous baseball player. **13.** Lately, the school board of Grady County, Georgia, which is near Jackie's birthplace, unanimously passed a motion to change the name of the Cairo High School baseball field to Jackie Robinson Field. **14.** Featuring a granite marker and bronze plaque, the field is dedicated to Jackie. **15.** Jackie Robinson, recognized by all as a brave man and gifted player, richly deserves all of these honors.

Modifying with Adjective Clauses and Appositives

Adjective Clauses

We discussed adjective clauses earlier in a section on subordinate clauses. An adjective clause is an important option when you want to modify a noun or pronoun in a sentence. Using an adjective clause instead of single-word adjectives or modifying phrases tends to place more emphasis on what you are saying about the noun or pronoun you are modifying. Consider the following sentences, for instance.

EXAMPLES

(adjective)   My **insensitive** neighbor plays his trombone all night long.

(adjective clause)   My neighbor, **who is insensitive,** plays his trombone all night long.

Using the adjective clause *who is insensitive* places more importance on the neighbor's insensitivity. Sometimes you need only single-word modifiers, but it is good to be aware of all of your choices for modifying words.
   Here is a brief review of adjective clauses.

1. Adjective clauses follow the noun or pronoun they modify.

2. Adjective clauses begin with the relative pronouns *who, whom, whose, which, that* (and sometimes *when* or *where*).

EXAMPLES

We returned the money to the *person* **who had lost it.** (*Who* introduces an adjective clause that modifies the noun *person.*)

I remember the *time* **when Homer and Hortense were married at the Spam factory.** (*When* introduces an adjective clause that modifies the noun *time.*)

Sidney decided to move to *Colorado,* **where his family used to spend summer vacations.** (*Where* introduces an adjective clause that modifies the noun *Colorado.*)

3. If the adjective clause provides information that is necessary to identify the noun or pronoun, do not set it off with commas.

EXAMPLE

The man **who was sitting next to my uncle at the banquet** is a famous sportswriter.

The information in this adjective clause is necessary to identify which man at the banquet is the famous sportswriter.

4. If the adjective clause provides information that is merely descriptive and is not necessary to identify the noun or pronoun, then set the clause off with commas.

EXAMPLE   Merlin Olsen, **who was an all-pro football player,** became a famous sportscaster.

Merlin Olsen's name already identifies him, so the adjective clause contains added but unnecessary information. Therefore, you need the commas.

We will discuss the rules for the use of commas with adjective clauses again in Chapter Five.

PRACTICE   Underline all adjective clauses and circle the words they modify. For further practice, try to determine which clauses need commas and add them where necessary.

1. The (woman) <u>who developed the new microchip</u> was from Vietnam.

2. *Beowulf* which is an Old English epic poem was written about 1000 A.D.

3. Anyone who even thinks about stealing my fried okra will seriously regret it.

4. Hurling which is a sport played primarily in Ireland is being considered for future Olympics.

5. Maurice Ravel who was a famous French composer wrote *Bolero* which became one of the most popular concert pieces of the twentieth century.

6. The frustrated contestant could not name the planet that was third from the sun.

7. Maurice Ravel asked Toots Thielemans who is a famous harmonica player to perform *Bolero* for the crowd.

8. The women who were arguing about the baby decided to ask Solomon for advice.

9. The plane that Chelsea had jumped from was circling 13,500 feet above Chula Vista where she went to high school.

10. Wolf Moonglow who was an exceptionally hirsute man was telling us about the time when he first began to study lycanthropy.

Appositives

Appositives give you another option for adding descriptive detail. An **appositive** is a noun or pronoun, along with any modifiers, that **renames** another noun or pronoun. The appositive almost always follows the word it refers to, and it is usually set off with commas.

Note how the following two sentences can be combined not only by adding an adjective clause but also by adding an appositive:

My neighbor plays the trombone all night long.

He is an insensitive man.

EXAMPLES   (adjective clause)   My neighbor, **who is insensitive,** plays his trombone all night long.

                (appositive)   My neighbor, **an insensitive man,** plays his trombone all night long.

In the appositive, the noun *man* renames the noun *neighbor.*

EXAMPLES   The wedding <u>ring</u>, a **<u>symbol</u>** of eternal love, dates back to 2800 B.C. in Egypt. (The noun *symbol* renames the noun *ring.*)

The huge <u>trout</u>, **the <u>one</u>** still in the river, would have made an impressive trophy on the wall of Harold's den. (**The pronoun** *one* renames the noun *trout.*)

The <u>honeymoon</u>, **a popular marriage <u>custom</u>,** comes from an ancient Northern European practice of stealing brides. (**The noun** *custom* renames the noun *honeymoon.*)

PRACTICE   Underline the appositives and circle the nouns or pronouns that the appositives rename.

1. The cell (phone), <u>a product of modern technology</u>, is an indispensable tool of many businesses.

2. Gothic cathedrals are often ornamented with gargoyles, grotesque sculptures of evil spirits.

3. Hera and Zeus, two powerful gods, often quarreled about his wandering eyes.

4. Harry Houdini, a famous American escape artist and magician, spent many years exposing fraudulent mediums and mind readers.

5. The one-armed man, Richard Kimble's elusive enemy, was recently seen playing the slot machines in Las Vegas.

6. Patrick Stewart, the former Captain Picard of the *U.S.S. Enterprise,* has also starred as Captain Ahab of the *Pequod.*

7. Whenever Elmo shows up, Cole, my only grandson, becomes all smiles.

8. D. H. Lawrence always kept in touch with John Thomas, a close childhood friend.

9. Miles Davis's *Kind of Blue*, perhaps the most famous jazz album, has just been reissued in a box that contains a tee shirt showing Miles.

10. Bill Liscomb was a pioneer in hang gliding, a popular sport among the Peter Pan crowd.

◎◎ PRACTICE Add an appositive or an adjective clause to each of the following sentences. Use commas when they are needed.

1. The sports car was parked near the school.

   The sports car that had been stolen last week was parked near the school.

2. Amelia Earhart vanished while flying over the Pacific Ocean.

   _____

   _____

3. Bruce Springsteen put on a great half-time show at the 2009 Super Bowl.

   _____

   _____

4. Wile E. Coyote carefully constructed the trap.

_____

_____

5. Angelina asked Brad to change the diapers of their latest child.

_____

_____

6. Spike Lee's film told a story about the Buffalo Soldiers of World War II.

_____

_____

7. Ewan McGregor might have groaned when he first read the stilted lines of Obi-Wan Kenobi.

_____

_____

8. Artists often depicted the gods and goddesses of ancient Rome in marble.

_____

_____

9. In *The Odyssey*, Homer also describes the voyage of Odysseus's son.

_____

_____

10. Mount Vesuvius still smolders over the ruins of Pompeii.

_____

_____

Section Two Review

1. **Adjective clauses** modify nouns and pronouns.

2. **Adjective clauses** follow the nouns or pronouns they modify.

3. **Adjective clauses** begin with *who, whom, whose, which, that* (and sometimes *when* or *where*).

4. **Adjective clauses** that contain information necessary to identify the words they modify are not set off with commas.

5. **Adjective clauses** that do not contain information necessary to identify the words they modify are set off with commas.

6. **Appositives** are words or word groups containing a noun or pronoun that renames another noun or pronoun in a sentence.

7. **Appositives** usually follow the nouns or pronouns they rename.

8. **Appositives** are usually set off with commas.

Exercise 2A

Underline all adjective clauses and appositives. Circle the words they modify or rename. Indicate whether the modifier is an appositive (AP) or an adjective clause (Adj). Add commas where necessary.

Adj 1. The body of (Abraham Lincoln) who was assassinated in 1865 was almost stolen from its grave in 1876.

_____ 2. Big Jim Kenealy the leader of an Illinois counterfeiting gang had recently been put out of business by the U.S. Secret Service.

_____ 3. Secret Service agents had arrested key members of his gang as well as the engraver who did Kenealy's most important work.

_____ 4. Kenealy developed a plan that would force the government to release his men.

_____ 5. He decided to kidnap Lincoln's body which was buried two miles outside of Springfield, Illinois.

_____ 6. After his death, Mary Todd Lincoln had taken her husband's body to Oak Ridge Cemetery where he was buried in an unguarded grave.

_____ 7. Kenealy who knew there was no Illinois law against stealing a body considered his plan foolproof.

_____ 8. However, Kenealy made one blunder a very serious mistake.

_____ 9. To steal the body, he recruited a helper an undercover agent of the Secret Service.

_____ 10. He decided upon November 7 the night after the national elections as the best time to dig up Lincoln's body.

_____ 11. He planned to use the excitement that accompanies all elections to cover his activities.

_____ 12. On November 8 his arrest was reported in the *Chicago Tribune* which ran the full story of his plot.

continued

_____**13.** Robert Todd Lincoln the President's oldest son hired attorneys to prosecute Jim

Kenealy.

_____**14.** The only crime that they were able to charge him with was conspiracy to steal

a coffin.

_____**15.** Kenealy who almost succeeded in stealing the body of President Lincoln received

a sentence of one year in the state penitentiary.

Exercise 2B

A. Add adjective clauses of your own to each of the sentences below. Make sure you use commas where necessary.

1. Chris likes to work on his old motorcycle.

   Chris likes to work on his old motorcycle, which he

   purchased last year from his brother.

2. Hellboy found his lost weapon on the sewer.

   _____

   _____

3. Sacajawea appears on a special edition dollar coin.

   _____

   _____

4. When the Berlin Wall fell, Helmut was able to secure a piece for Inga.

   _____

   _____

5. In the northeast corner of Montana, a group of wolves was pursuing a bear.

   _____

   _____

6. The United States reluctantly entered World War I at the request of England and France.

   _____

   _____

7. The Battle of Bull Run was won by the South.

   _____

   _____

continued

    8. The actor Mark Wahlberg was once an underwear model and a rap singer.

_____

_____

B. Add appositives of your own to the sentences below. Make sure you use commas where necessary.

    9. The pilot landed the burning airplane in a muddy field.

The pilot, an eighty-five-year-old grandmother, landed the

burning airplane in a muddy field.

    10. Peter Pan and the children frustrated Captain Hook.

_____

_____

    11. On his iPhone, Steve was listening to *How I Became a Millionaire*.

_____

_____

    12. *Battleship Galactica* is the favorite show of Neil Armstrong.

_____

_____

    13. "The Troubles" have worried Fergal since he left Ireland.

_____

_____

    14. The rain in Italy falls mainly in the mountains.

_____

_____

continued

15. Sister Mary Cecilia and Father Hadrian watched the film *Doubt*.

_____

_____

Exercise 2C

Underline all adjective clauses and circle the words they modify. Underline all appositives and circle the words they rename. Add commas where necessary.

1. Many English-speaking people are surprised when they discover the number of everyday (words) <u>that are drawn from different mythologies.</u> **2.** For example, the names of several of our weekdays—Tuesday, Wednesday, Thursday, and Friday—derive from Norse mythology.

3. Tuesday and Thursday refer to Tiu the Norse god of war and Thor the Norse god of thunder.

4. Wednesday refers to Woden who was the king of the Norse gods and Friday refers to Frigga the Norse goddess of love. **5.** Other common words are derived from Greek mythology. **6.** For instance, the word *tantalize* refers to Tantalus who was a king condemned to Hades as a punishment for his crimes. **7.** In Hades he was forced to stand below fruit that was just beyond his reach and in water that he could not drink. **8.** Another common Greek word in our language is *atlas* which refers to a map of the world. **9.** As a mythological figure, Atlas was a Titan who was condemned to support the heavens on his shoulders. **10.** Finally, Roman mythology which in many ways parallels Greek mythology is another source of many English words. **11.** For example, the month of January is named after Janus the Roman god with two faces. **12.** Janus whose two faces allowed him to watch two directions at once was the Roman god of doorways. **13.** June another of the many months that refer to Roman mythology is named after Juno the goddess of marriage and childbirth. **14.** These examples are just a few of the hundreds of English words that reflect the many mythologies of the world.

Misplaced and Dangling Modifiers

In Chapter Two, when you combined clauses to form various sentence types, you learned that joining clauses improperly can lead to comma splices and fused sentences. As you can probably guess, adding modifiers to sentences leads to an entirely new set of problems. In some cases, these problems are a bit more complicated than those caused by comma splices and fused sentences, but with a little practice, you should have no trouble at all handling them.

Misplaced Modifiers

Misplaced modifiers are exactly what their name says they are—modifiers that have been "misplaced" within a sentence. But how is a modifier "misplaced"? The answer is simple. If you remember that a modifier is nearly always placed just before or just after the word it modifies, then a misplaced modifier must be one that has been mistakenly placed so that it causes a reader to be confused about what it modifies. Consider the following sentence, for example:

EXAMPLE   Albert said **quietly** to move away from the snake.

Does the modifier *quietly* tell us how Albert said what he said, or does it tell us how we should move away from the snake? Changing the placement of the modifier will clarify the meaning.

EXAMPLES   Albert **quietly** said to move away from the snake. (Here, the word modifies the verb *said*.)

Albert said to move **quietly** away from the snake. (Here the word modifies the verbal *to move*.)

Sometimes finding the correct placement of a modifier can be a bit difficult. Let's look at a few other typical examples.

Misplaced Words

Any modifier can be misplaced, but one particular group of modifiers causes quite a bit of trouble for many people. These words are *only, almost, just, merely,* and *nearly*. Consider, for example, the following sentences:

EXAMPLES   By buying her new computer on sale, Floretta **almost** saved $100.

By buying her new computer on sale, Floretta saved **almost** $100.

As you can see, these sentences actually make two different statements. In the first sentence, *almost* modifies *saved*. If you *almost* saved something, you did *not* save it. In the second sentence, *almost* modifies *$100*. If you saved *almost* $100, you saved $85, $90, $95, or some other amount close to $100.

Which statement does the writer want to make—that Floretta did *not* save any money or that she *did* save an amount close to $100? Because the point was that she bought her computer on sale, the second sentence makes more sense.

To avoid confusion, be sure that you place all of your modifiers carefully.

EXAMPLES

(incorrect)	Her piano teacher encouraged her **often** to practice.
(correct)	Her piano teacher **often** encouraged her to practice.
(correct)	Her piano teacher encouraged her to practice **often**.
(incorrect)	Sophia **nearly** drank a gallon of coffee yesterday.
(correct)	Sophia drank **nearly** a gallon of coffee yesterday.

PRACTICE   Underline and correct any misplaced words in the following sentences. Some of the sentences may be correct.

1. During breakfast, Marshall ~~nearly~~ drank a *nearly* whole quart of orange juice.

2. The poet standing at the curb dejectedly stared at the rejection letter in his hand.

3. The bullfighter knew that he had only one chance to win the heart of the señorita.

4. The sinister-looking man who had been sitting in the corner silently got up and left the room.

5. By the time he had almost fallen ten thousand feet, the skydiver was wondering if he should open his chute.

6. Peyton Farquhar nearly crept to the edge of the trees before he saw the Union soldiers.

7. Because she had eaten a large lunch, Aracela just decided to order a small dinner salad.

8. Because she was worried about her health, Shawna asked Fernando frequently to take her to the gym.

9. The world-famous prevaricator would only invite the gullible to his dinner party.

10. Susan Boyle almost surprised everyone in the building when she started to sing.

Misplaced Phrases and Clauses

The phrases and clauses that you studied earlier in this chapter are as easily misplaced as individual words. Phrases and clauses often follow the words they modify.

✺ EXAMPLES	(prepositional phrase)	The driver **in the blue sports car** struck an innocent pedestrian.
	(present participial phrase)	The dog **chasing the car** barked at the bewildered driver.
	(past participial phrase)	They gave the bicycle **donated by the shop** to the child.
	(adjective clause)	Lucia gave the money **that she had borrowed from her sister** to the homeless woman.

In each of the above sentences, the modifier follows the word it modifies. Notice what happens when the modifier is misplaced so that it follows the wrong word.

✺ EXAMPLES The driver struck an innocent pedestrian **in the blue sports car.**

The dog barked at the bewildered driver **chasing the car.**

They gave the bicycle to the child **donated by the shop.**

Lucia gave the money to the homeless woman **that she had borrowed from her sister.**

Obviously, misplaced phrases and clauses can create rather confusing and sometimes even humorous situations. Of course, not all phrases and clauses follow the words they modify. Many occur before the word they refer to.

| ✺ EXAMPLES | (past participial phrase) | **Angered by the umpire's poor call,** Dana threw her bat to the ground. |
| | (present participial phrase) | **Hoping to win the debate,** Cyrus practiced three hours every day. |

Regardless of whether the modifier appears before or after the word it modifies, the point is that you should place modifiers so that they clearly refer to a specific word in the sentence.

◎◎ PRACTICE   Underline and correct any misplaced phrases and clauses in the following sentences. Some of the sentences may be correct.

1. The doctor set the leg of the dog <u>that had been broken in the accident.</u>

   The doctor set the dog's leg that had been broken in the accident.

2. Marco Polo presented the golden chest to the Pope filled with exotic spices.

   _____

   _____

3. Artemis shot the arrow at the frightened stag using her strong bow.

   _____

   _____

4. The astronauts on Mars were monitored by personnel at NASA who were sitting in a space rover on the surface of the planet.

   _____

   _____

5. My German shepherd lunged at the skunk, which sleeps at the foot of my bed, when it entered our garage.

   _____

   _____

6. *Full Metal Jacket* has become a classic film about the Vietnam War directed by Stanley Kubrick.

   _____

   _____

7. Homer daydreamed about Hortense chewing on his plug of tobacco.

_____

_____

8. The space aliens stared at the herd of sheep with cone-shaped heads and

large oval eyes before they fired their weapons.

_____

_____

9. My mother loved the film *Milk*, but my uncle did not, praising its honest

handling of the life of a brave man.

_____

_____

10. The Lewis and Clark expedition finally arrived at the Pacific Ocean, which

had been gone for months.

_____

_____

Dangling Modifiers

A **dangling modifier** is an introductory phrase (usually a verbal phrase) that
lacks an appropriate word to modify. Since these modifiers usually represent
some sort of action, they need a **doer** or **agent** of the action represented.
   For example, in the following sentence the introductory participial phrase
"dangles" because it is not followed by a noun or pronoun that could be the
doer of the action represented by the phrase.

EXAMPLE   **Driving madly down the boulevard,** the horse just missed being hit and
killed.

The present participial phrase *Driving madly down the boulevard* should be followed by a noun or pronoun that could logically do the action of the phrase. Instead, it is followed by the noun *horse*, which is the subject of the sentence. Was the horse "driving"? Probably not. Therefore, the modifying phrase "dangles" because it has no noun or pronoun to which it can logically refer. Here are some more sentences with dangling modifiers.

EXAMPLES

Nearly exhausted, the game was almost over.
(Was the *game* exhausted?)

After studying all night, the test wasn't so difficult after all.
(Did the *test* study all night?)

To impress his new girlfriend, Dominic's Chevrolet was polished.
(Did the *Chevrolet* want to impress Dominic's girlfriend?)

As you can see, you should check for dangling modifiers when you use introductory phrases.

PRACTICE

In the following sentences, indicate whether the modifying phrases are correctly used by writing either C for correct or D for dangling modifier in the spaces provided.

_____D_____ **1.** Hurrying to work, Ofelia's briefcase fell into a puddle.

_____ **2.** Wiping tears from her eyes, the story of Hansel and Gretel always upset the old witch.

_____ **3.** Delighted by his graphic novel, Rocco grinned broadly.

_____ **4.** To become invisible, the enclosed disappearance cream must be applied to the body.

_____ **5.** Determined to ruin his plans, Joe's bottle of poisoned wine was hidden by his mother-in-law.

Correcting Dangling Modifiers

You can correct a dangling modifier in one of two ways.

1. <u>Rewrite the sentence so that the introductory modifier logically refers to the subject of the sentence it introduces.</u>

EXAMPLES

Nearly exhausted, I hoped the game was almost over.
(*I* was nearly exhausted.)

After studying all night, **Lucilla** passed the test easily.
(*Lucilla* studied all night.)

To impress his new girlfriend, **Dominic** polished his Chevrolet.
(*Dominic* wanted to impress his girlfriend.)

2. Change the introductory phrase to a clause.

◎◎ EXAMPLES

Because I was nearly exhausted, I hoped the game was almost over.

After Lucilla had studied all night, she passed the test easily.

Dominic wanted to impress his girlfriend, so he polished his Chevrolet.

NOTE: Do not correct a dangling modifier by moving it to the end of the sentence or by adding a possessive noun or pronoun to a sentence. In either case, it will still "dangle" because it lacks a **doer** or **agent** that could perform the action of the modifier.

◎◎ EXAMPLES

(incorrect)	After searching for three weeks, the lost watch was finally found. (There is no doer for *searching*.)
(still incorrect)	The lost watch was finally found **after searching for three weeks.** (There still is no logical doer.)
(still incorrect)	After searching for three weeks, Alfredo's lost watch was finally found. (Adding the possessive form *Alfredo's* does not add a doer of the action.)
(correct)	After searching for three weeks, Alfredo finally found his watch. (The noun *Alfredo* can logically perform the action—*searching*—of the modifying phrase.)
(correct)	After Alfredo had searched for three weeks, he finally found his watch. (Here again, the doer of the action is clear.)

◎◎ PRACTICE

Underline and correct any dangling modifiers in the following sentences. Some of the sentences may be correct.

1. Delighted by the victory, the champagne and caviar were quickly

consumed.

Delighted by the victory, the coach and her team quickly

consumed the champagne and caviar.

2. Disappointed by his 3,098th failure, the rock of Sisyphus rolled back down the hill.

_____

_____

3. After telling the lie, Pinocchio's nose began to grow.

_____

_____

4. To make his ideas clear, Plato decided on the cave metaphor.

_____

_____

5. Examining their hearts, the lives of the newly dead were judged by Osiris.

_____

_____

6. Concerned about her students' dangling modifiers, Leanne's new lesson plan began to take shape.

_____

_____

7. To balance the stone at the top of the hill, it was secured with duct tape by Sisyphus.

_____

_____

8. Huffing and puffing as hard as he could, the house of bricks would not blow down.

_____

_____

9. Startled by the sudden explosion, the summer sky was filled with cranes and egrets.

_____

_____

10. To ask for more food, the bowl was lifted into the air.

_____

_____

Section Three Review

1. A **misplaced modifier** is a modifier that has been mistakenly placed so that it causes the reader to be confused about what it modifies.

2. Commonly misplaced words are *only, almost, just, merely,* and *nearly.*

3. Place modifying phrases and clauses so that they clearly refer to a specific word in a sentence.

4. A **dangling modifier** is an introductory phrase (usually a verbal phrase) that lacks an appropriate word to modify. Since these modifiers usually represent some sort of action, they need a **doer** or **agent** of the action represented.

5. You can correct a dangling modifier in one of two ways.

   a. Rewrite the sentence so that the introductory modifier logically refers to the subject of the sentence it introduces.

   b. Change the introductory phrase to a clause.

6. Do not correct a dangling modifier by moving it to the end of the sentence or by adding a possessive noun or pronoun.

Exercise 3A

A. Underline and correct any misplaced words in the following sentences. Some sentences may be correct.

1. After <u>nearly</u> chasing Trigger for four hours, Roy was almost out of breath.

   After chasing Trigger for nearly four hours, Roy was

   almost out of breath.

2. Clement only traded five of his virtues for defects.

   _____

   _____

3. We had expected a large crowd, but half a dozen people merely showed up.

   _____

   _____

4. Once he got his new high-definition television, Archie Bunker almost watched conservative talk shows every night.

   _____

   _____

5. As he passed the ragged beggar, Scrooge just placed one penny in his hat.

   _____

   _____

B. Underline and correct any misplaced phrases or clauses in the following sentences. Some of the sentences may be correct.

6. As Elise sat down in the bus, she looked over at the man in the next seat <u>with the huge</u> <u>ears</u>.

   As Elise sat down in the bus, she looked over at the

   man with the huge ears in the next seat.

Exercise 3A

continued

7. Percival found the grail but failed to ask the right question that everyone was looking for.

   _____

   _____

8. The scientists took a side trip to see the dolphins arguing in favor of stem cell research.

   _____

   _____

9. The taxi driver saw the police officer stop a jaywalker who had just written him a ticket for speeding.

   _____

   _____

10. In calculus class the student did not notice the professor standing behind him texting his girlfriend.

    _____

    _____

C. Underline and correct any dangling modifiers in the following sentences. Some of the sentences may be correct.

11. Angered by the booing of the <u>fans</u>, bats and helmets came flying out of the Dodger dugout.

    Angered by the booing of the fans, the Dodger players threw bats and helmets out of the dugout.

    _____

continued

12. Before exiting Iraq, pick up all of those plastic water bottles.

13. Visiting Graceland for the tenth time, Homer's belief that Elvis was still alive grew

even stronger.

14. To purchase the new software for my iMac, a trip to the Apple Web site is required.

15. Thinking about the message from the ghost, a plan was devised by Hamlet.

Exercise 3B

Underline and correct any misplaced or dangling modifiers in the following sentences. Some of the sentences may be correct.

1. Before leaving for their cross-country trip, the silver was placed in their safety deposit box.

   Before leaving for their cross-country trip, the McDonalds put their silver in their safety deposit box.

2. Rob barbecued the yellowtail and then took a drink from a bottle of Gatorade that he had caught on his fishing trip.

3. Marley wagged his tail and looked up lovingly at his master hanging his tongue out.

4. Drinking the cup of hemlock, Socrates accepted the verdict of the Athenian jury.

5. Although Peter Piper had hoped to pick a bushel of pickled peppers, he merely picked a peck of them.

6. A grizzly bear stood on its hind legs with yellow fangs and roared at us.

Exercise 3B

continued

7. Sherrie's dog, Abby, only asks her to change the cats' box if the stink becomes too extreme.

_____

_____

8. After memorizing the manual for your new laptop, send me your apology by e-mail.

_____

_____

9. The bodybuilder stopped to look at the Monarch butterfly lifting weights in his backyard.

_____

_____

10. Refusing to give up her seat, Rosa Parks's actions helped to start the civil rights movement of the 1950s and 1960s.

_____

_____

11. Diana gave the cute rabbit to her favorite wood nymph that she had found nesting in her garage.

_____

_____

12. To get to the cabin, you only need to follow a few simple directions.

_____

_____

13. Intrigued by her coy smile, the *Mona Lisa* is viewed by thousands of tourists every year.

_____

_____

Exercise 3B

continued

14. Bruno almost had given all of his gold chains away before he realized how valuable they were.

_____

_____

15. Armand drove his new Italian sports car wearing a red beret to his French girlfriend's house to impress her.

_____

_____

Exercise 3C

Correct any dangling or misplaced modifiers in the following paragraph.

1. My kindergarten teacher Ms. Madden, was <u>almost</u> cruel to me my entire first year at school. **2.** Ms. Madden terrified me, who resembled the Wicked Witch of the West. **3.** Playing with the other students, her abuse started when I fell off one of the tricycles my first week in school. **4.** Coming into the classroom to seek comfort, she glared at me. **5.** Her lips almost looked white as she pressed them together. **6.** She just threw me into a closet bleeding from my hands and knees. **7.** Another incident when she showed no pity toward me will nearly be imprinted forever on my memory. **8.** Unwrapping a peanut-butter-and-jelly sandwich at snack time, she suddenly came up behind me and snatched it violently from my hands. **9.** She almost encouraged everyone to come over and watch me licking the jelly off my sandwich. **10.** To ridicule me, rude comments about my family and race were made. **11.** Finally, tired of her abuse, I decided to fight back. **12.** One day, when our class had just finished story time for no apparent reason, Ms. Madden came up and grabbed my skin to pinch me, but I pinched her first. **13.** Consequently, I was tied to a chair by Ms. Madden wearing a brown paper bag on my head. **14.** Remaining this way for the rest of the day, Ms. Madden had no mercy on me. **15.** One day my mother made a surprise visit to the school, and, dragging me along the floor by the hair, she caught Ms. Madden red-handed. **16.** Suspended by the school, my mother and father and I were finally satisfied.

Sentence Practice: Using Participial and Infinitive Phrases, Appositives, and Adjective Clauses

In this chapter, you have become aware of the many choices you have when you want to modify words in your sentences. Your options range from single-word modifiers to modifying phrases to subordinate clauses. Let's explore some of the possibilities with the following sentence.

> The beautiful dalmatian looked hungrily at the thick steaks cooking on the grill and quietly begged the chef for a bite.

By changing various modifiers, you can express the sentence in several other ways. For instance, *The beautiful dalmatian*, with its single-word modifier *beautiful* describing *dalmatian*, could be changed into an appositive.

> The dog, **a beautiful dalmatian,** looked hungrily at the thick steaks cooking on the grill and quietly begged the chef for a bite.

This version tends to emphasize the beauty of the dog.

If you change the part of the sentence that contains the verb *looked* to a present participial phrase, you will get a different effect.

> **Looking hungrily at the thick steaks cooking on the grill,** the beautiful dalmatian quietly begged the chef for a bite.

This version places a bit more emphasis on the dog's hungry look.

Another alternative is to change the present participial phrase *cooking on the grill* to an adjective clause.

> The beautiful dalmatian looked hungrily at the thick steaks **that were cooking on the grill** and quietly begged the chef for a bite.

As you can see, the choices are many, and good writers often try several versions of a sentence before deciding on the one that best expresses their ideas. Experimenting with your sentences in this way is part of the fun and the challenge of writing.

The exercises in this section are designed to give you practice in using various types of modifiers when you compose your sentences.

Sentence Combining Exercises

Using your knowledge of modifying phrases and clauses, combine the following lists of sentences according to the directions. Avoid dangling and misplaced modifiers. Add commas where necessary.

⚙️ **EXAMPLE**   Combine these sentences into one sentence. Use sentence a as a present participial phrase. Use sentence b as an appositive.

    a. Elvira hoped to win the Los Angeles Marathon.
    b. Elvira is a world-class runner.
    c. Elvira practiced running on the sand dunes.
    d. The sand dunes were in the deserts of Southern California.

Hoping to win the Los Angeles Marathon, Elvira, a world-class runner, practiced running on the sand dunes in the deserts of Southern California.

1. Combine the following sentences into one sentence. Use sentence a as an appositive. Use sentence c as an adjective clause.

    a. Tinnitus is a constant ringing sensation in the ear.
    b. Tinnitus is the result of a disturbed auditory nerve.
    c. The auditory nerve sends sound signals to the brain.

    _____

    _____

    _____

2. Combine the following sentences into one sentence. Use sentence a as a present participial phrase. Use sentence c as an adjective clause.

    a. Halley's comet passes close to the earth every seventy-six years.
    b. Halley's comet is a ball of rock and ice.
    c. Halley's comet has been recorded by historians since 240 B.C.E.

    _____

    _____

    _____

Sentence Combining Exercises

continued

3. Combine the following sentences into one sentence. Use sentence a as an appositive. Use sentence c as an appositive. Use sentence d as an adjective clause. Use sentence e as an adverb clause.

    a. "The real McCoy" is an expression meaning "the real thing."
    b. "The real McCoy" most likely comes from Kid McCoy.
    c. Kid McCoy was the welterweight champion boxer in 1898.
    d. He started to call himself Kid "the Real" McCoy.
    e. He called himself Kid "the Real" McCoy because he had so many imitators.

4. Combine these sentences into one sentence. Use sentences c and d as appositives.

    a. Goldfish swallowing was started by Lothrop Withington, Jr.
    b. It was started in 1939.
    c. It was one of the most unusual fads of the 20th century.
    d. Lothrop Withington, Jr., was a Harvard freshman.

5. Combine the following sentences into one sentence. Use sentence a as an introductory adverb clause. Use sentence b as an adjective clause. Use sentence d as an infinitive phrase.

    a. Withington boasted to friends that he had once eaten a live fish.
    b. His friends attended college with him.
    c. His friends dared him.
    d. The dare was to eat another one.

Sentence Combining Exercises

continued

6. Combine the following sentences into one sentence. Use sentence a as a present participial phrase. Use sentence d as an adjective clause.

   a. Withington accepted the challenge.
   b. He agreed to meet on March 3.
   c. He would meet them in the student dining hall.
   d. He would eat a live goldfish.

   _____

   _____

   _____

7. Combine the following sentences into one sentence. Use sentence c as an appositive phrase. Use sentence d as an adjective clause.

   a. The date arrived.
   b. Withington stood before a crowd of students.
   c. Withington was a natural actor.
   d. The students had heard about the challenge.
   e. Withington grabbed a goldfish from a bowl.

   _____

   _____

   _____

8. Combine the following sentences into one sentence. Use sentence a as a present participial phrase.

   a. He held the fish by its tail.
   b. Withington slowly lowered it into his mouth.
   c. He chewed it for a moment.
   d. He then swallowed it.

   _____

   _____

   _____

Sentence Combining Exercises

continued

9. Combine these sentences into one sentence. Use sentence a as an infinitive phrase. Use sentence c as an adjective clause.

   a. He completed his performance.
   b. Withington pulled out a toothbrush.
   c. He used it to clean his teeth.
   d. Then he said, "The scales caught a bit on my throat."

   _____

   _____

   _____

10. Combine the following sentences into one sentence. Use sentence a as an introductory prepositional phrase. Use sentence c as a past participial phrase.

   a. It was that spring.
   b. College students across the country were gulping down goldfish.
   c. The students were worried about exams.
   d. They were ready for any diversion.
   e. They were gulping as many as forty-two goldfish at one sitting.

   _____

   _____

   _____

Essay and Paragraph Practice: Using Examples

Assignment

In the first two chapters of this text, you have written paragraphs about an event and a place. Such writing is usually called "narrative" or "descriptive" because it either narrates (tells about) an event or describes a place. In this chapter you will write an **expository** paragraph or essay (your instructor will decide which one). Expository writing **explains** a topic or idea to a reader, or it **informs** the reader about a topic or idea. The topic of an expository paragraph or essay can range from explaining how to conduct an experiment in chemistry to analyzing the causes of World War II. In fact, most of the writing you will do in college classes will be expository.

One common type of expository writing is the paragraph or essay that relies on examples to make its point. If you look at Exercises 1C (page 162), 2C (page 174), and 3C (page 191) of Chapter Three, you will see that they all rely on examples to support the statements made in the topic sentences. Exercise 1C gives examples of cities that have honored Jackie Robinson. Exercise 2C gives examples of English words that are drawn from mythology. And Exercise 3C gives examples of the cruelty of a teacher.

Supporting your ideas with examples is a powerful way to help your readers understand your point. Examples allow your readers to see your topic at work in real-life situations, and they show your readers that your topic is based on reality. Of course, examples are also important when you take tests. Your ability to back up general answers with specific examples can show an instructor that you have understood and mastered the material you have been studying.

For this chapter, your assignment is to write a paper that uses several *specific examples* to support a statement made in a topic sentence or a thesis statement. Develop your paper from one of the following prewriting suggestions or from an idea suggested by your instructor.

Prewriting to Generate Ideas

Whether you are writing a paragraph or an essay, the prewriting techniques are the same. Use freewriting, brainstorming, and clustering to develop ideas from the topic suggestions that follow. Look for topics that you can illustrate with specific, detailed examples of your own.

Prewriting Application: Finding Your Topic

Read the following topic suggestions before you begin to prewrite. Not all of them will apply to you. Find the suggestions that interest you the most and then spend five or ten minutes freewriting on each of them. Try not to settle for a topic that seems only mildly interesting. Instead, look for that "Aha!" experience, the emotional reaction that identifies a topic that really moves you.

1. Give examples of *one* particular personality characteristic of your own. Are you a hard-working, "Type A" personality? Do you overeat when you experience stress, anger, or boredom? Are you sometimes too outspoken? Are you overly impulsive? Choose <u>one</u> personality characteristic of your own and illustrate it with examples.

2. Give examples of *one* particular personality characteristic of someone you know. Choose someone close to you—a family member, a close friend, or someone you work with or have known for a while. Identify *one* of that person's personality characteristics, and then illustrate it with examples.

3. Have you ever found that at times telling a lie is the ethical, responsible thing to do? Have you ever told a lie to protect someone from danger or from unnecessary pain? Use specific examples to illustrate times when lying seemed to you to be the correct, responsible behavior.

4. Take any simple statement that you know to be true and illustrate it with specific examples. Consider ideas like these:

   Last year's rains damaged many homes in my hometown.

   The food served in some restaurants can have appalling things happen to it while it is still in the kitchen.

   At last year's comic convention I was introduced to some of the weirdest people that I have ever seen.

   The Sun City Senior Center is full of people who have led exciting, adventurous lives.

   Some people treat their pets as if they were people.

5. Have you ever experienced intolerance or bigotry because of your race, gender, religious beliefs, or age? Write a paper in which you use specific examples to illustrate what has happened to you.

6. People sometimes say that the simplest things in life are the most valuable. If you agree, use specific examples to illustrate the truth of that statement in your own life.

7. Choose a sport, activity, or hobby with which you are familiar. Use specific examples to illustrate something that you know to be true about it.

8. Use examples to illustrate an idea about something that you own: your car, an animal, your computer, your clothing.

9. Choose a statement that people commonly believe to be true and use examples to show why it is or is not true in your life. Here are some examples:

   Whatever can go wrong will go wrong.

   Sometimes help can come from the most unlikely places.

   If you try hard enough, you will succeed.

   You can't tell who your real friends are until you need help.

10. Choose a technological device—the computer, cell phone, answering machine, fax machine, etc.—and use examples to illustrate your attitude toward it.

Choosing and Narrowing the Topic

As you choose your topic, remember that a more specific focus will result in a better paper than a more general focus. For example, don't try to give examples of a topic as general as *problems in the United States*. There are hundreds of possible examples of such a general topic, so all you would be able to do is briefly list a few of them, without going into detail about any. On the other hand, a more focused topic, such as *problems caused by my father's excessive drinking,* could certainly be supported by several detailed, descriptive examples.

Writing a Topic Sentence

If your assignment is to write a single paragraph, use your prewriting to decide upon a narrowed topic and a limited central point. Then write a topic sentence that can be supported with examples. Examine your topic sentence closely. Not all statements suggest that examples will follow. Consider the following sentences. Which would cause a reader to expect examples as support? Which would not?

⊚⊚ EXAMPLES

1. Last summer I had a chance to visit Toronto, Canada.

2. Many people on the corner of Queen and Peter streets in Toronto, Canada, looked as if they had stepped directly out of the 1960s.

Sentence 1 merely states a fact. It does not cause one to expect examples. Sentence 2 would cause a reader to expect examples of the people on Queen and Peter streets.

⊚⊚ EXAMPLES

3. Some of my best friends today used to be some of my worst enemies.

4. One of my best friends recently made a very unwise decision.

Sentence 3 causes one to expect examples of friends who used to be enemies. Sentence 4 would cause a reader to expect an explanation of the decision and why it was unwise, but it does not suggest that several examples will follow.

Prewriting Application: Working with Topic Sentences

Identify the topic sentences in Exercises 1C (page 162), 2C (page 174), and 3C (page 191). Then identify the topic and the central point in each topic sentence.

Prewriting Application: Evaluating Topic Sentences

Write "No" before each sentence that would not make a good topic sentence *for this assignment*. Write "Yes" before each sentence that would make a good one. Using ideas of your own, rewrite the unacceptable topic sentences into topic sentences that might work.

_____ **1.** I have many different personality characteristics.

_____

_____

_____ **2.** Computers are supposed to be convenient, time-saving machines, but mine has brought me nothing but trouble.

_____

_____

_____ **3.** People who believe that money can't buy happiness have obviously never met my uncle.

_____

_____

_____ **4.** Basketball has been my favorite sport for as long as I can remember.

_____

_____

_____ **5.** After having owned a horse for ten years, I have decided that my particular horse has to be one of the stupidest animals alive.

_____

_____

_____ **6.** Whenever I go to a garage sale or a swap meet, I end up buying some absolutely useless item.

_____

_____

_____ **7.** My paragraph is about why Idaho holds such pleasant memories for so many people.

_____

_____

_____ **8.** My best friend's parties always seem to turn into near riots.

_____

_____

_____ **9.** Our country is a wonderful place to live, but it has many serious problems that need to be resolved.

_____

_____

_____ **10.** My father believes that we should never lie, but sometimes his honesty is so painful it is almost cruel.

_____

_____

Prewriting Application: Talking to Others

Once you have decided on a topic and a preliminary topic sentence, you need to develop your examples. A good way to do so is to tell three or four other members of your class why your topic sentence is true. Think of yourself as an attorney before a jury. You must provide the evidence—the examples—to support the central idea in your topic sentence.

For example, if your topic is that your father's honesty borders on cruelty, convince the other people in your group with brief, specific examples. Consider these questions as you discuss your topics.

1. Exactly where and when does each example occur? Have the place and time of each instance been clearly identified?

2. Can you visualize the examples? Are the people mentioned in the example identifed by name or by relationship? Are physical features specifically named or described?

3. What point do these examples reveal? Should the topic sentence be revised to express that point more clearly?

4. Are you convinced? Have enough examples been provided to illustrate the topic idea? Should any of the examples be more convincing?

5. Which example should be used first in the paper? Last?

Organizing Examples

Examples can be organized a number of ways. Sometimes a **chronological order** is best, arranging examples according to *when* they occurred. Sometimes a **spatial order** would work well, arranging examples by *physical location*. Many times an **emphatic order** should be used, arranging examples from *least to most important* (or, sometimes, from most to least important).

Prewriting Application: Organizing Examples

First, arrange the following examples in chronological order, numbering them 1, 2, 3, 4, 5. Then arrange them in spatial order. Then arrange them in emphatic order. If you prefer one arrangement over another, explain why.

Topic Sentence: My father thinks that the junk he buys at swap meets and garage sales makes terrific household decorations.

_____   He bought a warped wooden tennis racket a few months ago for five dollars and nailed it above our front door. He thinks it makes our house look "sporty."

_____   On the hallway wall is a cuckoo clock that he bought last Saturday. The bird is missing one of its wings, and the clock will not keep correct time anymore. He thought it was a real bargain because he got the clock for one dollar.

_____   Upstairs in our guest bedroom is a faded velvet picture of Elvis Presley and another one of some dogs playing poker. He bought them last year for ten dollars each.

_____   When we used to live in Big Bear, California, he spent $75 for a huge moth-eaten moose head that turned out to be crawling with bugs that infested our whole house. It's now mounted over the fireplace in the living room.

_____   Two plastic pink flamingos are stuck into our front lawn. Dad bought them the weekend we moved into this house. He says they add "character" to our home.

Writing the Paragraph

Write the first draft of your paragraph. Your first sentence should be your preliminary topic sentence. After writing the topic sentence, write the examples that illustrate your point. Devote several sentences to each example and be as specific and as detailed as you can in each of those sentences.

Using Transitions

Transitions are words, phrases, or clauses that let the reader know when you are moving from one idea or example to another. They are essential for clear writing because they help your readers follow your train of thought. Since you will be writing several examples in one paragraph for this assignment, you need to let your readers know when one example has ended and another is beginning. Use common transitional phrases such as those below to introduce each new example:

for example	to illustrate
for instance	another example of

Notice how transitional words and phrases are used to introduce examples in Exercise 2C, page 174.

EXAMPLES   **For example,** the names of several of our weekdays—Tuesday, Wednesday, Thursday, and Friday—derive from Norse mythology.

Other common words derive from Greek mythology.

For instance, the word *tantalize* refers to Tantalus, who was a king condemned to Hades as a punishment for his crimes.

Finally, Roman mythology, which in many ways parallels Greek mythology, is another source of many English words.

For example, the month of January is named after Janus, the Roman god with two faces.

Writing Application: Identifying Transitional Sentences

Examine Exercises 1C (page 162) and 3C (page 191). In each paragraph, identify the transitions that introduce each example.

Rewriting and Improving the Paragraph

1. Once your first draft is complete, read it over to determine how you can improve the examples you have used. In particular, try to make the examples as specific and as concrete as you can. Use actual names of people and places and refer to specific details whenever possible.

2. As you read your draft, make sure you can tell where each of your examples ends and the next begins. Revise your transitional sentences as needed to make them clearer.

3. If your preliminary topic sentence can be improved so that it more accurately states the central point of your paragraph, change it now.

4. Examine your draft for sentences that can be combined using participial phrases, appositives, infinitive phrases, or adjective clauses. Combine such sentences the way you did in the Sentence Combining Exercises.

Rewriting Application: Responding to Writing

Read the following paragraph. Then respond to the questions following it.

I Enjoy H_2O to Relax

Whenever I feel stressed, I find that I can relax best if I am near the water. For example, as a teenager living in San Bernardino, I would drive many miles into the local foothills of the mountains, where a small river or a large stream called Lytle Creek was located in the little town of Applewhite. I would walk down between the trees and then over all of the rocks to find a place where I would sit for hours. I enjoyed watching the water rush by because it made me become very relaxed. Then, in the late 1980s, I moved to San Diego County. My first apartment was in Escondido, and times were troubled and stressful nearly every day, yet I was able to find comfort by driving to Lake Dixon. After several weekend trips I began taking this drive at all different times of the week. Usually alone, but sometimes with my boys, I would go to the lake and feed the ducks or just fish from the shore. Now, living in San Marcos, I prefer the ultimate water experience by relaxing at the beach. During most of my quick trips, I drive down Del Dios Highway and across the railroad tracks into Solana Beach parking lot. I walk down the large ramp and sit on the sand or walk along the shoreline to the cave. Watching the water really washes away any troubles that I brought with me. It seems to clear my head and to bring a warm feeling of contentment to my soul. In conclusion, no matter whether the water is a stream, lake, or ocean, its appearance and its soothing sounds take away all of my stress and troubles.

1. Identify the topic sentence. State its topic and central idea. Is it an effective topic sentence? Why or why not?

2. Identify the transitional sentences that introduce each example.

3. Are the examples specific? Point out which words in each example identify specific places or things.

4. Which words in each example would you make still more specific?

5. Which example is the most effective? Why? Which one would you improve? How?

Proofreading

Before you do the final editing of your paper, revise it one more time. If the topic sentence needs work, improve it now. Check the examples. Are they as specific and descriptive as they can be? Add transitional sentences between examples. Wherever you can, combine related sentences using subordinate clauses as well as participial and infinitive phrases.

Now edit the paper. Check your draft for any of the following errors:

- Sentence fragments

- Comma splices

- Fused sentences

- Misplaced modifiers

- Dangling modifiers

- Misspelled words

Prepare a clean final draft, following the format your instructor has requested. Before you turn in your final draft, proofread it carefully and make any necessary corrections.

Moving from Paragraph to Essay

All of the assignments so far have asked you to write single paragraphs, but most college classes will ask you to produce essays consisting of several paragraphs.

Writing an essay is not really much different from writing a paragraph. An essay focuses on and develops one central idea, just as a paragraph does. The central idea of an essay is called its **thesis statement.**

The main difference between an essay and a paragraph is that the supporting material in an essay is longer and more complicated, so it needs to be separated into different body paragraphs, each with its own **topic sentence.**

Recognizing Essay Form

An essay consists of an introductory paragraph, one or more body paragraphs, and a concluding paragraph.

- The *introductory paragraph* includes the **thesis statement** (usually as the last sentence of the first paragraph).

- Each *body paragraph* starts with a **topic sentence** that supports the thesis statement. The central idea of each body paragraph is supported with **facts, examples, and details.**

- The *concluding paragraph* brings the essay to a close, often by restating the central idea of the essay.

Introductory Paragraph

Introductory sentences
ending with a
thesis statement

Body Paragraphs

Topic sentence
supported with
facts, examples, and details

Topic sentence
supported with
facts, examples, and details

> **Topic sentence**
>
> supported with
>
> facts, examples, and details

Concluding Paragraphs

> Concluding sentences
>
> bringing the essay
>
> to a close

Choosing and Narrowing a Thesis Statement

A **thesis statement** states the topic and the central idea of an entire essay, just as a topic sentence states the topic and central idea of a paragraph. Like a topic sentence, a thesis statement needs to be narrowed and focused so that it does not try to cover too much material in a short essay.

Consider the following sentences. Which is narrowed enough to function as a thesis statement in a brief essay?

EXAMPLES

1. Many people have problems when they move to a new place.

2. Immigrants face many obstacles when they move to the United States.

3. Immigrants who do not yet speak English will encounter several obstacles when they try to get a job in the United States.

Sentence 1 is much too broad for any essay at all. Both sentences 2 and 3 could work as thesis statements, but sentence 3 will work better in a brief essay because it is narrowed to the topic of *Immigrants who do not yet speak English,* and its central point is focused on *obstacles when they try to get a job.* An essay with this thesis statement would devote a separate body paragraph to each obstacle to getting a job. Each body paragraph would then include examples of one or more immigrants who encountered that obstacle.

Writing the Essay

An essay takes more time to write than a paragraph, but the writing process itself is very similar.

- Generate topic ideas as well as supporting material by freewriting, brainstorming, and clustering.

- Focus your material on one central idea, expressed in a thesis statement.

- Divide your supporting material (examples, facts, details) into separate body paragraphs.

- Arrange your body paragraphs into a logical order, such as a chronological, spatial, or emphatic order.

- Write your first draft without worrying too much about the quality of your writing. Focus more on getting your ideas onto paper. You can improve them later.

Rewriting and Improving the Essay

Once you have a complete draft, consider these questions as you revise your paper.

- Do your opening sentences introduce the topic in a way that will interest a reader?

- Is your thesis sufficiently narrowed? Is it placed at the end of the introductory paragraph?

- Does each paragraph open with a topic sentence that clearly supports the thesis statement?

- Are the supporting facts and examples in each paragraph specific and clear?

- Does each paragraph contain enough examples?

- Are transitions used to move clearly from one idea to another?

- Does the conclusion close the essay in an interesting way?

Application: Working with Essay Form

Read the following student essay and answer the questions at the end.

Lying

My parents are two of the most honest people I have ever met. Ever since I can remember, they have told me that "Honesty is the best policy." My father says that lying only leads to more lying and that telling the truth is exactly the right thing to do. The problem is that I don't think they are right. There are times when the right thing to do is to tell a lie.

For example, sometimes lying can mean the difference between survival and disaster. I have a friend with two daughters, ages three and five. When her husband deserted her, she needed to find a job fast. But there was one problem. Every place where she applied asked if she had ever been convicted of a crime. She told the truth that she had been convicted of selling marijuana years ago, and she was politely shown out the door at Sears, Target, and Wal-Mart. It didn't matter that she hasn't used drugs or alcohol

---

now for over seven years. She needed to feed her children, so on her next job application she lied and got the job. I would have lied too.

Lying is also the right thing to do when you need to spare people any unnecessary pain in an emotional time. For instance, when I was in high school, a friend of mine named Melody died in a car accident, and the police believed drugs were involved. The parents refused to believe that their little girl would ever have taken drugs, but they didn't know everything about their daughter. Several of her friends and I knew that Melody had been using marijuana for a while. She had even tried cocaine a few times, but when her parents talked to us, we told them that she had never tried drugs. What good would telling the truth have done? It would only have hurt her parents more. So we lied.

I've also found that telling the truth can sometimes cause trouble among friends. There have been plenty of times when I have prevented a fight by not telling one friend what another one said about him or her. I've prevented these situations when I felt that the argument between the two was not worth fighting over.

I know that lying is not usually the right answer to a problem. But sometimes honesty isn't either. It seems to me that a person has to think about each situation and not live his life by general rules that don't always apply.

1. Underline the thesis statement. Is it sufficiently narrowed for a brief essay? Explain your response.

2. Now underline each topic sentence. Each topic sentence should clearly refer to and support the thesis statement. Explain how each one does so.

3. Look at the introductory sentences before the thesis statement. What function do they serve?

4. Look at the examples in each body paragraph. Which examples are the strongest? Why? Which are the weakest? Why?

5. Consider the organization of the three body paragraphs. Should it be changed at all? Explain why or why not.

6. Look at the concluding paragraph. Does it close the essay effectively? Why or why not?

Proofreading

As with all of your papers, proofread your essay carefully before you submit it.

Chapter 3 Practice Test

I. Review of Chapters One and Two

A. In the following sentences, identify the underlined words by writing one of the following abbreviations above the words: noun (N), pronoun (Pro), verb (V), adjective (Adj), adverb (Adv), conjunction (Conj), or preposition (Prep).

1. The <u>soldiers</u> and marines in Iraq <u>dress</u> differently from their counterparts in Vietnam.

2. The soldiers and marines in Iraq <u>always </u>look the same, <u>with</u> nothing extra added or written on their uniforms.

3. In Vietnam, the soldiers and marines were <u>blatantly</u> informal, with all kinds of things written on their <u>dirty</u> helmets and sweat-stained flak jackets.

4. The troops <u>in</u> Vietnam were mostly draftees, <u>so</u> many of them did not want to be there.

5. The troops in Iraq <u>are </u>an all-volunteer army <u>who</u> consider themselves professional.

B. In the following sentences, underline the subjects once and the complete verbs twice. Put parentheses around all prepositional phrases.

6. Albert Einstein never liked his mathematics classes during his time in school.

7. Will Queequeg or Tashtego learn how to harpoon in time?

8. Captain Ahab came on deck and addressed his crew.

9. In our English classes, we study irregular verbs; however, linguists call them "strong" verbs.

10. After Thetis dipped her son in the river, she dried him with a towel.

C. Compose sentences of your own according to the instructions.

11. Write a simple sentence with one subject, two verbs, and at least one prepositional phrase.

_____

_____

12. Write a compound sentence. Use a coordinating conjunction and appropriate punctuation to join the two clauses.

_____

_____

continued

13. Write a complex sentence that starts with a subordinate clause. Use appropriate punctuation.

_____

_____

14. Write a complex sentence that uses the subordinator *who*.

_____

_____

15. Write a compound-complex sentence. Use the conjunction *so* and the subordinator *when*.

_____

_____

D. Identify the following items as being correct (C), fused (F), comma splice (CS), or fragment (Frag). Then correct the errors. If a sentence is correct, do nothing to it.

_____**16.** The famous American writer John Updike died this year, appropriately, *The New Yorker* devoted an entire issue to him.

_____

_____

_____**17.** Alexander Skarsgard, who plays one of the main characters in the HBO series *Generation Kill*.

_____

_____

_____**18.** When she looked into Krishna's mouth, she saw the entire universe.

_____

_____

continued

_____ **19.** Arnold Vosloo performed well in *The Mummy*, however no one could take the place of Lon Chaney, Jr.

_____

_____

_____ **20.** Ishmael was baffled he could not see the relationship between a coffee shop and *Moby Dick*.

_____

_____

II. Chapter Three

A. Underline all infinitive and participial phrases and circle the words that they modify.

21. Rounding the tip of South America, Magellan headed into the Pacific.

22. In celebration of his new position, Steve's wife and daughters bought a gift certificate to give to him after dinner.

23. Not everyone was happy for the man elected President in the recent elections.

24. The sword hanging on the wall once belonged to King Arthur.

25. The package to give to the mail carrier is sitting by the front door.

B. Add infinitive or participial phrases to the following sentences at the places indicated. Use the verbs in parentheses.

26. The treasure map ^ was almost impossible to read. (discover)

_____

_____

27. ^ Blanche dimmed all of the lights. (conceal)

_____

_____

continued

28. The commercials ^ cost a great deal of money. (show)

_____

_____

29. Clyde thought that Bonnie's plan ^ was a good one. (steal)

_____

_____

30. ^ the paramedics rushed her to the hospital. (look)

_____

_____

C. Underline the adjective clauses and appositives in the following sentences and circle the words they modify.

31. Fritz Perls, a famous psychotherapist, developed the concept of Gestalt therapy.

32. The arrow that William Tell shot split the apple.

33. Cochise, who was a great Apache leader, resisted attempts to move his tribe from

Arizona to New Mexico.

34. Cole was heartbroken because he had lost his blanket, a camouflage-colored binky.

35. *Slumdog Millionaire*, which was filmed in Mumbai, won an Oscar for best picture.

D. Add adjective clauses or appositives to the following sentences and punctuate them correctly.

36. Romeo drove his new car to the costume party.

_____

_____

continued

37. *Sex and the City* must have been good for the shoe and clothing industry.

_____

_____

38. DNA analysis has helped to solve many crimes.

_____

_____

39. Even though many other puppets encouraged him, Elmo refused to go near the garbage can.

_____

_____

40. Sophocles discussed his new play with his wife.

_____

_____

E. Underline and then correct any dangling or misplaced modifiers in the following sentences. Do nothing if a sentence is correct.

41. Rocco read the short story to the creative writing class that he had found in his attic.

_____

_____

42. Running out the door, Cynthia almost forgot her briefcase.

_____

_____

continued

43. Digging deep into his demented memory, the crucial turning point came to The Joker.

_____

_____

44. To get from here to there, asking Mark Twain for directions is recommended.

_____

_____

45. Ms. Schmidt only bought the 1988 Mercedes for two thousand dollars.

_____

_____

46. Thinking it was a peace offering, the Trojan Horse was wheeled into the city.

_____

_____

47. The column of army ants terrified Homer and Hortense, swarming over the sweet

potato pie, who were both afraid of bugs.

_____

_____

48. Scratching his head in frustration, Aesop's imagination could not think of a tale to tell.

_____

_____

continued

49. Drifting down the river at night and hiding during the day, Huck and Jim wondered

if they would ever reach Cairo.

_____

_____

50. Two young boys who were whispering to each other quietly crept toward their

unsuspecting sister.

_____

_____

Lining Up the Parts of a Sentence

The Careful Writer

As you have probably already noticed, effective writing is less a matter of inspiration and more a matter of making innumerable choices and paying careful attention to detail. Strictly speaking, every word in each of your sentences represents a specific choice on your part. Good writers carefully choose words and their positions in sentences, not only to be grammatically correct but also to make their writing clear and concise.

Although close attention to detail alone will not ensure good writing, it does have a number of advantages. The most important reason for you to take care in your writing is to make certain that you communicate your ideas clearly. As you can see from having worked through the last chapter, if your sentences contain misplaced or dangling modifiers, your reader will sometimes be confused about what you mean. In addition, a clear and careful piece of writing in itself creates a good impression, just as a well-tended lawn does. You have probably already found that people are often judged by their writing. If your writing is carefully thought out and presented with an attention to correctness and detail, it will be taken seriously.

Making sure that your sentences are correctly constructed and checking to see that your modifiers clearly and logically modify the right words are two ways of taking care in your writing. In this chapter we will discuss a few others: paying attention to the special relationship between those two most important parts of your sentences, the subjects and verbs; making sure that the pronouns you use are in their correct forms; and checking the connection between your pronouns and the words they stand for.

Subject–Verb Agreement

One reason you need to be able to identify subjects and verbs accurately is that the form of the verb often changes to match the form of its subject. If the subject of your sentence is singular, your verb must be singular. If the subject is plural, your verb must be plural. This matching of the verb and its subject is called **subject–verb agreement.**

You need to pay special attention to subject–verb agreement when you use present tense verbs. **Most present tense verbs that have singular subjects end in "s." Most present tense verbs that have plural subjects do not end in "s."** Here are some examples.

Singular	*Plural*
The dog barks.	The dogs bark.
He walks.	They walk.
It is.	They are.
The man has.	The men have.
She does.	They do.

Notice that in each case the verb ends in "s" when the subject is singular. This rule can be confusing because an "s" at the end of a <u>noun</u> almost always means that the noun is plural, but **an "s" at the end of a <u>verb</u> almost always means it is singular.**

☺☺ PRACTICE

Change the subjects and verbs in the following sentences from singular to plural or from plural to singular. You may need to add *a, an,* or *the* to some of the sentences.

1. At night, the mockingbirds sing too loudly.

   At night, the mockingbird sings too loudly.

2. The toy poodle escapes from the yard nearly every day.

   _____

3. My friends often visit me at school.

   _____

4. The text message has made everything even worse.

   _____

5. His explanations always confuse the entire class.

Identifying Subjects: A Review

1. <u>Make sure you accurately identify the subject.</u> Sentences usually contain several nouns and pronouns.

EXAMPLE   The **boys** from the private **school** on the other **side** of **town** often use our gymnasium.

This sentence contains five nouns, but only *boys* is the subject.

2. <u>Remember that a noun or pronoun that is part of a prepositional phrase cannot be the subject.</u>

EXAMPLE   **Each** of the children takes a vitamin with breakfast.

The subject is *Each*, not *children*, because *children* is part of a prepositional phrase.

3. <u>Indefinite pronouns can be subjects.</u> The indefinite pronouns are listed on page 5.

EXAMPLE   **Everyone** sitting at the tables under the trees has a picnic lunch.

Subject–Verb Agreement: Points to Know

1. <u>Two subjects joined by *and* are plural.</u>

EXAMPLES
```
          S             S      V
```
The **boy** <u>and</u> his **dog were** far from home.

```
 S        S     V
```
Ham <u>and</u> **rye make** a delicious combination.

2. <u>However, if a subject is modified by *each* or *every*, it is singular.</u>

EXAMPLES
```
          S      S                V
```
<u>Every</u> **boy** and **girl** at the party <u>was</u> **given** a present to take home.

```
          S          S            V
```
<u>Each</u> **envelope** and **piece** of paper <u>has</u> the name of the company on it.

3. The following indefinite pronouns are singular.

EXAMPLES

anybody	either	neither	one
anyone	everybody	nobody	somebody
anything	everyone	no one	someone
each	everything	nothing	something

EXAMPLES

$\quad$ S $\qquad\qquad\qquad$ V
Each of the band members **has** a new uniform.

$\quad$ S $\qquad\qquad\qquad$ V
Everyone sitting under the trees **is** part of my family.

4. A few nouns and indefinite pronouns, such as *none, some, all, most, more, half,* or *part* may sometimes be considered plural and sometimes singular, depending on the prepositional phrases that follow them. If the object of the preposition is singular, treat the subject and verb as singular. If the object of the preposition is plural, treat the subject and verb as plural.

EXAMPLES

$\qquad\qquad\qquad\qquad$ S $\qquad$ V
(singular) $\quad$ **None** of the cake **is** left.

$\qquad\qquad\qquad\qquad$ S $\qquad$ V
(plural) $\quad$ **None** of the people **are** here.

PRACTICE

Place an "S" above the subjects and underline the correct verb form in the parentheses.

$\qquad\qquad\qquad\qquad\qquad$ S $\qquad\qquad$ S
1. In the writing lab, a teacher and a student (was <u>were</u>) working on a piece of writing.

2. The rooster adopted by our neighbor's children (crows crow) at dawn every day.

3. Every firefighter and police officer in the city (has have) brought an item to the auction.

4. A plate of possum pie and a bowl of collard greens (sounds sound) like a great way to start the day.

5. Some of the bike riders from the southern towns (wear wears) brightly colored scarves to the convention.

6. Each glass bottle and plastic container (was were) recovered from the trash and recycled.

7. Somebody from one of our local schools (has have) won the prestigious Peacock scholarship.

8. The movie's soundtrack and pacing (appeals appeal) to me more than its plot and characterization.

9. A squirrel with two cats chasing it (was were) running down the street.

10. Most of the earth's surface (is are) covered by water.

---

5. <u>When subjects are joined by *or* or *nor*, the verb agrees with the closer subject.</u> If one subject is singular and one is plural, place the plural subject closer to the verb to avoid awkwardness.

EXAMPLES

(singular subjects)   Neither **Alberto** nor his **brother knows** what to do.

(plural subjects)   Either the **actors** or the **screenwriters have decided** to strike.

(singular and)   Neither **Alberto** nor his **sisters were** at last night's
(plural subjects)   concert.

NOTE: When you have helping verbs in a sentence, the helping verb—not the main verb—changes form.

EXAMPLES

Does Alberto or his **brother** want to go fishing?

Have the **actors** or **screenwriters** decided to strike?

6. <u>Collective nouns usually take the singular form of the verb.</u> Collective nouns represent groups of people or things, but they are considered singular. Here are some common collective nouns.

audience	crowd	herd
band	family	jury
class	flock	number
committee	government	society
company	group	team

EXAMPLES

The **audience was** delighted when the curtain slowly rose to reveal the orchestra already seated.

My **family goes** to Yellowstone National Park every summer.

7. The relative pronouns *that, which,* and *who* may be either singular or plural. When one of these pronouns is the subject of a verb, you will need to know which word it refers to before you decide whether it is singular or plural.

EXAMPLES

(singular)   I bought the <u>peach</u> **that was** ripe.

(plural)   I bought the <u>peaches</u> **that were** ripe.

(plural)   Colleen is one of the <u>students</u> **who are** taking flying lessons.

(singular)   Colleen is the only <u>one</u> of the students **who is** taking flying lessons.

PRACTICE   Place an "S" above the subjects and underline the correct verb forms in the parentheses.

1. Neither the money nor my excuses for the accident (pleases <u>please</u>)

   Mr. Hernandez.

2. A family of porcupines (has have) taken up residence in my cellar.

3. Rory is one of the dogs that (plays play) Frisbee so well.

4. Neither Angelina nor Jennifer (knows know) that Madonna plans to adopt

   a child.

5. His pet albino porcupine or his three striped iguanas (seem seems) to take

   all of Al's attention.

6. That crowd of people at the end of the pier (belongs belong) to the Polar

   Bear Club.

7. Henry is the only citizen in Concord who (refuses refuse) to pay taxes.

8. (Has Have) the eggplant casserole or the vegetarian omelet been added to

   tomorrow's menu?

9. The speeches that Senator Cassius makes (impress impresses) the people

   each time.

10. Esperanza is one of the triathletes who (does do) not know how to swim.

8. A few nouns end in "s" but are usually considered singular; they take the singular form of the verb. These nouns include *economics*, *gymnastics*, *mathematics*, *measles*, *mumps*, *news*, *physics*, and *politics*.

EXAMPLES

                    S   V

World **economics** <u>has</u> been an important international issue for years.

     S   V

Gymnastics <u>is</u> one of the most popular events in the Olympics.

9. When units of measurement for distance, time, volume, height, weight, money, and so on are used as subjects, they take the singular verb form.

EXAMPLES

        S   V

Two **teaspoons** of sugar **was** all that the cake recipe called for.

      S V

Five **dollars** <u>is</u> too much to pay for a hot dog.

10. In a question or in a sentence that begins with *there* or *here*, the order of the subject and verb is reversed.

EXAMPLES

    V   S

Was the **bus** on time?

    V   S

Is there a squeaking **wheel** out there somewhere?

      V   S

There **is** an **abundance** of wildflowers in the desert this spring.

     V   S

Here **are** the **keys** to your car.

11. The verb must agree only with the **subject**.

EXAMPLE

             S   V

Our biggest **problem is** termites in the attic.

The singular verb form *is* is correct here because the subject is the singular noun *problem*. The plural noun *termites* does not affect the form of the verb.

PRACTICE

Place an "S" above the subjects and underline the correct verb forms in the parentheses.

          S

1. Mathematics (<u>remains</u> remain) one of the hardest subjects for students.

2. Fifteen inches of rain (fall falls) in Murrieta every winter.

3. The topic at today's meeting (is are) the six chickens I keep in my backyard.

4. The news of Demeter's missing daughter (has have) cast a shadow across the land.

5. Gymnastics (does do) not interest Antonio nearly as much as competitive ice fishing.

6. After deliberating for three days, the jury in the Mallory trial (has have) not yet reached a verdict.

7. Five ounces of gold (sells sell) for nearly $5,000 today.

8. Here, alive and well-fed, (is are) the two-headed horned toad and the legless lizard from the pet store down the street.

9. Esther's favorite hobby (requires require) paper clips and pots of glue.

10. Ten miles of unpaved road (lies lie) between my house and the beach.

Section One Review

1. In the present tense, when the subject is a singular noun or a singular pronoun, the verb form usually will end in "s."

2. **Subject–verb agreement:** points to know

    a. Two subjects joined by *and* are plural.

    b. If a subject is modified by *each* or *every,* it is singular.

    c. Indefinite pronouns are usually singular.

    d. Sometimes indefinite pronouns like *some, half,* or *part* are considered plural, depending on the prepositional phrases that follow them.

    e. When subjects are joined by *or* or *nor,* the verb agrees with the closer subject. If one subject is singular and one is plural, place the plural subject closer to the verb to avoid awkwardness.

    f. When a collective noun, such as *family* or *group,* is the subject, the singular form of the verb is used.

    g. The relative pronouns *that, which,* and *who* may be either singular or plural, depending upon the word the pronoun refers to.

    h. A few nouns, such as *economics* or *news,* end in "s" but are usually considered singular.

    i. When the subject is a unit of measurement, such as distance, weight, or money, the singular form of the verb is used.

    j. In a question or in a sentence that begins with *there* or *here,* the verb will often come before the subject.

    k. The verb must agree only with the **subject.**

Exercise 1A

Circle the subjects and underline the correct verb forms in the parentheses.

1. (Anyone) with plaid pants and pink shoes (<u>was</u> were) let into the golf tournament free.

2. Neither the police officer nor the two firefighters (knows know) what to do with the Cheshire cat in the tree.

3. Both his mother and his uncle (has have) been puzzled by Hamlet's behavior.

4. Near the Christmas tree at the back of the stage (stands stand) Clara and Herr Drosselmeyer.

5. Of all the subjects Angela is studying, economics (interest interests) her the most.

6. An alligator carrying two babies on its back (floats float) slowly through the Everglades.

7. Six hundred tons of wheat (was were) not enough to feed the victims of the drought.

8. A little pig with two of his friends (loves love) his new house of straw.

9. (Has Have) the committee decided what to do about that troll under the bridge?

10. Every lost boy and evil pirate on the island (enjoys enjoy) the stories that Wendy reads.

11. According to the report, high school gymnastics (cause causes) more injuries than football.

12. Everybody on both shores of the river (wants want) to help rebuild the levee.

13. Two weeks with his daughter Regan (was were) too much for Lear and his men.

14. A family of hedgehogs (has have) moved into our boathouse.

15. Everyone from both baseball teams (is are) invited to the party after the game.

Exercise 1B

Correct any subject–verb agreement errors in the following sentences. If a sentence is correct, do nothing to it. To check your answers, circle the subjects.

1. Neither (Horatio) nor (Fortinbras) ~~want~~ *wants* to clean up the mess.

2. In spring every one of the trees in our yard fill with leaves.

3. Each mountain and river were surveyed by Lewis and Clark.

4. Our nation's troubled economics are the topic of the President's address.

5. The winged statue with no head and the portrait of the woman with the enigmatic smile appears in the museum.

6. Mrs. Hutchinson is one of the villagers who supports the lottery.

7. A herd of bison often wander through Hayden Valley in Yellowstone National Park.

8. Do either Cupid or Eros plan to attend the Valentine's Day party?

9. Benvolio and another member of the Montague family has decided to go to the party.

10. Benedict Arnold is one of the colonists who has secretly decided to support the British.

11. Fernando and his car club travels to Mammoth Lakes each spring.

12. As the days grow longer, nearly everyone in my neighborhood begin to spend more time outdoors.

13. Five hundred feet of kite string have been found tangled in Charlie Brown's tree.

14. There is a man in clown suit and a boy dressed like a duck standing in Bruce's grapefruit orchard.

15. Two gallons of hot sauce were added to the recipe at the last minute.

Exercise 1C

Correct all subject–verb agreement errors. Not all sentences will contain errors.

1. One divorce in our family ~~have~~ *has* had many unpleasant consequences. 2. Everyone in my family, including my aunts and uncles, were affected when my grandparents decided to divorce.

3. One of the most glaring effects of their divorce are my grandparents' financial difficulties.

4. Now that the divorce is final, the assets that once belonged to both of them has been divided.

5. As a result, both my grandmother and my grandfather struggles to pay rent on separate apartments. 6. My grandmother, who hasn't worked in years, now work as a secretary for a realty company. 7. These financial problems causes bitterness between my grandmother and grandfather. 8. Another unfortunate result of their divorce are the many awkward situations at family get-togethers. 9. Today my grandmother won't even come to a family event if my grandfather plan to attend. 10. Without both of them there, everybody feel rather sad.

11. Finally, their divorce seem to have created dissension in the family. 12. When my grandparents argue, my grandfather always ask my mother and her brothers and sisters to agree with him. 13. If some of them takes the other side, he feels angry. 14. There has been many instances when he even yells at some of them. 15. Clearly, my grandparents' divorce have damaged our family. 16. I hope there is no future separations among my family members.

SECTION 2

Pronoun Agreement and Reference

Pronoun–Antecedent Agreement

Because pronouns stand for or take the place of nouns, it is important that you make it clear in your writing which pronouns stand for which nouns. The noun that the pronoun takes the place of is called the **antecedent.** **Pronoun–antecedent agreement** refers to the idea that a pronoun must match or "agree with" the noun that it stands for in **person** and in **number.**

Person

Person in pronouns refers to the relationship of the speaker (or writer) to the pronoun. There are three persons: **first person, second person,** and **third person.**

1. **First person** pronouns refer to the person speaking or writing:

Singular	Plural
I	we
me	us
my, mine	our, ours

2. **Second person** pronouns refer to the person spoken or written to:

Singular	Plural
you	you
your	your
yours	yours

3. **Third person** pronouns refer to the person or thing spoken or written about:

Singular	Plural
he, she, it	they
him, her, it	them
his, her, hers, its	their, theirs

Because nouns are always in the third person, pronouns that refer to nouns should also be in the third person. Usually this rule poses no problem, but sometimes writers mistakenly shift from third to second person when they are referring to a noun.

EXAMPLE   When a new **student** first enters the large and crowded registration area, **you might** feel confused and intimidated.

In this sentence, *you* has mistakenly been used to refer to *student*. The mistake occurs because the noun *student* is in the third person, and the pronoun *you* is in the second person. There are two ways to correct the sentence:

1. You can change the second person pronoun *you* to a third person pronoun.

EXAMPLE   When a new **student** first enters the large and crowded registration area, **he or she** might feel confused and intimidated.

2. You can change the noun *student* to the second person pronoun *you*.

EXAMPLE   When **you** first enter the large and crowded registration area, **you** might feel confused and intimidated.

Here's another incorrect sentence.

EXAMPLE   Most **people** can stay reasonably healthy if **you** watch **your** diet and exercise several times a week.

One way to correct this sentence is to change *you* to *they* and *your* to *their* so that they agree with *people*.

EXAMPLE   Most **people** can stay reasonably healthy if **they** watch **their** diets and exercise several times a week.

PRACTICE   Correct any errors in pronoun person in the following sentences. When you correct the pronoun, you also may need to change the verb.

1. When a person first attends a college class, ~~you~~ *he or she* might feel nervous.

2. Most people are naturally uncomfortable when you are in a new environment.

3. A new student should try to arrive at the campus early, especially if you want to find a parking place.

4. When my daughter left home for her first class, you could see she was worried.

5. After the first week or so, you get used to the new routine.

Number

Errors in number are the most common pronoun–antecedent errors. To make pronouns agree with their antecedents in **number**, use singular pronouns to refer to singular nouns and plural pronouns to refer to plural nouns. The following guidelines will help you avoid errors in number.

1. Use plural pronouns to refer to words joined by *and* unless the words are modified by *each* or *every*.

EXAMPLE   General Ulysses S. Grant and General Dwight D. Eisenhower led their armies to victory.

2. Use singular pronouns to refer the following indefinite pronouns.

anybody	either	neither	one
anyone	everybody	nobody	somebody
anything	everyone	no one	someone
each	everything	nothing	something

EXAMPLES   **Everything** was in **its** place.

Neither of the girls wanted to give up **her** place in line.

One of the fathers was yelling loudly at **his** son throughout the game.

NOTE: In spoken English, the plural pronouns *they, them,* and *their* are often used to refer to the antecedents *everyone* or *everybody*. However, in written English, the singular pronoun is still more commonly used.

EXAMPLE   **Everybody** at the game cheered for **his** favorite team.

3. In general, use singular pronouns to refer to collective nouns.

EXAMPLE   The **troop** of soldiers had almost reached **its** camp when the blizzard started.

4. When antecedents are joined by *or* or *nor*, use a pronoun that agrees with the closer antecedent.

EXAMPLE   Neither **Chris** nor **Craig** wanted to spend his Saturday mowing the lawn.

NOTE: If one antecedent is singular and one is plural, place the plural antecedent last to avoid awkwardness. If one antecedent is female and one is male, rewrite the sentence to avoid awkwardness.

EXAMPLES

(awkward)   Either the **members** of the council or the **mayor** will send **his** regrets.

(rewritten)   Either the **mayor** or the **members** of the council will send **their** regrets.

(awkward)   Either **Mary** or **Ruben** will lend you **his** watch.

(rewritten)   You may borrow a watch from either Mary or Ruben.

PRACTICE

Correct any pronoun–antecedent errors in the following sentences. When you correct a pronoun, you may also need to change the verb.

1. If an accountant wants to do a good job, *he or she needs* ~~you need~~ to be careful and precise.

2. Everybody at the prison was angry when they were required to lie flat on the ground.

3. When parents read a story by the Brothers Grimm, you might scare your children.

4. The team from Atlanta was surprised when a fan objected to its "tomahawk chop."

5. Neither Galileo nor Copernicus could keep their eyes focused on the ground.

6. Someone with gray hair wants to read their poetry at the department meeting.

7. No one could tell us where the dog had misplaced its tail.

8. When a tourist visits Yosemite, you should not approach the bison.

9. Either Croesus or the Rockefellers left their dinner plates in my sink.

10. An immigrant from another country is often surprised when they see the size of a typical restaurant serving in the United States.

Sexist Language

In the past it was traditional to use masculine pronouns when referring to singular nouns whose gender could be either masculine or feminine. A good example is the sentence *A **person** should stop delivery of **his** newspaper before **he** leaves on a trip of more than a few days.* Although the noun *person* could be either masculine or feminine, masculine pronouns like *he* or *his* tended to be used in a case like this one.

Because women make up over 50 percent of the English-speaking population, they have been justifiably dissatisfied with this tradition. The problem is that the English language does not contain a singular personal pronoun that can refer to either sex at the same time in the way that the forms of *they* can.

The solutions to this problem can prove awkward. One of the solutions is to use feminine pronouns as freely as masculine ones to refer to singular nouns whose gender could be masculine or feminine. Either of the following sentences using this solution is acceptable.

EXAMPLES

A **person** should stop delivery on **her** newspaper before **she** leaves on a trip of more than a few days.

A **person** should stop delivery on **his** newspaper before **he** leaves on a trip of more than a few days.

Another solution is to change *his* to *his or her* and *he* to *he or she*. Then the sentence would look like this:

EXAMPLE

A **person** should stop delivery on **his or her** newspaper before **he or she** leaves on a trip of more than a few days.

As you can see, this solution does not result in a very graceful sentence. An alternative is to use *her/his* and *she/he*, but the result would be about the same. Sometimes a better solution is to change a singular antecedent to a plural one and use the forms of *they*, which can refer to either gender. That would result in a sentence like this:

EXAMPLE

People should stop delivery of **their** newspapers before **they** leave on a trip of more than a few days.

This sentence is less awkward and just as fair. Finally, in some situations, the masculine pronoun alone will be appropriate, and in others the feminine pronoun alone will be. Here are two such sentences:

EXAMPLES

Each of the hockey players threw **his** false teeth into the air after the victory. (The hockey team is known to be all male.)

The last runner on the relay team passed **her** opponent ten yards before the finish line. (All members of the relay team are female.)

Whatever your solutions to this problem, it is important that you be logical and correct in your pronoun–antecedent agreement in addition to being fair.

Unclear Pronoun Reference

Sometimes, even though a pronoun appears to agree with an antecedent, it is not clear exactly which noun in the sentence is the antecedent. And sometimes a writer will use a pronoun that does not clearly refer to any antecedent at all. The following two points will help you use pronouns correctly.

1. A pronoun should refer to a specific antecedent.

EXAMPLE   Mr. **Mellon** told **Larry** that **he** could take a vacation in late August.

In this sentence, *he* could refer to *Mr. Mellon* or to *Larry.* To correct this problem, you can eliminate the pronoun.

EXAMPLE   Mr. Mellon told Larry that **Larry** could take his vacation in late August.

Or you can revise the sentence so that the pronoun clearly refers to only one antecedent.

EXAMPLES   Mr. Mellon told **Larry** to take **his** vacation in late August.

OR

Mr. Mellon told Larry, "Take your vacation in late August."

Here is another example:

EXAMPLE   Every time **Patricia** looked at the **cat, she** whined.

In this sentence, the pronoun *she* could refer to *Patricia* or the *cat.* The pronoun reference needs to be clarified.

EXAMPLES   **Patricia** whined every time **she** looked at the cat.

OR

The **cat** whined every time Patricia looked at **her.**

PRACTICE   Revise the following sentences so that each pronoun refers to a specific antecedent.

1. Julio told his roommate that his new contact lenses were at the optometrist's office.

   Julio said to his roommate, "Your new contact lenses are at the optometrist's office."

2. When Abbott told Costello the names of the baseball players, he became very confused.

_____

_____

3. During the trip Michelle Obama spent time with Queen Elizabeth, and she did not act very friendly.

_____

_____

4. When Gary introduced his in-laws to his parents, he hoped they would not reveal his secret.

_____

_____

5. The famous archer shot an arrow through the apple on his son's head, and then he sold it on eBay.

_____

_____

2. Pronouns should not refer to implied or unstated antecedents. Be especially careful with the pronouns *this, that, which,* and *it.*

EXAMPLE

My baseball coach made us go without dinner if we lost a game; **this** was unfair.

In this sentence, there is no specific antecedent for the pronoun *this* to refer to. The following sentence clarifies the pronoun reference.

EXAMPLE

My baseball coach made us go without dinner if we lost a game; **this punishment** was unfair.

Sometimes a pronoun refers to a noun that is only implied in the first part of the sentence.

EXAMPLE

Mrs. Brovelli is a poet, **which** she does some of every day.

In this sentence, *which* apparently stands for "writing poetry," which is implied in the noun *poet*; however, there is no specific noun for the pronoun *which* to stand for. The faulty pronoun reference can be cleared up in several ways.

EXAMPLES   Mrs. Brovelli is a poet, and **she writes** poetry every day.

Mrs. Brovelli is a poet **who writes** poetry every day.

PRACTICE   Revise the following sentences so that each pronoun refers to a specific, not an implied or unstated, antecedent. To correct the sentence, you may have to eliminate the pronoun altogether.

1. I have always resisted learning how to serve oysters, which annoys my roommate.

   My resistance to learning how to serve oysters annoys

   my roommate.

2. The king shepherd barked all night when our neighbors were having a party, which made me call the police.

   _____

   _____

3. There were many pieces of glass on the kitchen floor, but Ibrahim had not broken it.

   _____

   _____

4. Rafiki was looking forward to watching the Padres play the Angels, but this wasn't what happened.

   _____

   _____

5. It rained all day Friday and then cleared up on Saturday, which ruined our plans.

   _____

   _____

Reflexive and Intensive Pronouns

The reflexive and intensive pronouns are those that end in *self* or *selves*. The singular pronouns end in *self*, and the plural ones end in *selves*.

Singular	*Plural*
myself	ourselves
yourself	yourselves
himself	themselves
herself	
itself	
oneself	

These are the only reflexive and intensive forms. Avoid nonstandard forms like *hisself, ourselfs, theirselves,* or *themselfs.*

The **reflexive pronouns** are used to reflect the action of a verb back to the subject.

EXAMPLE   Amos gave **himself** a bloody nose when he tried to slap a mosquito.

The **intensive pronouns** emphasize or intensify a noun or another pronoun in the sentence.

EXAMPLE   Let's have **Estella Cordova herself** show us how to cross-examine a witness in court.

To help you use intensive and reflexive pronouns correctly, remember these three points.

1. Do not use a reflexive pronoun unless it is reflecting the action of a verb back to a subject.

2. Do not use an intensive pronoun unless the sentence contains a noun or pronoun for it to emphasize or intensify.

3. In general, do not use a reflexive or intensive pronoun where a personal pronoun is called for. For example, reflexive and intensive pronouns are never used as subjects.

EXAMPLES   (incorrect)   Tim's mother and **myself** often go shopping together on Saturdays.

(correct)   Tim's mother and **I** often go shopping together on Saturdays.

(incorrect)   The other employees at the restaurant gave Carmen and **myself** large bouquets of flowers on the anniversary of our first year there.

(correct)   The other employees of the restaurant gave Carmen and **me** large bouquets of flowers on the anniversary of our first year there.

⟲⟳ PRACTICE   Correct any errors in the use of reflexive or intensive pronouns in the following sentences.

1. We decided to redecorate the den ~~ourself.~~ *ourselves.*

2. Lorenzo, a misanthrope, prefers to spend his days by hisself.

3. Homer and Hortense sent a dehydrated Spam omelet to ourselves for Christmas.

4. Whenever Fergal and myself have time, we meet for lunch at the Market Street Café.

5. After three gigs in a row, Pam and Eric finally had a weekend to themself.

⟲⟳ PRACTICE   Correct any errors in pronoun reference or in the use of reflexive and intensive pronouns in the following sentences.

1. I used to paint landscapes, but I do not like ~~it~~ *painting them* anymore.

2. Brent wondered if Frances and himself would make it to Hawaii this year.

3. My accountant filled in my tax return in pencil, and he took a large deduction for jelly doughnuts. This made the government suspicious.

4. Jose Luis apologized to his brother, but he was still angry.

5. When Thor himself arrived at the scene, a bolt of lightning fell from the clouds.

6. I could test my model boat in the pool, but it is not clean.

7. I have always enjoyed the genius of Picasso, which I saw two of at the museum.

8. John and Yoko spent some time by theirselves after their famous "bed-in" in Amsterdam.

9. Bean stuck a peppermint stick in his nose and broke it.

10. Charlotte Brontë told Emily that Anne's new novel was not as well-written as hers.

Section Two Review

1. The **antecedent** is the word a pronoun stands for.

2. A pronoun must agree with its **antecedent** in **person** and in **number.**

3. Use a plural pronoun to refer to antecedents joined by *and*.

4. Use a singular pronoun to refer to an **indefinite pronoun.**

5. Use a singular pronoun to refer to a **collective noun.**

6. When antecedents are joined by *or* or *nor,* use a pronoun that agrees with the closer antecedent.

7. Make sure a pronoun refers to a specific antecedent in its sentence or in the previous sentence.

8. Be sure that your pronoun does not refer to an implied or unstated antecedent.

9. A **reflexive pronoun** reflects the action of a verb back to the subject.

10. An **intensive pronoun** emphasizes or intensifies a noun or pronoun in the sentence.

11. Do not use a reflexive or intensive pronoun when a personal pronoun is called for.

Exercise 2A

Underline the correct pronouns in the parentheses.

1. Ms. Pelican likes to watch the 11 o'clock news, but Mr. Pelican doesn't consider (<u>it</u>/them) interesting.

2. Everyone who passes through airport security is asked to take off (his or her/their/your) shoes.

3. Habitat for Humanity was honored by the mayor for (its/their) philanthropic work in the community.

4. Either the *Niña,* the *Pinta,* or the *Santa Maria* had used up all of (its/their) fresh water.

5. Anyone who wants to compete for the scholarships must submit (his or her/their) applications by midnight.

6. Even though my brother offered to help, we decided to build the sand castle by (ourself/ourselfs/ourselves).

7. If a driver hears an ambulance or a police siren, (you/he or she/they) should pull over to the side of the road.

8. We have spent hours training our dogs, yet neither the rat terrier nor the papillon will come when we call (it/them).

9. Someone had told us that Mammoth Mountain was situated near a volcano, but we did not take (her/their) warning seriously.

10. As each visitor arrived, Homer offered (him or her/them) a tin of anchovies.

11. Icarus had tried to find a way out of the labyrinth by (hisself/himself) many times.

12. When a traveler passes the House of Usher, (you/he or she/they) should ignore the horrible shrieks coming from the second-story windows.

13. The bee outside my window or the spider on the wall will soon find (its/their) way into my new story.

14. As the boat crossed the River Lethe, one of the passengers lost (his/their) memory.

15. Every sumo wrestler threw salt into the ring before (his/their) match began.

Exercise 2B

Correct all errors in pronoun usage in the following sentences. Do nothing if the sentence is correct.

he or she

1. When a player has lost three games in a row, ~~you~~ can become rather frustrated.

2. When AIG offered large bonuses to their top-performing employees, the public was outraged.

3. Anyone in this town can pay their taxes at the coffee shop.

4. A colony of beavers is doing their best to build a dam across Murrieta Creek.

5. Neither Pinocchio nor Cyrano knew if their nose would keep growing.

6. When a citizen meets the queen, you should bow or curtsy, whichever is appropriate.

7. No one would join them, so Cameron and John decided to sail to Hawaii by theirselves.

8. Lance Armstrong is the best cyclist, which is my favorite sport.

9. The volcanologist asked my brother and myself if we had ever heard of Pompeii.

10. Priscilla told Rosalie that her mother had just been announced as this week's lottery winner.

11. There was not enough food, and it had started to rain, but this did not worry Felicitas.

12. Only one of the Seven Wonders of the Ancient World remains, which is hard to believe.

13. If a person quietly approaches that cave, you might see a monster with one eye.

14. Elton John, Eminem, and Dolly Parton performed together at the concert, which confused many people.

15. When Dante saw the sign above the entrance, he knew that Virgil and himself were in trouble.

Exercise 2C

Correct any errors in pronoun agreement or reference in the following paragraph.

1. Until recent years, a common practice of a newly married man was to lift his bride over the threshold of their new home. **2.** Few people know that this results from a number of ancient traditions. **3.** Perhaps the most ancient of them all is the tradition of marriage-by-capture. **4.** In many primitive societies, when a man wanted a woman from another tribe, you would seize them if they wandered too far from the protection of home. **5.** He would then force her to accompany himself back to his own tribe, and you would do battle with members of her tribe who tried to stop you. **6.** In this case, the connection to the bridegroom who picks up their bride and carries her into a new home is clear. **7.** This also comes from Roman times, when people believed that the threshold was guarded by both a good spirit and an evil spirit. **8.** The Romans believed that it would try to trip the bride as she stepped across the threshold, thus bringing bad luck to the groom and herself. **9.** To prevent this, each newly married man would carry their bride over the threshold. **10.** Finally, the practice of lifting your bride over the threshold was influenced by one other Roman tradition. **11.** Many Romans believed that something evil would happen if the bride placed their left foot across the threshold first. **12.** Since neither the groom nor the bride wanted to start the marriage out on the wrong foot, the groom would lift you over the threshold. **13.** Today, many newly married couples still practice this.

Pronoun Case

Pronouns, like verbs, can appear in a variety of different forms, depending on how they function in a sentence. For example, the pronoun that refers to the speaker in a sentence may be written as *I, me, my,* or *mine.* These different spellings are the result of what is called **pronoun case.**

The three pronoun cases for English are the **subjective,** the **objective,** and the **possessive.**

Subjective Case

Singular	*Plural*
I	we
you	you
he, she, it	they
who	who

Objective Case

Singular	*Plural*
me	us
you	you
him, her, it	them
whom	whom

Possessive Case

Singular	*Plural*
my, mine	our, ours
your, yours	your, yours
his, her, hers, its	their, theirs
whose	whose

Subjective Pronouns

The subjective pronouns are *I, we, you, he, she, it, they,* and *who.* They are used in two situations.

1. Subjective pronouns are used as subjects of sentences.

⊚ EXAMPLES

   S

I will return the car on Monday.

   S

They are trying to outwit me.

2. Subjective pronouns are used when they follow linking verbs. Because the linking verb <u>identifies</u> the pronoun after it with the subject, the pronoun must be in the same case as the subject.

EXAMPLES

S

It was **she** who won the award for being the best-dressed mud wrestler. (The subjective pronoun *she* is <u>identified</u> with the subject *it* by the linking verb *was.*)

S

That was I you saw rowing across the lake yesterday.

S

It was **they** who caused the huge traffic jam.

Objective Pronouns

The **objective pronouns** are *me, us, you, him, her, it, them,* and *whom.* They are used in three situations.

1. Objective pronouns are used as objects of prepositions.

EXAMPLES

Sally loved the chrysanthemums that Mr. Kim had given <u>to her</u>.

The difficulties <u>between Samantha and me</u> continued into the fall.

2. Objective pronouns are used as direct objects of action verbs. The noun or pronoun that receives the action of the action verb is called the **direct object.**

For example, in the simple sentence *Tuan visited Serena yesterday,* the verb is *visited,* an action verb. The direct object of *visited* is *Serena* because *Serena* receives the action of the verb *visited.* If you substitute a pronoun for *Serena,* it must be the objective pronoun *her—Tuan visited **her** yesterday.*

EXAMPLES

Brenda married **him** on March 7, 1987.

Last summer Joan beat **me** at tennis every time we played.

Both classes helped clean up the park, and the city rewarded **them** with a picnic.

3. Objective pronouns are used as indirect objects. The **indirect object** indicates **to whom or for whom (or to what or for what) an action is directed,** but the prepositions *to* and *for* are left out.

EXAMPLES

(prepositional phrase)   He threw the ball **to her.**

(indirect object)   He threw **her** the ball.

In the first sentence, *her* is the object of the preposition *to*. In the second sentence, the *to* is omitted and the pronoun is moved, making *her* the indirect object. In both sentences, the direct object is *ball*. Here are other examples.

EXAMPLES   She had already given **me** two chances to make up for my mistakes.

The architect showed **them** a picture of how the new city hall would look.

PRACTICE   In the blanks, identify the underlined pronouns as subjective (sub) or objective (obj).

_____*sub*_____   **1.** On Saturday, <u>we</u> will leave for our trip to the Mardi Gras.

_____   **2.** Many words of praise were offered to <u>him</u> after his performance.

_____   **3.** Is <u>he</u> the one who stole your cotton candy?

_____   **4.** Emily felt lonely and left out, so Esteban gave <u>her</u> his seat.

_____   **5.** Please give <u>them</u> this check for one million dollars.

_____   **6.** The Loch Ness Monster was on their minds as <u>they</u> submerged.

_____   **7.** He is the man <u>whom</u> we saw standing in the alley.

_____   **8.** For six months Ceres had to wait for <u>her</u>.

_____   **9.** Because <u>he</u> was a quadruped, he had to buy two pairs of shoes.

_____**10.** The dentist told <u>us</u> to floss more often.

Possessive Pronouns

The **possessive pronouns** are *my, mine, our, ours, your, yours, his, her, hers, its, their, theirs,* and *whose*. They are used in two situations.

1. Possessive pronouns are used as adjectives to indicate possession.

EXAMPLES   The old sailor had turned up **his** collar against the wind.

The weary travelers shuffled off to **their** rooms.

The polar bear constantly paced up and down **its** enclosure.

NOTE: The contraction *it's* means "it is." The word *its* is the only possessive form for *it*. (In fact, you do not use apostrophes with any of the possessive pronouns.)

2. Some possessive pronouns indicate possession without being used as adjectives. In this case, they may be used as subjects or objects.

EXAMPLE   I had to borrow Zan's flashlight because **mine** was lost.

Here the possessive pronoun *mine* is the subject of its clause.

EXAMPLE   The Chin house is large, but **yours** is cozy.

In this example, *yours* is the subject of its clause.

EXAMPLE   He didn't have any change for a phone call because he had given **his** to the children begging on the street.

Here the possessive pronoun *his* is a direct object.

Common Sources of Errors in Pronoun Case

Compound Constructions

Compound subjects and objects often cause problems when they include pronouns. If your sentence includes a compound construction, be sure to use the correct pronoun case.

EXAMPLES

(compound subject)	Sandra and <u>she</u> will return the car on Monday.
(compound after linking verb)	That was **my friend and** <u>I</u> whom you saw on the news.
(compound object of a preposition)	They awarded first-place trophies **to both Dolores and** <u>me</u>.
(compound direct object)	Julio's boss fired **Mark and** <u>him</u> yesterday.
(compound indirect object)	She had already given <u>him and me</u> two chances to make up our minds.

In most cases, you can use a simple test to check whether you have chosen the right pronoun case when you have a compound construction. Simply remove one of the subjects or objects so that only one pronoun is left. For example, is this sentence correct? *Our host gave **Erin and I** a drink.* Test it by dropping **Erin and.** *Our host gave **I** a drink.* Now you can see that the *I* should be *me* because it is an object (an indirect object). The correct sentence should read: *Our host gave **Erin and me** a drink.*

PRACTICE   Underline the correct pronoun in the parentheses.

1. My brother and (I/me) enjoy our dune buggies.

2. Just between you and (I/me), their plans for the party will never succeed.

3. Without Dionysius and (she/her), the party won't be any fun.

4. Aritakis enjoyed the gyros that Placido and (he/him) had made.

5. When Dorothy told Auntie Em and (I/me) her story, we started to laugh.

6. Brent and (she/her) decided to watch *Slumdog Millionaire*.

7. The vice squad stopped Manuela and (he/him) for interdigitation.

8. This year's winners of the best-dressed award are Clifford and (she/her).

9. Chuck Berry smiled when Keith Richards and (she/her) asked him for an autograph.

10. At the end of the war, Victor Frankl and (he/him) were released from the concentration camp.

Who and *Whom*

When to use *who* or *whom* is a mystery to many writers, but you should have no problem with these pronouns if you remember two simple rules.

1. Use the subjective pronoun *who* or *whoever* if it is used as the subject of a verb.

2. Use the objective pronoun *whom* or *whomever* if it is not used as the subject of a verb.

EXAMPLES   After leaving the airport, I followed the man **who** had taken my bags. (*Who* is the subject of *had taken*.)

The letter was sent to the person **whom** we had decided to hire. (*Whom* is not the subject of a verb.)

Please give the money to **whoever** needs it. (*Whoever* is the subject of *needs*.)

PRACTICE Underline the correct pronoun in the parentheses.

1. The people (who/<u>whom</u>) we saw at the concert were having a good time.

2. Leonardo is painting a woman (who/whom) has a very subtle smile.

3. The witness claimed to recognize the suspect, (who/whom) she had never really seen before.

4. Charles Darwin would explain his theory to (whoever/whomever) would listen.

5. The police were prepared to arrest (whoever/whomever) the dog licked first.

Comparisons

When a pronoun is used in a comparison, you often need to supply the implied words in order to know what pronoun case to use. For example, in the sentence *My brother cannot skate as well as I,* the implied words are the verb *can skate: My brother cannot skate as well as I [can skate].*

EXAMPLE The police officer allowed my friend to leave the scene sooner than **me.**

You can tell that *me* is the correct case in this sentence when you supply the implied words:

The police officer allowed my friend to leave the scene sooner than [she allowed] me [to leave].

PRACTICE Underline the correct pronoun in the parentheses.

1. Oscar never drives as fast as (<u>I</u>/me).

2. Julio is my best friend, but he talks more to my sister than to (I/me).

3. Chris thought she was as triskaidekaphobic as (he/him).

4. Andrea knew Clyde would not care for her plants as well as (she/her).

5. When they became engaged, the happy couple told William sooner than (I/me).

Appositives

As you will remember from Chapter Three, an appositive is a word group containing a noun or pronoun that renames another noun or pronoun. When the appositive contains a **pronoun** that does the renaming, be sure that the pronoun is in the same case as the word it renames.

EXAMPLE Some team members—Joe, Frank, and **I**—were late for practice.

Here *I* is in the subjective case because the appositive *Joe, Frank, and I* renames the word *members*, the subject of the sentence.

EXAMPLE When the show is over, please send your review to the producers, Mark and **her**.

Here *her* is in the objective case because the appositive *Mark and her* renames *producers*, the object of the preposition *to*.

PRACTICE Underline the correct pronoun in the parentheses.

1. Alejandro was disappointed when the authors—Elena, Serena, and (he/him)—were not paid well.

2. The teacher gave automatic A's to two students, Natasha and (I/me).

3. Kalisha was disappointed that her teammates, Cameron and (he/him), had given up.

4. The award money was shared among three people—Carlos, Monica, and (she/her).

5. The last people to arrive—Celeste, Annamaria, Lawrence, and (I/me)—were told to sit in the back of the room.

PRACTICE Underline the correct pronoun form in the parentheses.

1. The tape will be broken by (whoever/whomever) crosses the finish line first.

2. Do you really think that she can swim as fast as (I/me)?

3. When the recession is at (its / it's) worst, (its / it's) time to buy stocks.

4. Did Jackson and (she / her) agree to bring the Brussels sprouts?

5. Petra decided that she would marry (whoever / whomever) her astrologer recommended.

6. Before the wedding, she also consulted two palm readers, Madame Sosostris and (he / him).

7. Send Narcissus and (he / him) this invitation to the self-reflection workshop.

8. Aphrodite worried that Ares was more attracted to Artemis than to (she / her).

9. Homer made a Spam sculpture of Elvis Presley, (who / whom) he has always admired.

10. During the war in Iraq, Ricardo and (she / her) were separated for more than a year.

Section Three Review

1. The **subjective pronouns** are used in two ways:

   a. As the subjects of sentences

   b. After linking verbs

2. The **objective pronouns** are used in three ways:

   a. As objects of prepositions

   b. As direct objects of action verbs

   c. As indirect objects

3. The **possessive pronouns** are used in two ways:

   a. As adjectives to modify nouns to indicate possession

   b. As subjects and objects

4. Some common sources of errors in pronoun case:

   a. Pronouns in compound constructions

   b. The use of the pronouns *who, whom, whoever,* and *whomever*

   c. Pronouns in comparisons

   d. Pronouns in appositives

Exercise 3A

Underline the correct pronoun form in the parentheses.

1. The baby seal was barking because it could not find (<u>its</u>/it's) mother.

2. The last piece of bacon was divided between Petunia and (I/me).

3. The $64,000 challenge for Eric and (she/her) was to name the thirteen original colonies.

4. Was it (she/her) to (who/whom) you sold your used golf clubs?

5. No one was more surprised than (I/me) to see Neptune rise from the waves in Ocean Beach.

6. Ask Larry and (they/them) if they know when the Gettysburg Address was delivered.

7. The fellows (who/whom) the Earps met at the OK Corral were soon sorry they had come.

8. Did Ahab ever explain to you and (she/her) why he was chasing the whale?

9. Walking through the maze, the Minotaur lost (its/it's) way.

10. It was (she/her) who insisted on reporting the theft to the police.

11. The prize goes to (whoever/whomever) throws a cow chip the farthest.

12. Loren was certain he had seen Meryl Streep and (she/her) on the Sunset Strip.

13. Two poets, T. S. Eliot and (she/her), discussed the merits of "The Love Song of J. Alfred Prufrock."

14. (Its/It's) hard to believe that your pet parrot can spell (its/it's) own name.

15. When they heard the buzz of the fly, Emily and (he/him) started closing the windows.

Exercise 3B

Correct any pronoun errors in the following sentences. Some sentences may not contain errors.

1. Alice likes mushrooms and white rabbits more than ~~me~~ *I*.

2. Do you think that Mephistopheles and he will reach an agreement?

3. Was that Dr. Frankenstein and his monster who you rented your castle to?

4. Moe gave Curly and I a noogie as we left the studio.

5. Peter Rabbit excitedly told his friends, Bugs and she, about the secret garden.

6. When its time to go, the Grim Reaper will approach you with its scythe.

7. Plato smiled philosophically at Bill and I as we stared at the shadows flickering across the screen.

8. All night long Rumpelstiltskin and she spun straw into gold.

9. The children who Homer visited in the hospital asked to see his cow chip award.

10. His friends had entered the room earlier than Larry, but Larry still completed the exam faster than them.

11. Between Horace and me was a deep chasm.

12. It's food was covered with ants, so it's not surprising the dog started to howl.

13. The first- and second-place ribbons for hallway whistling were awarded to Bruce and him.

14. The iconoclasts whom were bothering Pollyanna and her were finally asked to leave.

15. When the Girl Scout cookies arrived, Martin and me knew exactly what to do.

Exercise 3C

Correct any errors in pronoun case in the following paragraph.

1. Urban legends—ironic, supernatural, or unbelievable accounts of real-life events—may be the result of the ordinary human emotions of the people ~~whom~~ *who* tell them. **2.** For example, one of my favorite urban legends clearly finds it's origin in the desire to get something for nothing. **3.** It was originally told to my brother and I by a local bank manager. **4.** Someone whom she knows has a friend who says that his wife and him paid only $1,500 for a $50,000 Porsche Targa. **5.** They paid so little because it had sat in the Mojave Desert for two weeks with the body of it's owner in it. **6.** My brother is more skeptical than me, but even he would like to believe that such an event could happen to him. **7.** Another urban legend is probably caused by our fear of the unknown, especially in dark, lonely places. **8.** According to this legend, a boy and a girl whom have parked in the woods are talking about a rumor that a one-armed man has been seen nearby. **9.** Friends have told the boy and she that he has attacked several people with his hook in the past few weeks while frothing at the mouth and yelling, "Bloody murder!" **10.** Frightened, the two leave the woods, but when they arrive home and get out of the car, they find a hook dangling from it's right front door. **11.** They are both terrified, but the boy is determined to find the man who tried to attack his girlfriend and he. **12.** He drives back to the woods and is never heard from again. **13.** Finally, an urban legend that my wife and me have heard several different versions of must be caused by a need to see people get what they deserve. **14.** In this one, an elderly woman whom lives in a downtown apartment with her blind husband finds her beloved cat dead one day. **15.** The old woman puts the body into a shopping bag, and her husband and her tearfully take a bus across town to a pet cemetery. **16.** On the trip, a teenage gang member, who is much stronger than them, grabs the bag, laughs at the woman, and jumps off the bus. **17.** According to almost every version told to my wife and I, when the thief looks into the bag, he is so startled that he falls backward into the path of a car. **18.** Clearly, urban legends like these are repeated because they express many of our unspoken desires and fears.

Sentence Practice: Using Transitions

Writers use certain words and phrases to indicate the relationships among the ideas in their sentences and paragraphs. These words and phrases provide links between ideas, leading a reader from one idea to another smoothly. They show relationships like time, addition, or contrast. Consider this paragraph from Rachel Carson's *Edge of the Sea:*

> **When** the tide is rising the shore is a place of unrest, with the surge leaping high over jutting rocks **and** running in lacy cascades of foam over the landward side of massive boulders. **But** on the ebb it is more peaceful, **for then** the waves do not have behind them the push of the inward pressing tides. There is no particular drama about the turn of the tide, **but presently** a zone of wetness shows on the gray rock slopes, **and** offshore the incoming swells begin to swirl **and** break over hidden ledges. **Soon** the rocks that the high tide had concealed rise into view and glisten with the wetness left on them by the receding water.

Because she is writing about a process, most of Rachel Carson's transitional words indicate a relationship in time (*when, then, presently, soon*). But she also uses transitional words that indicate contrast (*but*), cause (*for*), and addition (*and*). As you can see, she uses these expressions to lead her readers smoothly from one idea to another.

The sentence combining exercises in this chapter are designed to give you practice in using transitional words and phrases to link your ideas. Try to use as many different ones as you can. For your convenience, here is a list of commonly used transitional words and phrases.

- Time: *then, soon, first, second, finally, meanwhile, next, at first, in the beginning*

- Contrast: *yet, but, however, instead, otherwise, on the other hand, on the contrary*

- Addition: *and, also, besides, furthermore, in addition, likewise, moreover, similarly*

- Cause–effect: *for, because, consequently, so, therefore, hence, thus, as a result, since*

- Example: *for example, for instance, that is, such as*

- Conclusion: *thus, hence, finally, generally, as a result, in conclusion*

PRACTICE   Add transitions to the following sentences.

1. Sometimes I am indecisive about the most trivial things. _____, this morning I spent fifteen minutes trying to decide whether to buy a cinnamon roll or a jelly doughnut.

2. California is known for its many beaches. _____, it has many excellent ski resorts.

3. Barbara and Greg have been very successful in their real estate careers. _____, they have raised five well-adjusted, happy children.

4. Only seven of our team members showed up for our weekend softball game. _____, we had to forfeit the game to the other team.

5. This afternoon I will probably jog for thirty minutes. _____, perhaps I will stay home and eat the last of my jelly doughnuts.

Sentence Combining Exercises

Combine the following sentences, using transitions as indicated in the directions.

☯ EXAMPLE   Combine these sentences into two sentences. Use transitions that indicate contrast, example, and addition. Underline your transitions.

     a. Herman knows he needs to lose weight.
     b. He is unable to resist the urge to eat ice cream.
     c. Yesterday he drank a low-fat fiber shake for lunch.
     d. After work he stopped at a 31 Flavors ice cream store.
     e. He ate a large chocolate sundae.

Herman knows he needs to lose weight, but he is unable to resist the urge to eat ice cream. For example, yesterday he drank a low-fat fiber shake for lunch, but after work he stopped at a 31 Flavors ice cream store and ate a large chocolate sundae.

1. Combine the following sentences into two sentences. Use transitions that indicate time and addition. Underline your transitions.

     a. At the grocery store, Andrew finds a cart that will not wobble.
     b. He heads to the bakery section for a fresh doughnut.
     c. He moves to the freezer aisle to find a gallon of strawberry ice cream.
     d. He ends up at the deli, where he orders a bagel covered with cream cheese.

_____

_____

_____

_____

2. Combine the following sentences into two sentences. Use transitions that indicate cause–effect and contrast. Underline your transitions.

     a. There are more holes in the mouthpiece of the common telephone than in the earpiece.
     b. People will cover their ears with the earpiece.
     c. People will move their mouths all over the place while speaking.
     d. The mouthpiece requires more holes.

_____

_____

_____

_____

continued

3. Combine the following sentences into two sentences. Use transitions that indicate cause–effect. Underline your transitions.

   a. Horse-drawn covered wagons used to be called "Conestogas."
   b. Conestogas were originally built in the Conestoga Valley of Pennsylvania.
   c. The Conestogas supplied cigars, among other things, to the pioneers.
   d. Cigars came to be called "stogies."

   _____

   _____

   _____

   _____

4. Combine the following sentences into three sentences, using transitions that show time relationships. Underline your transitions.

   a. Brenda finished reading *Romeo and Juliet*.
   b. Brenda folded her laundry.
   c. Brenda made a list of tasks she had to complete by Monday.
   d. Brenda worked on her poem.
   e. It was very late.
   f. Brenda watched *The Late Show with David Letterman*.

   _____

   _____

   _____

   _____

continued

5. Combine the following sentences into two sentences. Use transitions that indicate cause–effect and example. Underline your transitions.

    a. Simon avoids his family.
    b. Whenever he visits his family, someone insults him.
    c. Last Christmas his mother said that he could pass for the Christmas turkey.
    d. He had gained twenty pounds.

    _____

    _____

    _____

    _____

6. Combine the following sentences into three or four sentences, using transitions that show time and cause–effect relationships. Underline your transitions.

    a. The holes in bread are made by bubbles of gas.
    b. Flour and water are mixed to form dough.
    c. A small amount of yeast is added.
    d. The yeast grows.
    e. The yeast gives off a gas.
    f. The gas bubbles up through the dough.
    g. The dough expands.

    _____

    _____

    _____

    _____

continued

7. Combine the following sentences into two sentences. Use transitions that indicate cause–effect and contrast. Underline your transitions.

   a. In ancient times, wedding guests threw wheat at a new bride.
   b. Wheat was a symbol of fertility and prosperity.
   c. In the first century B.C.E., Roman bakers began to cook the wheat into small cakes.
   d. Wedding guests did not want to give up the custom of throwing wheat.
   e. They threw the wedding cakes instead.

   _____

   _____

   _____

   _____

8. Combine the following sentences into three sentences. Use transitions that indicate cause–effect and contrast. Underline your transitions.

   a. Many drunk people drive home.
   b. They believe that drinking coffee before they leave will sober them up.
   c. Drinking coffee will do nothing to make a drunk person less drunk.
   d. A good sleep, plenty of liquids, and enough time will remedy the effects of alcohol.

   _____

   _____

   _____

continued

9. Combine the following sentences into three sentences. Use transitions that show contrast and addition.

   a. The song "Chopsticks" was not named after the Chinese eating implement.
   b. It was named after the chopping motions the hands have to make to play it.
   c. A Chinese composer did not write the little waltz.
   d. A British girl wrote it.
   e. She made up the instructions to play it with both hands turned sideways to imitate a chopping motion.

   _____

   _____

   _____

   _____

   _____

10. Combine the following sentences into three sentences. Use transitions that indicate example, cause–effect, and addition. Underline your transitions.

    a. Many superstitions have unusual origins.
    b. It is considered bad luck to walk under a ladder.
    c. A ladder leaning against a wall forms a triangle.
    d. Many ancient societies believed that a triangle was a place sacred to the gods.
    e. Walking through a triangle defiled that space.

    _____

    _____

    _____

Essay and Paragraph Practice: Explaining Causes and Effects

Assignment

In Chapter Three you wrote an expository paper that used examples as support. Such an organization—one that calls for a listing of examples to support an idea—is very common in college papers and tests. Another common assignment is one that asks you to explain the **causes** or the **effects** of something. In an American history class, for example, you might be asked to explain the causes of the South's failure to win the Civil War. Or in a psychology class you might be asked to explain the long-term effects that physical abuse can have on children.

A paper that focuses on causes explains *why* a certain event might have occurred or why people do what they do. On the other hand, a paper that focuses on effects explains what has *resulted* or might result from an event, action, or behavior. In this chapter, Exercise 1C (page 228) explains the effects of a divorce in the family; Exercise 2C (page 242) explains the causes of the tradition of a groom carrying a bride across the threshold; and Exercise 3C (page 254) explains the causes of some urban legends. Each of these paragraphs states the purpose of the paragraph (to explain causes or effects) in a topic sentence and then presents several specific causes or effects.

Your assignment is to write a paper that explains *either* the causes *or* the effects of a topic with which you are personally familiar. Develop your paper from one of the suggestions below or from an idea suggested by your instructor.

Prewriting to Generate Ideas

Prewriting Application: Finding Your Topic

Use prewriting techniques of freewriting, brainstorming, or clustering to decide which of the following topic ideas interests you. Write for five or ten minutes on several of these suggestions. Don't stop writing once you find one topic that might work. Try out several of them before you make a decision.

Analyzing Causes

1. Why do you or do you not admire, respect, or trust a particular person?

2. Why are you doing well or poorly in a particular course?

3. Why did your or your parents' marriage or relationship fail, or why is it a success?

4. Why was your childhood or some other period the best or worst time of your life?

5. Why did you move from one place to another?

6. Why did you buy the particular car or other item that you did?

7. Why are you attending a particular college?

8. Why did you make an important decision?

9. Why did a particular experience affect you the way it did?

10. Why will you never go to *that* restaurant, hotel, beach, or lake again?

Analyzing Effects

1. What were the effects of an important decision that you made?

2. What were the effects of your move to a new place?

3. What were the effects of your being an only child, or an oldest child, or a youngest child, or of growing up in a large family?

4. What are the effects of stress upon the way you act, feel, or think?

5. What were the effects upon you of a major change in your life—having a child? getting married? changing jobs? experiencing a divorce?

6. What have been the effects of a serious compulsion or addiction to drugs, alcohol, gambling, or overeating upon someone you know or upon his or her loved ones?

7. What have been the effects of mental, emotional, or physical abuse upon you or someone you know?

8. What have been the effects of discrimination or prejudice upon you or someone you know? (Discrimination might involve race, gender, age, sexuality, or religion.)

9. What have been the effects upon you and/or upon your family of working and/or raising a family and attending school at the same time?

10. What have been the effects upon you of some major change in your lifestyle or values?

Choosing and Narrowing the Topic

Once you have settled on several possible topics, consider these points as you make your final selection.

- Choose the more limited topic rather than the more general one.

- Choose the topic about which you could develop several causes or effects. Avoid topics that involve only one or two causes or effects.

- Choose the topic about which you have the most experience or knowledge.

- Choose the topic in which you have the most personal interest. Avoid topics about which you don't really care.

Writing a Thesis Statement or Topic Sentence

If your assignment is to write a single paragraph, you will open it with a topic sentence. If you are writing a complete essay, you will need a thesis statement at the end of your introductory paragraph. In either case, you will need a clear statement of the topic and central idea of your paper.

Prewriting Application: Working with Topic Sentences

Identify the topic sentences in Exercises 1C (page 228), 2C (page 242), and 3C (page 254). Then identify the topic and the central point in each topic sentence.

Prewriting Application: Evaluating Thesis Statements and Topic Sentences

Write "No" before each sentence that would not make an effective thesis statement or topic sentence for a paper explaining causes or effects. Write "Yes" before each sentence that *would* make an effective one. Identify each effective sentence as introducing a paper about causes or effects. Using ideas of your own, rewrite each ineffective sentence into one that might work.

_____   **1.** My father's generosity, sensitivity, and openness have made him into the most important person in my life.

_____

_____

_____   **2.** I divorced my husband on June 30 of last year.

_____

_____

_____

_____ 3. Although I loved living in Boulder, Colorado, several events over the past few years helped me to decide that it was time to move.

_____

_____

_____ 4. Whenever I let myself worry too much about my job, school, or family responsibilities, everyone that I love is affected by my strange behavior.

_____

_____

_____ 5. My life has changed in many ways since I was young.

_____

_____

_____ 6. Many students at our local high school use marijuana, methamphetamines, and even cocaine.

_____

_____

_____ 7. Telling my parents that I was gay was one of the best decisions that I ever made.

_____

_____

_____ 8. Growing up as an only child helped me to become an independent, decisive, and responsible person.

_____

_____

_____ **9.** My new computer, which uses all the latest technology, came loaded with my favorite games and word processing software.

_____

_____

_____

_____ **10.** Attending a college away from home has caused me to become a much better person in a number of ways.

_____

_____

Prewriting Application: Talking to Others

Form a group of three or four people and tell one another what topic you have chosen and whether you plan to discuss causes or effects. Use the following guidelines to discuss your papers.

1. What is the topic of the paper? Will the paper focus on causes or effects?

2. What causes or effects will be included? Can they be more specific and descriptive? Can they be explained more clearly?

3. What other causes or effects could be included? Are there any less obvious but more interesting ones?

4. Are you convinced? Have enough causes or effects been provided to illustrate the topic idea? Should any of them be explained or described more thoroughly?

5. Which cause or effect should the paper open with? Which should it close with?

Organizing Causes and Effects

Chronological and **emphatic** arrangements are perhaps the most common ways to organize several causes or effects. If you are explaining what caused you to stop smoking, a chronological arrangement would list the most remote causes first and move to the most recent causes. On the other hand, an emphatic arrangement would involve deciding which cause was the most significant one and saving it until last.

Writing the Essay

If your assignment is to write a complete essay:

- Place your **thesis statement** at the end of the introductory paragraph.

- Write a separate **body paragraph** for each cause or effect that you intend to discuss.

- Open each body paragraph with a **topic sentence** that identifies the specific cause or effect.

- Within each body paragraph, use **specific facts and details** to explain and support your ideas.

Writing the Paragraph

If your assignment is to write a single paragraph:

- Open it with a **topic sentence** that clearly identifies the topic and central idea of the paragraph.

- Use **clear transitions** to move from one cause or effect to the next.

- Use **specific facts and details** to explain and support your ideas.

Writing Application: Identifying Transitional Words, Phrases, and Sentences

Examine Exercises 1C (page 228), 2C (page 242), and 3C (page 254). Identify the transitions that introduce each new cause or effect. Then identify any other transitions that serve to connect ideas between sentences.

Rewriting and Improving the Paper

1. Revise your sentences so that they include specific and concrete details. As often as possible, use actual names of people and places. Refer to specific details whenever possible.

2. Add or revise transitions wherever doing so will help clarify your movement from one idea to another.

3. Improve your preliminary thesis statement (if you are writing an essay) or your preliminary topic sentence (if you are writing a single paragraph) so that it more accurately states the central point of your paper.

4. Examine your draft for simple sentences that can be combined to make compound, complex, or compound-complex sentences. Watch also for sentences that can be combined using participial phrases, appositives, infinitive phrases, or adjective clauses.

Rewriting Application: Responding to Paragraph Writing

Read the following paragraph. Then respond to the questions following it.

Changing Careers

Two years ago, after serving for over twenty-five years in the United States Navy, I decided that it was time to move on to new and better things, and I have never regretted that decision. One of the most pleasant effects of retiring from the military has been not having to endure any more family separations. While in the Navy, I spent most of my career aboard ship and made many six-month deployments or had to stand duty every four or five days when not on deployment. Now that I have more time to spend with my family, I have joined a family bowling league and have time to attend school events that my children are participating in. Another effect of leaving the military is that I am able to get involved with community activities because I know that I won't be moving to another city in two or three years. During one period of my career my family and I lived in San Francisco two years, Norfolk, Virginia, three years, and then San Diego. Now that I don't plan to move within two or three years, I have joined the Parent/Teachers' Association at my son's school, become an active member in the local Boy Scout troop, and become a board member of my homeowners' association. Finally, by working fewer hours than I did when I was in the Navy, I have the opportunity to go to school. I am able to use the Montgomery G.I. Bill to supplement my income while in school and obtain a degree in Business Management. My wife and I agree that we made the right decision to leave the military when I did. The week after I retired, the ship I had been stationed on made an unexpected nine-month deployment to Somalia. I obtained a good civil service job after I retired, and my supervisor allows me to attend school in the mornings and work in the afternoons and weekends.

---

1. Identify the topic sentence. State its topic and central idea. Is it an effective topic sentence? Can you tell whether the paper will focus on causes or effects?

2. How many causes or effects are mentioned in this paper? Identify them.

3. Identify the transitional sentences that introduce each cause or effect. What other transitions are used between sentences in this paragraph?

4. What parts of each cause or effect could be made still more specific?

5. Consider the organization of the paragraph. Would you change the order of the causes or effects? Explain why or why not.

Rewriting Application: Responding to Essay Writing

Read the following essay. Then respond to the questions at the end of it.

A New Person

I used to be the kind of person who only thought of herself. I wanted to make a lot of money, party every weekend, and just have fun. I was probably the most self-centered person you have ever met. But in the past two years I have really changed. I have started to think about other people before I think about myself. I am happy that I am becoming a different person, but the causes of my change have been painful.

I think my change started when my boyfriend left me last year. We had been together for five years, ever since we graduated from Oceanside High School. Even though we fought a lot, I was sure that we would eventually get married and be together forever. So I was stunned and really hurt when he told me goodbye. He told me I was the most selfish person he had ever met. I was furious for a long time after that, but I kept thinking about what he had said. I began to think that maybe he was right. Maybe I was selfish.

I have also changed because of people I have met at Palomar College. When I decided to go back to school, I just wanted to get my degree and be left alone. I thought I was smarter than everyone else, so I hardly ever talked to anyone in my classes. By the end of my first semester, I was really lonely. It seemed as if everyone but me had made friends and was having fun. So I tried an experiment. I started asking people around me in class how they were doing, and if they were having trouble I offered to help.

That was really a big step for me. By the end of the year, I had several new friends, and two of them are still my best friends today.

The biggest cause of my new attitude, however, came when I took a part-time job at Vista Convalescent Care. I had never worked with old people before, and I dreaded the idea of changing bedpans and cleaning up after them. But after a few weeks I really started to like the people I was taking care of, and I began to see that making them feel good made me feel good too. One little old lady in particular became my friend. Her name was Rita Gonzalez, and she had Alzheimer's. Whenever I came into her room, she was always so happy because she thought I was her daughter. Her real daughter never visited her, so I took her place, and Rita and I spent lots of afternoons together. She taught me to forget about my own problems, so when she died last month, I was heartbroken, but I was also very grateful to her.

I think I am a much better person today than I used to be, and I hope I will not forget these experiences. They have been painful, but they have taught me how to think about other people before I think about myself. I like who I am today, and I could not say that a few years ago.

1. Identify the thesis statement. State its topic and central idea. Is it an effective thesis statement? Can you tell whether the paper will focus on causes or effects?

2. Identify each topic sentence. State its topic and central idea. Does each topic sentence clearly introduce one specific cause or effect?

3. What transitional words introduce each new body paragraph?

4. Does the essay use a chronological or emphatic organization? Would you change the order of the paragraphs? Why or why not?

5. Is each cause or effect explained clearly and fully? If you would improve any, explain how you would do so.

Proofreading

When proofreading your paper, watch for the following errors:

- Sentence fragments
- Comma splices
- Fused sentences
- Misplaced modifiers
- Dangling modifiers
- Incorrect subject–verb agreement
- Incorrect pronoun case
- Incorrect pronoun–antecedent agreement or pronoun reference
- Misspelled words

Prepare a clean final draft, following the format your instructor has requested. Before you turn in your final draft, proofread it carefully and make any necessary corrections.

Chapter 4 Practice Test

I. Review of Chapters One, Two, and Three

A. Underline all subjects once and complete verbs twice. Place all prepositional phrases in parentheses.

1. The block of ice in the old freezer contained a frozen alien from outer space.

2. After the romantic had praised the beauty of nature, the realist decided to mow the lawn.

3. Spring had arrived, so the birch trees would soon have new leaves.

4. The son gathered the wax and the feathers and took them to his father.

5. Every Wednesday someone would buy a box of doughnuts and place them on the shelf near the door.

B. Correct any fragments, fused sentences, or comma splices in the following sentences. Do nothing if the sentence is correct.

6. Persephone, asking her mother if she should eat the pomegranate.

    _____

    _____

7. Calamity Jane loved Wild Bill Hickok she claimed to have given birth to his child.

    _____

    _____

8. The salmon, swimming swiftly upstream, did not see the bear, which flicked many of them out of the water with its huge paw.

    _____

    _____

9. Neil Armstrong made his historic statement, however, he left out one small word.

    _____

    _____

continued

10. After Babe Ruth had eaten seven hotdogs and drunk a bucket of beer.

_____

_____

C. At the places indicated, add adjective clauses, appositives, infinitive phrases, or participial phrases to the following sentences as directed in the parentheses. Use commas where they are needed.

11. The minnow stared at the barracuda ^ . (adjective clause)

_____

_____

12. Brittany glared at the umpire ^ as she returned to the dugout. (appositive)

_____

_____

13. ^ Arthur prepared to pull the sword from the stone. (participial phrase)

_____

_____

14. Jenna trained her African gray parrot ^ whenever the doorbell would ring. (infinitive phrase)

_____

_____

15. The black Ford Expedition ^ nearly hit the red-and-white Yaris. (participial phrase)

_____

_____

continued

D. Correct any dangling or misplaced modifiers in the following sentences. Do nothing if the sentence is correct.

16. Rocco saw his favorite kitten dash into the street while playing badminton with his daughter.

_____

_____

17. The earthquake was so strong that it almost damaged every building in the city.

_____

_____

18. Pulling tiredly on their oars, the trip was nearly over.

_____

_____

19. The man with no name ignored the stagecoach dreaming of the open prairie.

_____

_____

20. Surprised by the flashing lights of the police car, Amy's new car slowly came to a stop.

_____

_____

II. Chapter Four

A. Underline the correct verb form in the parentheses.

21. Each earthworm, cricket, and toad in our backyard (has have) crawled or hopped into

our family room.

22. In the past few years, gymnastics (seems seem) to have become very popular.

23. Here (is / are) the black lipstick and green eye shadow you ordered from Macy's.

Chapter 4 Practice Test

continued

24. The panel of judges (decide/decides) which sculpture gets the prize.

25. Neither Dr. Cuddy nor Dr. Wilson (knows/know) what to do about their friend's odd behavior.

B. Correct any subject–verb agreement errors in the following sentences. Do nothing if the sentence is correct.

26. An old dog and a cat with torn ears goes through the garbage each night.

27. Anything you might need to buy and sell houses successfully are easily found on the Internet.

28. One hundred dollars seems like a fair price for my collection of broken roof tiles.

29. Do Jules Verne or H. G. Wells have anything to say about this phenomenon?

30. The man wearing seven gold medals at the boys' swim meet remind me of someone famous, but I can't remember who.

C. Underline the correct pronouns in the parentheses.

31. Someone left (her their) knife in the library, and I think it was Mrs. Peacock.

32. If a climber wants to tackle K2, (you/he or she/they) should first ask why it is called "the Savage Mountain."

33. For the rest of their lives, Hester and Dimmesdale kept their secret to (themself/theirselves/themselves).

34. The army crossed the Alps on (its their) way to Italy.

35. Every child in the audience clapped (his or her/their) hands enthusiastically.

D. Correct any pronoun errors in the following sentences. Do nothing if the sentence is correct.

36. The Africanized honey bees have established a hive near the black bear's den, which worries Mark's mother.

37. Whenever Elvis visited Ringo, he complained about today's music.

38. Joe was certain the Chargers were heading for the Super Bowl, but this did not happen.

continued

39. Everyone who heard about the "Orphan Train" wanted to know why they had never learned about it in history class.

40. Although many neighbors asked for their recipe, Ben and Jerry decided to keep their secret ice cream formula to theirselves.

E. Underline the correct pronoun in the parentheses.

41. Spam Lite, the miracle weight-loss food, was delivered to Bill and (I/me).

42. Jenna headed for San Francisco once Danny and (she/her) had loaded the U-Haul.

43. Cesar knew he needed to train the dog's owners, Kelly and (he/him), not the dog itself.

44. I was angry because our employer gave Margarita a bigger raise than (I/me).

45. Hester, (who/whom) borrowed some needles and thread from me, seems to be working hard on her project.

F. Correct any pronoun errors in the following sentences. Do nothing if the sentence is correct.

46. When it's mate disappeared into the cave, the chained dog began to howl.

47. The Flash could not add nearly as fast as them, so he lost the math contest.

48. Do you want Tom and him to help you paint that fence?

49. Between Achilles and I, we met about thirty thousand Trojans that day.

50. When the reception was over, Darla gave Keiko and I the leftover ice cream and cake.

Using Punctuation and Capitalization

Chapter 5

When we speak to people face to face, we have a number of signals, aside from the words we choose, to let them know how we feel. Facial expressions—smiles, frowns, grimaces—convey our emotions and attitudes. Tone of voice can tell a listener whether we feel sad or lighthearted or sarcastic about what we are saying. Hand gestures and other body language add further messages to the communication. In fact, experts tell us that these nonverbal communications make up over 80 percent of the messages in a conversation.

When we write in order to communicate with a reader, we must make up for that eighty percent of lost, nonverbal communication by using the writing signals that we know. Some of the most important signals in writing are the punctuation marks. They signal whether we are making a statement or asking a question. They indicate the boundaries of our sentences. They determine much of the rhythm and emotion of our writing.

If you are able to use punctuation effectively, you have a powerful tool to control how your writing affects your readers. If you do not know the basic rules of punctuation, you run the risk of being misunderstood or of confusing your readers. In this chapter we will discuss the essential rules of punctuation, not just so that your writing will be correct but, more importantly, so that you will be able to express your ideas exactly the way you want them to be expressed.

Using Commas

The comma gives writers more trouble than any of the other punctuation marks. Before printing was developed, commas came into use to tell readers when to put in a slight pause when they were reading aloud. Now, although the placement of the comma does affect the rhythm of sentences, it also conveys many messages that are more important than when to pause. Because the comma is such an important punctuation mark and because it can be troublesome to you if you don't know how to use it correctly, we take it up first. You are already familiar with several of its uses.

Comma usage can be explained by four general rules:

1. Use commas before coordinating conjunctions that join main clauses to form a compound sentence.

2. Use commas between elements in a series.

3. Use commas after introductory elements.

4. Use commas before and after interrupters.

Commas in Compound Sentences

1. When joining two main clauses with one of the coordinating conjunctions to form a compound sentence, use a comma before the conjunction.

◎◎ EXAMPLES
I don't know her, **but** I like her already.

The tableware in the restaurant was exquisite, **and** the food was some of the best I have ever tasted.

We had to remove the huge eucalyptus tree, **or** its encroaching roots would have undermined our happy home.

2. When conjunctions join other parts of a sentence, such as two words, two phrases, or two subordinate clauses, do not put commas before the conjunctions.

◎◎ EXAMPLE
Every morning that scoundrel has a drink **and** then thoroughly beats his poor dog.

No comma is needed before *and* because it does not join two main clauses. Instead, it joins the verbs *has* and *beats.*

◎◎ EXAMPLE
I decided to visit France because I had never had a chance to see that country **and** because my travel agent was able to offer me a special discount on the trip.

No comma is needed before *and* because it joins two subordinate clauses, not two main clauses.

PRACTICE   Add commas to the following sentences where necessary.

1. Homer bought the Spam‚and Hortense cooked it for him.

2. The jetliner crash-landed in the Hudson River but everyone was rescued.

3. The hounds searched under the dinner table but could find no hush puppies.

4. The archeologist left for northern New Mexico for he wanted to see the Pre-Puebloan ruins.

5. He wanted to record his findings so he brought his camera equipment along.

Commas with Elements in a Series

1. When listing three or more elements (words, phrases, clauses) in a series, separate them by commas. When the last two elements are joined by a coordinating conjunction, a comma before the conjunction is optional.

EXAMPLES

(words)   The gazpacho was cold, spicy, and fresh.

(phrases)   In the mountains, he had been thrown by his horse, bitten by a snake, and chased by a bear.

(clauses)   To rescue the koala, the firefighters brought a ladder, the police brought a rope, and the mayor brought a speech.

2. When using two or more adjectives to modify the same noun, separate them with commas if you can put *and* between the adjectives without changing the meaning or if you can easily reverse the order of the adjectives.

EXAMPLES   She eagerly stepped into the comforting, cool water.

A stubborn, obnoxious boll weevil is ruining my cotton patch.

Note that you could easily use *and* between the above adjectives. (The water is *comforting* and *cool;* the boll weevil is *stubborn* and *obnoxious*.) You could also reverse the adjectives (the *cool, comforting water* or the *obnoxious, stubborn* boll weevil).

3. On the other hand, if the adjectives cannot be joined by *and* or are not easily reversed, no comma is necessary.

EXAMPLE

A bureaucrat wearing a **black leather jacket** and a smirk strode into the auditorium.

Notice how awkward the sentence would sound if you placed *and* between the adjectives (*a black and leather jacket*) or if you reversed them (*a leather black jacket*).

PRACTICE

Insert commas between main clauses joined by a coordinating conjunction and between items in a series.

1. The bill was only $10.50 so Vera paid it in cash.

2. My red-beans-and-rice dish contains red beans a ham hock cayenne pepper tomato sauce and many other secret ingredients found only in New Orleans.

3. Martin finished the ninety-five items grabbed a hammer and nailed them to the church door.

4. The realistic convincing performance by Mickey Roark in *The Wrestler* was amazing.

5. The Super Bowl crowd was ecstatic for Bruce Springsteen had put on a scintillating performance.

6. The dirty unkempt man stumbled into camp and the first thing he wanted was a Popsicle.

7. The new President was an imposing and charismatic person but was sometimes upstaged by his equally impressive wife.

8. You may embrace a geocentric view of the universe if you wish or you may accept the heliocentric model.

9. Sam called Bill loaded his pickup with fishing gear went by Starbucks and headed for the lake.

10. The courageous proud Cherokee Chief Tsali surrendered to save the rest of his people in the Smoky Mountains.

Commas with Introductory Elements

When you begin a sentence with certain introductory words, phrases, or clauses, place a comma after the introductory element.

1. Use a comma after the following introductory words and transitional expressions.

Introductory Words		Transitional Expressions
next	similarly	on the other hand
first	nevertheless	in a similar manner
second	therefore	in other words
third	indeed	for example
moreover	yes	for instance
however	no	in fact
		in addition
		as a result

EXAMPLES   **First,** we will strike at the heart of the matter and then pursue other clichés.

For example, let's all stand up and be counted.

2. Use a comma after introductory prepositional phrases of five or more words. However, you may need to use a comma after shorter introductory prepositional phrases if not doing so would cause confusion.

EXAMPLES   **After a long and thrilling nap,** Buster went looking for a cat to chase.

After dinner we all went for a walk around the lake.

In spring, time seems to catch up with small furry animals.

Without the comma, this last sentence might look as if it begins *In springtime.*

3. Use a comma after all introductory infinitive and participial phrases.

EXAMPLES   **Blackened with soot,** the little boy toddled out of the smoldering house.

Begging for her forgiveness, Homer assured Hortense that they would never run short of Spam again.

To break in your new car properly, drive at varying speeds for the first one thousand miles.

4. Use a comma after introductory adverb subordinate clauses.

EXAMPLES   Because Umberto played the tuba so well, he was awarded a music scholarship.

As soon as he arrived on shore, Columbus claimed the land for Spain.

Although it was raining furiously, Freida ran six miles anyway.

PRACTICE   Insert commas after introductory elements.

1. First, I will tell you about my relative who fought at the Alamo.

2. On board the Santa Maria in 1492 Columbus and his crew were relieved to find that the world is not flat.

3. Saving for six months Bill Gates was able to buy an iPhone 3GS.

4. While they were completing the transaction for the iPhone the Apple salesperson asked Gates for a picture identification.

5. Yes Freud named some of his psychological observations after people in Greek myths.

6. Approaching the crash site Matt Scudder slowed to a stop.

7. As the artist looked up at the ceiling he hoped the Pope would like it.

8. After scrupulously examining the body Dr. Scarpetta decided the larvae had been laid at 8:00 yesterday.

9. In order to create a romantic atmosphere Juliet played Louis Armstrong's "A Kiss to Build a Dream On" for Romeo.

10. To find the Holy Grail Perceval spent years wandering throughout Europe and Great Britain.

Commas with Interrupters

Sometimes certain words, phrases, or clauses will interrupt the flow of thought in a sentence to add emphasis or additional information. These interrupters are enclosed by commas.

1. Use commas to set off parenthetical expressions. Common parenthetical expressions include *however, indeed, consequently, as a result, moreover, of course, for example, for instance, that is, in fact, after all, I think,* and *therefore.*

EXAMPLES

The answer, **after all,** lay right under his left big toe.

That big blue bird by the feeder is, **I think,** one of those unruly Steller's jays.

She is, **moreover,** a notorious misspeller of the word *deceitful.*

NOTE: Whenever a parenthetical expression introduces a second main clause after a semicolon, the semicolon takes the place of the comma in front of it.

EXAMPLE

Yes, you may eat your snails in front of me; **after all,** we are old friends.

PRACTICE

Use commas to set off any parenthetical elements in the following sentences.

1. The red Mustang, after all, did signal before turning left.

2. Wynton Marsalis on the other hand knows more about jazz than any other living person I know.

3. Marsalis went to Juilliard School of Music and plays trumpet; moreover he plays both classical and jazz trumpet excellently.

4. Wynton incidentally has a father who plays jazz piano, a brother who plays saxophone, and another brother who plays percussion.

5. John Hancock detested signing his name; for instance he hesitated to sign one of the famous documents of history.

---

2. Use commas to set off nonrestrictive elements. Nonrestrictive elements are modifying words, phrases, or clauses that are not necessary to identify the words they modify. They include adjective subordinate clauses, appositives, and participial phrases.

Adjective Clauses

(See pages 84–87 if you need to review adjective clauses.) If the information in an adjective clause <u>is not necessary to identify the word it modifies</u>, it is called a **nonrestrictive clause,** and it is enclosed in commas.

🌀 EXAMPLE   Ms. Erindira Sanchez, **who is president of that company,** began twenty years ago as a secretary.

Because the name of the person is used, the adjective clause is not necessary to identify which woman began twenty years ago as a secretary, so the commas are needed.

However, if her name is not used, the adjective clause is a **restrictive** one <u>because the woman is not already identified</u>. In this case, the commas are not necessary.

🌀 EXAMPLE   The woman **who is president of that company** began twenty years ago as a secretary.

The following are additional examples of nonrestrictive clauses.

🌀 EXAMPLE   My oldest brother, **who is a park ranger,** showed me his collection of arrowheads.

Because a person can have only one oldest brother, the brother is already identified, and the adjective clause is <u>not needed to identify him</u>, making it nonrestrictive.

🌀 EXAMPLE   His home town, **which is somewhere in northeastern Indiana,** wants him to return for its centennial celebration.

A person can have only one home town, so the adjective clause is nonrestrictive.

🌀 PRACTICE   In the following sentences, set off all nonrestrictive clauses with commas.

1. La Paloma, which is an old theater near my house, is my favorite place to

   see films.

2. The use of steroids by baseball players which is in the news almost every

   day threatens to damage the reputation of the sport.

3. Claudius who was the brother of the murdered King Hamlet met an ironic

   death.

4. The man who had poisoned his brother was poisoned himself.

5. The *Titanic* which was supposed to be one of the safest ships ever built

sank on its maiden voyage.

Participial Phrases

(See pages 152–153 if you need to review participial phrases.) Participial phrases that <u>do not contain information necessary to identify the words they modify</u> are nonrestrictive and are therefore set off by commas. Restrictive participial phrases do not require commas.

⊙⊙ EXAMPLE   (nonrestrictive)   The President, **seeking to be reelected,** traveled throughout the country making speeches and kissing babies.

Because we have only one president, the participial phrase *seeking to be reelected* is nonrestrictive. It is not necessary to identify who is meant by *President*.

⊙⊙ EXAMPLE   (restrictive)   The woman **sitting by the door** is a famous surgeon.

Sitting by the door is a restrictive participial phrase because it is necessary to identify which woman is the famous surgeon.

⊙⊙ EXAMPLE   Foxworth, **discouraged by years of failure,** decided to buy a pet chimpanzee.

Discouraged by years of failure is a nonrestrictive past participial phrase. It is not necessary to identify Foxworth.

⊙⊙ PRACTICE   In the following sentences, set off nonrestrictive participial phrases with commas.

1. Paul Groves‚ worrying about his friend's mental state‚ offered to build a

deck for him.

2. The woman living in the redwood tree was eventually forced to come down.

3. Rosa Parks determined not to sit at the back of the bus was instrumental in

beginning the civil rights movement.

4. Dustin Hoffman playing Willy Loman in *Death of a Salesman* revealed the

complexity of Arthur Miller's famous character.

5. Bill's daughter frightened by his condition called 911.

Appositives

(See page 165 if you need to review appositives.) Appositives usually contain information <u>not necessary to identify the words they modify</u> and are therefore nonrestrictive. Set them off with commas.

EXAMPLES   Natalie's mother, **a lawyer in Boston,** will be coming to visit her soon.

Kleenex, **a household necessity,** was invented as a substitute for bandages during World War I because of a cotton shortage.

Parker took his stamp collection to Mr. Poindexter, **a noted stamp expert.**

PRACTICE   In the following sentences, set off all appositives with commas.

1. The Tickled Trout, a nearby seafood restaurant, attracts many customers.

2. Persephone stared at the pomegranate the only fruit in sight.

3. Eros the son of the goddess Aphrodite plays all sorts of tricks on mortals.

4. One of the Roman versions of Eros is Cupid the angelic-looking creature with a bow and arrow.

5. The hummingbirds at my house an extremely picky group refuse to drink at my feeder.

---

3. <u>Use commas to separate most explanatory words from direct quotations.</u>

EXAMPLES   Mr. Jones asked, "Where are you going?"

"I will arrive before dinner is over," **he remarked.**

"Tonight's dinner," **he said,** "will be delayed."

NOTE: Do not use commas to separate explanatory words from a partial direct quotation.

EXAMPLE   He described the clouds as "ominous, dark, and threatening."

4. <u>Use commas to set off words of direct addresses.</u> If a writer addresses someone directly in a sentence, the word or words that stand for that person or persons are set off by commas. If the word or words in direct address begin the sentence, they are followed by a comma.

☉☉ EXAMPLES   And now, **my good friends,** I think it is time to end this conversation.

Mr. Chairman, I rise to a point of order.

I would like to present my proposal, **my esteemed colleagues.**

5. Use commas to set off dates and addresses. If your sentence contains two, three, or more elements of the date or address, use commas to set off these elements. The following sentences contain two or more elements.

☉☉ EXAMPLES   We visited Disneyland on **Monday, June 5,** in order to avoid the weekend rush.

We visited Disneyland on **Monday, June 5, 2005,** in order to avoid the weekend rush.

Celia has lived at **3225 Oliver Street, San Diego,** for five years.

Celia has lived at **3225 Oliver Street, San Diego, California,** for five years.

Celia has lived at **3225 Oliver Street, San Diego, California 92023,** for five years.

NOTE: The zip code is not separated from the state by a comma.

The following sentences contain only one element.

☉☉ EXAMPLES   We visited Disneyland on **Monday** in order to avoid the weekend rush.

Celia has lived at **3225 Oliver Street** for five years.

☉☉ PRACTICE   In the following sentences, use commas to set off explanatory words for direct quotations, words in direct address, and dates and addresses that have two or more elements.

1. Hester, have you lived at 4590 A Street, Salem, Massachusetts, for the past two years?

2. The package that was mailed on Friday September 13 1875 from Transylvania Ohio never made it to Carlsbad California.

3. Hellboy's girlfriend smiled and said "Red is the color of my true love's hair."

4. The multicolored togas arrived at The Debauchery 415 Cicero Street Rome Arkansas on the day before Saturnalia began.

5. Throw the ball Peyton.

PRACTICE   Use commas to set off parenthetical expressions, nonrestrictive elements, explanatory words for direct quotations, words in direct address, and dates and addresses that have two or more elements.

1. Placido, for instance, is rarely seen without a coffee cup.

2. A misanthrope who is a person who dislikes other people is usually not well liked.

3. *The Tell-Tale Tart* a novel by Dulcinea Baker will soon be a movie.

4. Mallory how many actors have played James Bond?

5. This year Easter occurs on April 12 2009 which is the first Sunday after the first full moon after the vernal equinox.

6. The missing coprolite was found on August 10 1954 in Rome Georgia.

7. Clint Eastwood accepting his latest Oscar wore a gun belt with a six-shooter in it.

8. "The spiders have arrived" said Harker "and I'm ready."

9. Mark Misanthrope for instance has not one single friend.

10. Clark please tell Scarlett who is a sensitive Southern belle that you apologize for using the word *damn*.

Section One Review

Rules for the Use of the Comma

1. <u>Use a comma before a coordinating conjunction that joins two main clauses.</u>

2. <u>Use commas to separate elements in a series.</u>

   a. Elements in a series may be words, phrases, or clauses.

   b. Two or more adjectives that modify the same noun may need to be separated with commas.

3. <u>Use a comma after an introductory element.</u> Introductory elements include:

   a. Introductory words

   b. Transitional expressions

   c. Prepositional phrases

   d. Verbal phrases

   e. Adverb clauses

4. <u>Use commas to separate interrupters from the rest of the sentence.</u> Interrupters include:

   a. Parenthetical expressions

   b. Nonrestrictive clauses

   c. Nonrestrictive participial phrases

   d. Appositives

   e. Explanatory words for direct quotations

   f. Words in direct address

   g. Dates and addresses with two or more elements

Exercise 1A

Add commas to the following sentences where necessary.

1. Satumo's father has high blood pressure,and his mother has asthma.

2. Arachna had long thin arms and legs but never considered herself unattractive.

3. She was however embarrassed about her red hourglass birthmark.

4. Rush Limbaugh a famous conservative radio personality made the cover of *The New Yorker* magazine as a crying infant smoking a cigar.

5. The hopeful man replied "The only way to get rid of a temptation is to give in to it."

6. The man in the previous sentence was stealing a quotation from Oscar Wilde who was famous for his wit.

7. Inside the wet crumpled piece of paper Carlton found a warning not to make any more three-point shots.

8. The television and film industries suffering from low ratings have decided to introduce 3-D.

9. Coming from the humblest of Irish conditions Seamus Heaney a contemporary poet was awarded the Nobel Prize for Literature.

10. Icarus you must gather a pound of feathers today.

11. Before Virgil entered the room full of geeks he checked his pocket protector.

12. The fearsome belligerent crowd on December 8 1857 supported slavery but that did not deter Abraham Lincoln who gave one of the most powerful speeches of his career.

13. Sofia was wise beyond her years; however she was unable to program the DVD player.

14. No the stock market crash in 2008 did not bother anyone who lives in Utopia Texas.

15. Sav-on which is a large drugstore chain has had a hard time procuring Band-Aids lately.

Exercise 1B

Add commas to the following sentences where necessary.

1. Over the last fifty years, many people have noticed that Mickey Mouse has only four fingers.

2. He has in fact only three fingers and one thumb on each hand.

3. Donald Duck Goofy and Minnie Mouse also have only four fingers each.

4. If you ever visit Disneyland in Anaheim California or Disney World in Orlando Florida look at the hands of the costumed characters.

5. Even Chip and Dale who are two cartoon chipmunks have only four fingers on each hand.

6. When cartoonists and animators are asked about this phenomenon they say that there is a good reason for it.

7. It is more convenient to draw four fingers than five and it also saves time.

8. In cartoons before the seventies each frame was painstakingly drawn by hand.

9. A team of cartoonists would perform this tedious tiring work for weeks on end.

10. Because the hand is difficult to keep in proportion to the rest of the body it is the most difficult part of the anatomy to draw.

11. Many artists have particular difficulty drawing individual fingers so Mickey was drawn with one finger missing.

12. Today's computerized animation which revolutionized the cartoon industry could replace the missing digit but no one is willing to change well-known cartoon characters.

13. Therefore most of the characters in cartoons by Disney Warner Brothers and other production companies still have only four fingers.

Exercise 1B

continued

14. Since more realistic animated characters usually have five fingers Snow White and Cinderella were spared this amputation.

15. No one knows for sure which of Mickey's fingers was severed for convenience but we hope it was not a major one.

Exercise 1C

In the following paragraph, add commas wherever they are needed.

1. Even though the United States and Mexico share a common border, the customs, activities, and traditions differ when they celebrate holidays. **2.** For example Independence Day is an important occasion for each country. **3.** On the Fourth of July in the United States people shoot off fireworks and they eat American food like hotdogs hamburgers potato salad potato chips and ice cream. **4.** Mexico on the other hand celebrates its independence over two days September 15 and 16. **5.** As students parade through the streets people blow horns throw confetti and wave flags. **6.** Ever since September 16 1810 the Mexican president has yelled "Viva Mexico!" from the Presidential Palace at exactly 12:00 A.M. **7.** Two other holidays Halloween in the United States and *Dia de los Muertos* in Mexico are also celebrated in differing ways. **8.** On the night of the American Halloween young children dress up in costumes and then they go door-to-door begging for candies. **9.** Similarly many American adults dress up in costumes and attend parties. **10.** In Mexico on *Dia de los Muertos* people take food to the dead clean tombstones and decorate the graves with flowers and candles. **11.** Instead of asking for candy Mexican children in some cities go around town asking for gifts of candles or money. **12.** Finally Easter celebrations in Mexico and the United States have both similarities and differences. **13.** People in the United States dress up quite formally to go to church and then the children hunt for decorated Easter eggs to put in their Easter baskets. **14.** Of course people in Mexico also dress up and go to church; in addition many of them reenact the crucifixion of Christ. **15.** Some things that will not be found in a Mexican Easter celebration however are Easter eggs and bunnies. **16.** Having spent several years in both cultures I can appreciate and enjoy the differences in these holiday celebrations.

Other Punctuation Marks

Punctuation would be simple if we could just include a page of punctuation marks at the end of a piece of writing and invite readers to sprinkle them about anywhere they choose. But if you want to be an effective writer, it helps a great deal to know how to use not only those troublesome commas but also all of the other marks of punctuation. In this section, we will take up end punctuation and the other punctuation marks.

The placement of punctuation marks can affect the meaning of a sentence profoundly. Here are a few examples.

In this sentence, the dog recognizes its owner.

EXAMPLE   A clever dog knows **its** master.

In this one, the dog is in charge.

EXAMPLE   A clever dog knows **it's** master.

In this sentence, we find a deliberately rude butler.

EXAMPLE   The butler stood by the door and called the **guests** names as they entered.

In this sentence, he is more mannerly.

EXAMPLE   The butler stood by the door and called the **guests'** names as they entered.

And in this sentence, we find a person who doesn't trust his friends.

EXAMPLE   Everyone **I know** has secret ambitions.

Add two commas, and you change the meaning.

EXAMPLE   Everyone, **I know,** has secret ambitions.

As you can see, punctuation marks are potent tools.

End Punctuation

The Period

1. The period is used at the end of a sentence that makes a statement or gives a command.

EXAMPLES   This rule is probably the easiest of all.

            Circle the subject in the above sentence.

2. The period is used with most abbreviations.

EXAMPLES   Mr., Mrs., Dr., A.D., Ph.D., U.S., St., Rd., Blvd., Sgt., Lt.

The Question Mark

1. The question mark is used at the end of sentences that ask questions.

EXAMPLES   Where have all the flowers gone?

Is the water hot yet?

2. A question mark is not used at the end of an indirect question.

EXAMPLES   (direct question)   Why is Emile going to the dance?

(indirect question)   I wonder why Emile is going to the dance.

The Exclamation Point

1. The exclamation point is used after words, phrases, and short sentences that show strong emotion.

EXAMPLES   Rats!

Not on your life!

Watch it, Buster!

Ouch! That hurt!

2. The exclamation point is not often used in college writing. For the most part, the words themselves should express the excitement.

EXAMPLE   Chased by a ravenous pack of ocelots, Cedric raced through the forest to his condo, bolted up his stairs, swiftly locked the door, and threw himself, quivering and exhausted, onto his beanbag chair.

PRACTICE   Use periods, question marks, and exclamation points in the following sentences.

1. Robinson wondered whether he would ever leave the island .

2. Have you fed Cerberus

3. The *Titanic* is sinking

4. The pitcher asked his catcher if he should throw a curve

5. Has Penelope been underground for six months yet

   6. What is a quark

   7. Help me

   8. Michael received his Ph D from Arizona State University

   9. Why did they leave the game so early

   10. After five days the fish wondered if it had worn out its welcome

---

Internal Punctuation

The Semicolon

   1. A semicolon is used to join two main clauses that are not joined by a coordinating conjunction. Sometimes a transitional word or phrase follows the semicolon.

   EXAMPLES   Thirteen people saw the incident; each one described it differently.

   All tragedies end in death; on the other hand, all comedies end in marriage.

   2. A semicolon can be used to join elements in a series when the elements require further internal punctuation.

   EXAMPLE   Before making his decision, Elrod consulted his banker, who abused him; his lawyer, who ignored him; his minister, who consoled him; and his mother, who scolded him.

   3. Do not use a semicolon to separate two phrases or two subordinate clauses.

   EXAMPLE   (incorrect)   I will pay you for the work when you return the tape deck that was stolen from our car; and when you repair the dented left fender.

The Colon

   1. A colon is used to join two main clauses when the second clause is an example, an explanation, or a restatement of the first clause.

   EXAMPLES   The past fifty years had been a time of turmoil: war, drought, and famine had plagued the small country.

   The garden was a delight to all insects: aphids abounded in it, ladybugs exulted in it, and praying mantises cavorted in it.

2. A colon is used when a complete sentence introduces an example, a series, a list, or a direct quotation. Often a colon will come after the words *follows* or *following.*

EXAMPLES

The paper explored the comic elements of three Melville novels: *Moby Dick, Mardi,* and *Pierre.*

The list of complaints included the following items: leaky faucets, peeling wallpaper, and a nauseating green love seat.

3. A colon is generally not used after a verb.

EXAMPLES

(incorrect)   At the store I bought: bread, eggs, and bacon.

(correct)   At the store I bought bread, eggs, and bacon.

PRACTICE   In the following sentences, add semicolons and colons where necessary.

1. You crack three eggs into the pan;then you stir them slowly.

2. The aspiring star did the following to prepare for his audition got disturbing tattoos all over his body, dyed his hair extravagant colors, and learned two chords on the guitar.

3. We seem to be running out of superheroes however, I am sure more will magically appear when needed.

4. The principal did not condone body piercing, tattoos, tight tops, or short skirts.

5. Brad hated one thing about fatherhood more than any other changing his baby's dirty diapers.

Quotation Marks

1. Quotation marks are used to enclose direct quotations and dialogue.

EXAMPLES

"When a stupid man is doing something he is ashamed of, he always declares that it is his duty."
                                        —George Bernard Shaw

Woody Allen said, "If my film makes one more person miserable, I've done my job."

2. Quotation marks are not used with indirect quotations.

EXAMPLES

(direct quotation)　　Fernando said, "I will be at the airfield before the dawn."

(indirect quotation)　Fernando said that he would be at the airfield before the dawn.

3. Place periods and commas inside quotation marks.

EXAMPLES

Flannery O'Connor wrote the short story "A Good Man Is Hard to Find."

"Always forgive your enemies—nothing annoys them so much," quipped Oscar Wilde.

4. Place colons and semicolons outside quotation marks.

EXAMPLES

Priscilla was disgusted by the story "The Great Toad Massacre": it was grossly unfair to toads and contained too much gratuitous violence.

Abner felt everyone should read the essay "The Shocking State of Okra Cookery"; he had even had several copies made just in case he found someone who was interested.

5. Place the question mark inside the quotation marks if the quotation is a question. Place the question mark outside the quotation marks if the quotation is not a question but the whole sentence is.

EXAMPLES

The poem asks, "What are patterns for?"

Did Mark Twain say, "Never put off until tomorrow what you can do the day after tomorrow"?

6. Place the exclamation point inside the quotation marks if the quotation is an exclamation. Place it outside the quotation marks if the quotation is not an exclamation but the whole sentence is.

EXAMPLES

"An earwig in my ointment!" the disgusted pharmacist proclaimed.

Please stop saying "It's time to leave"!

PRACTICE

Add semicolons, colons, and quotation marks to the following sentences.

1. Dante said, "I like this place, but I would like to leave now"; however, Virgil told him that no one was allowed to leave.

2. Batman was afraid of losing his significant other to the district attorney moreover, he had lately developed a fear of heights.

3. Who was it who said, Give me Spam, okra, hush puppies, and rhubarb pie, or give me nothing?

4. My favorite Mae West quotation is this one When I'm good, I'm very good, but when I'm bad, I'm better.

5. Coltrane looked at Davis and said, Tell me a few of my favorite things.

6. Where should I hide the letter? asked Edgar.

7. Was it Mark Twain who said, I believe that our Heavenly Father invented man because he was disappointed in the monkey?

8. Ironman screamed, Get me some rust preventative!

9. Humpty fell off the wall and broke he could not understand why all the king's men were calling for Super Glue.

10. Oscar Wilde once said, Consistency is the last refuge of the unimaginative.

The Apostrophe

1. <u>Apostrophes are used to form contractions.</u> The apostrophe replaces the omitted letter or letters.

I am	I'm	did not	didn't
you are	you're	is not	isn't
it is	it's	were not	weren't
they are	they're	will not	won't
does not	doesn't	cannot	can't

2. <u>Apostrophes are used to form the possessives of nouns and indefinite pronouns.</u>

   a. Add *'s* to form the possessive of all singular nouns and all indefinite pronouns.

EXAMPLES

(singular nouns)	The **girl's** hair was shiny.
	Charles's car is rolling down the hill.
(indefinite pronouns)	**Everyone's** watch was affected by the giant magnet.
(compound words)	Mr. Giuliano left on Monday to attend his **son-in-law's** graduation.
(joint possession)	**Vladimir and Natasha's** wedding was long and elaborate.

   b. Add only an apostrophe to form the possessive of plural nouns that end in *s*. However, add *'s* to form the possessive of plural nouns that do not end in *s*.

EXAMPLES

(plural nouns that end in *s*)

The **Joneses'** cabin had been visited by an untidy bear.

We could hear the three **friends'** conversation all the way down the hall.

(plural nouns that do not end in *s*)

During the storm the parents were concerned about their **children's** safety.

   c. Expressions referring to time or money often require an apostrophe.

EXAMPLES

Please give me one **dollar's** worth.

Two **weeks'** vacation is simply not enough.

3. Do not use apostrophes with the possessive forms of personal pronouns.

Incorrect	*Correct*
her's	hers
our's	ours
their's	theirs

NOTE: *It's* means "it is." The possessive form of *it* is *its*.

PRACTICE   Add apostrophes (or *'s*) to the following sentences where necessary.

1. Everyone was looking for Alices rabbit; he wouldnt come when we

    called him.

2. Mr. Lewis sense of propriety was bothered by Mr. Clarks rude remarks.

3. Did you see Mr. Audubons new bird illustration?

4. My brother was just let go from his job with only two days severance pay.

5. Jorges computer wasnt working, so he threw it into his fathers garage.

6. Its a shame that the meteor shower wont be visible from here.

7. Hed nearly reached the border when the cars engine blew.

8. He had one weeks free stay at his father-in-laws hotel.

9. Staring over the rim of Sylvias soup bowl was a cockroach.

10. The childrens favorite bedtime story was the one about the man with the

     hatchet.

PRACTICE   Write sentences of your own according to the instructions.

1. Write a complete sentence in which you use the possessive form of *women*.

   The women's basketball team is now playing in

   the semifinals.

2. Write a complete sentence in which you use the possessive form of *Thomas*.

   _____

   _____

3. Write a complete sentence in which you use the possessive form of *mother-in-law*.

   _____

   _____

4. Write a complete sentence in which you use the possessive form of a plural word.

   _____

   _____

5. Write a complete sentence in which you use the possessive form of *Ms. Lewis* and the contraction for *did not*.

   _____

   _____

Section Two Review

1. Use a **period** at the end of sentences that make statements or commands.

2. Use a **period** to indicate most abbreviations.

3. Use a **question mark** at the end of sentences that ask questions.

4. Do not use a **question mark** at the end of an indirect question.

5. Use an **exclamation point** after exclamatory words, phrases, and short sentences.

6. Use the **exclamation point** sparingly in college writing.

7. Use a **semicolon** to join two main clauses that are not joined by a coordinating conjunction.

8. Use a **semicolon** to separate elements in a series when the elements require further internal punctuation.

9. Do not use a **semicolon** to separate two phrases or two subordinate clauses.

10. Use a **colon** to join two main clauses when the second main clause is an example, an explanation, or a restatement.

11. Use a **colon** to introduce an example, a series, a list, or a direct quotation.

12. Do not use a **colon** to introduce a series of items that follows a verb.

13. Use **quotation marks** to enclose direct quotations and dialogue.

14. Do not use **quotation marks** with indirect quotations.

15. Place periods and commas inside **quotation marks.**

16. Place colons and semicolons outside **quotation marks.**

17. If a quotation is a question, place the question mark <u>inside</u> the **quotation marks.** If the quotation is not a question, but the whole sentence is, place the question mark <u>outside</u> the quotation marks.

18. If the quotation is an exclamation, place the exclamation point <u>inside</u> the **quotation marks.** If the quotation is not an exclamation, but the whole sentence is, place the exclamation point <u>outside</u> the quotation marks.

19. Use **apostrophes** to form contractions.

20. Use **apostrophes** to form the possessives of nouns and indefinite pronouns.

Exercise 2A

Add periods, question marks, exclamation points, semicolons, colons, quotation marks, and apostrophes (or 's) to the following sentences as necessary.

1. The firefighter shouted, "Watch out!"

2. Picassos girlfriends wondered why his depictions of women were so weird

3. Wont it be cloudy tomorrow asked Icarus

4. Tony Sopranos request included these items some antipasto, a loaf of Sicilian bread, a big plate of ravioli with pesto sauce, and some candied olives

5. The baseball players best friend asked if he had sought his mother-in-laws advice

6. One of Ben Jonsons lines about Shakespeare is He was not of an Age but for all time

7. Whose turn is it to play asked Miles

8. The Yankees let the Southerners escape from Gettysburg therefore, Lincoln was very angry

9. Did Thoreau write, As if you could kill time without injuring eternity

10. Igor Timidsky, Ph D, wouldnt board the airplane without his lucky rabbits foot.

11. Lincolns wife battled depression however, she was a charming, witty, and intelligent first lady.

12. When Leonard Cohens son heard his fathers song, he asked his father who his mother really was

13. Didnt people worry about Kirks volatile personality

14. The lookout on the ships highest mast shouted, There goes Moby Dick

15. Lawrence Putnam, M D , went to Afghanistan with these items goggles, water purifying tablets, a Swiss Army knife, and a dozen boxes of chocolate

Exercise 2B

Add periods, question marks, exclamation points, semicolons, colons, quotation marks, apostrophes (or *'s*), and commas to the following sentences where necessary.

1. The lobsters were bound for Rudy's Fish House, 591 Triton Street, Kansas City, Kansas.

2. All aboard yelled the conductor as the train prepared to leave the station

3. Did Jackson Pollock really paint that or are you just joking

4. The students did not respond to Fergals knock-knock jokes however they woke up when he started imitating Queen Elizabeth

5. Mark Twain said Im opposed to millionaires but it would be dangerous to offer me the position

6. There aint no way to find out why a snorer cant hear himself snore said Tom Sawyer

7. The Queen placed her arm on Michelle Obamas back therefore it was not improper for Ms Obama to place her arm on the Queens back

8. Dont you think the custom of taking off ones hat indoors is somewhat outmoded

9. The man at the fair asked Do you think you can knock down all three bottles

10. Drop that cotton candy right now hollered the police officer

11. The groups agent said Youll need the following to succeed in this business tattoos on both forearms a scar on one cheek tight leather pants ear plugs and little sensitivity to music

12. Lady Macbeth asked her friends valet where the soap and water were

13. Eros asked Romeo Doesnt Juliet have my bow

14. The childrens babysitter arrived with these items a gallon of ice cream two bugles a jump rope and one set of earplugs

15. Bruce Springsteens band was ready to leave the stage after its performance at the Super Bowl however the enthusiastic crowd wouldnt let it leave

Exercise 2C

In the following paragraph, correct any errors in the use of periods, exclamation points, question marks, semicolons, colons, quotation marks, or apostrophes.

1. King Lear, the central character in Shakespeare's *The Tragedy of King Lear,* and Willy Loman, the protagonist in Arthur Miller's *Death of a Salesman,* are similar characters in some ways. **2.** For instance, both character's mistakenly believe that their favorite child no longer loves them, therefore, they respond with anger and resentment. **3.** Lears three daughters are: Goneril, Regan, and Cordelia. **4.** Goneril and Regan insincerely flatter Lear, Cordelia refuses to do so. **5.** When Lear asks her what she will say to show her love, she replies: Nothing, my lord as a result, Lear disinherits her. **6.** Willy Loman also think's he has lost the love of his son Biff. **7.** In one scene he addresses Biff this way You vengeful, spiteful mutt! **8.** Then, just a few lines later, he realizes that Biff actually love's him. **9.** Lear and Loman are also similar: in that both seem to be losing their minds. **10.** From the very start of the play, there is evidence that Lears' thoughts are not rational. **11.** Even his closest counselor tells Lear he is acting foolishly, however, the king will not listen. **12.** By the middle of the play: Lear seems completely mad! **13.** Similarly, Willy Loman is having trouble distinguishing between: reality and fantasy. **14.** Willy constantly drifts into scene's from his past; or talks to his dead brother. **15.** Finally, both main characters are abandoned by children they thought were loyal to them. **16.** Lear is stripped of all his dignity by Goneril and Regan therefore, he ends up wandering through a raging storm with the court fool. **17.** Willy Loman is abandoned by his son Happy; who leaves him in the bathroom of a restaurant. **18.** When a woman remind's Happy about Willy, Happy makes this unsettling statement No, that's not my father. He's just a guy. **19.** In many ways these two plays are quite different, however, the two main characters' have some remarkable similarities.

Titles, Capitalization, and Numbers

The rules regarding titles, capitalization, and numbers are not, perhaps, as critical to clear writing as the ones for the punctuation marks discussed in the previous two sections. In fact, you can forget to capitalize at all without losing the meaning of what you are writing. So why should you learn to apply these rules correctly? The answer is simple. You should know how to apply them for the same reason you should know whether it is appropriate to slap a person on the back or to kiss him on both cheeks when you are first introduced. **How people write** says as much about them as **how they act.** Your ability to apply the rules presented in this section, as well as in other sections, identifies you as an educated person.

Titles

1. <u>Underline or place in italics the titles of works that are published separately, such as books, magazines, newspapers, and plays.</u>

   - Books: <u>Huckleberry Finn</u>, <u>Webster's Dictionary</u>

   - Plays: <u>Hamlet</u>, <u>Death of a Salesman</u>

   - Pamphlets: <u>How to Paint Your House</u>, <u>Worms for Profit</u>

   - Long musical works: Beethoven's <u>Egmont Overture</u>, Miles Davis's <u>Kind of Blue</u>

   - Long poems: <u>Paradise Lost</u>, <u>Beowulf</u>

   - Newspapers and magazines: <u>The New York Times</u>, <u>Newsweek</u>

   - Films: <u>The Aviator</u>, <u>Chicago</u>

   - Television and radio programs: <u>Morning Edition</u>, <u>American Idol</u>

   - Works of art: Rembrandt's <u>Night Watch</u>, <u>Venus de Milo</u>

EXAMPLES   Hortencia has subscriptions to <u>Newsweek</u> and <u>The New Yorker</u>.

The Los Angeles Chamber Orchestra played Bach's <u>Brandenburg Concerto Number Five</u>.

2. <u>Use quotation marks to enclose the titles of works that are parts of other works, such as articles, songs, poems, and short stories.</u>

   - Songs: "Honeysuckle Rose," "Yesterday"

   - Poems: "Stopping by Woods on a Snowy Evening," "The Waste Land"

- Articles in periodicals: "Texas Air's New Flak Attack," "Of Planets and the Presidency"
- Short stories: "Paul's Case," "Barn Burning"
- Essays: "A Modest Proposal," "Once More to the Lake"
- Episodes of radio and television programs: "Tolstoy: From Rags to Riches," "Lord Mountbatten: The Last Viceroy"
- Subdivisions of books: "The Pulpit" (Chapter Eight of *Moby Dick*)

⊚⊙ EXAMPLES

The professor played a recording of Dylan Thomas reading his poem "After the Funeral."

Many writing textbooks include Jonathan Swift's essay "A Modest Proposal."

⊚⊙ PRACTICE

In the following sentences, correct any errors in the use of titles.

1. On the plane I sat next to a priest reading Dan Brown's novel <u>The Da Vinci Code</u>.

2. In Langston Hughes's short story Salvation, a boy ironically loses his faith while participating in church services.

3. Robert Frost's poem The Road Not Taken is one of his most well known works.

4. Before Bud read his copy of the magazine Wired, he decided to eat dinner.

5. The movie The Wizard of Oz mixes both black-and-white and color photography.

Capitalization

1. <u>Capitalize the personal pronoun *I*.</u>

⊚⊙ EXAMPLE

In fact, **I** am not sure **I** like the way you said that.

2. <u>Capitalize the first letter of every sentence.</u>

⊚⊙ EXAMPLE

The road through the desert was endlessly straight and boring.

3. <u>Capitalize the first letter of each word in a title except for *a*, *an*, and *the*,</u> <u>coordinating conjunctions, and prepositions.</u>

   NOTE: The first letter of the first word and the first letter of the last word of a title are always capitalized.

   ■ Titles of books: <u>Moby Dick</u>, <u>Encyclopaedia Britannica</u>

   ■ Titles of newspapers and magazines: <u>People</u>, <u>Cosmopolitan</u>, <u>Los Angeles Times</u>

   ■ Titles of stories, poems, plays, and films: "The Lady with the Dog," "The Road Not Taken," <u>Othello</u>, <u>Gone with the Wind</u>

4. <u>Capitalize the first letter of all proper nouns and adjectives derived from</u> <u>proper nouns.</u>

   ■ Names and titles of people: Coretta Scott King, Mr. Birch, Mayor Golding, President Roosevelt, Cousin Alice, Aunt Bea

   ■ Names of specific places: Yosemite National Park, Albuquerque, New Mexico, London, England, Saudi Arabia, Rockefeller Center, London Bridge, Elm Street, Venus, the Rio Grande, the Rocky Mountains, the Midwest

   NOTE: Do not capitalize the first letter of words that refer to a direction (such as "north," "south," "east," or "west"). Do capitalize these words when they refer to a specific region.

EXAMPLES

Texas and Arizona are in the **Southwest.**

The police officer told us to drive **east** along the gravel road and turn **north** at the big pine tree.

   ■ Names of national, ethnic, or racial groups: Indian, Native-American, Spanish, Irish, Italian, African-American

   ■ Names of groups or organizations: Baptists, Mormons, Democrats, Republicans, American Indian Movement, Boy Scouts of America, Indianapolis Colts, U.S. Post Office

   ■ Names of companies: Ford Motor Company, Montgomery Ward, Coca-Cola Bottling Company

   ■ Names of the days of the week and months of the year but not the seasons: Thursday, August, spring

   ■ Names of holidays and historical events: Memorial Day, the Fourth of July, the French Revolution, the Chicago Fire

   ■ Names of <u>specific</u> gods and religious writings: God, Mohammed, Talmud, Bible

5. <u>The names of academic subjects are not capitalized unless they refer to an ethnic or national origin or are the names of specific courses.</u> Examples include mathematics, political science, English, History 105.

🌀 PRACTICE

Correct any errors in the use of titles or capitalization.

1. In february, the San Diego Symphony will present a series of concerts of Mozart's works.

2. michelle obama received a signed copy of toni morrison's latest novel a mercy.

3. born in lorain, ohio, ms. morrison has been on the cover of many magazines, including time.

4. uncle elvis was playing bruce springsteen's song born in the u.s.a. when I told him john updike had died.

5. a number of men and women from boise, idaho, participated in operation desert storm and are now continuing to fight in the war in iraq.

6. during the christmas holidays, one can see beautiful decorations in santa fe and albuquerque.

7. in california, the native american tribes are having a legal battle with the state government over gambling.

8. at the barnes and noble bookstore, I found the film of shakespeare's play macbeth.

9. charlie showed marisa his collection of t.v. guide magazines.

10. the mervyn's store on oak street is closing at the beginning of summer.

Numbers

The following rules about numbers apply to general writing rather than to technical or scientific writing.

1. Spell out numbers that require no more than two words. Use numerals for numbers that require more than two words.

EXAMPLES   Last year it rained on only **eighty-four** days.

In 1986 it rained on more than **120** days.

2. Always spell out a number at the beginning of a sentence.

EXAMPLE   **Six hundred ninety** miles in one day is a long way to drive.

3. In general, use numerals in the following situations:

- Dates: August 9, 1973   30 C.E.   110 A.D.

- Sections of books and plays: Chapter 5, page 22
  Act 1, scene 3, lines 30–41

- Addresses: 1756 Grand Avenue
  Hemostat, Idaho 60047

- Decimals, percents, and fractions: 75.8   30%, 30 percent   1/5

- Exact amounts of money: $7.95 $1,300,000

- Scores and statistics: Padres 8 Dodgers 5   a ratio of 6 to 1

- Time of day: 3:05   8:15

NOTE: Round amounts of money that can be expressed in a few words can be written out: *twenty cents, fifty dollars, one hundred dollars.* Also, when the word *o'clock* is used with the time of day, the time of day can be written out: *seven o'clock.*

4. When numbers are compared, are joined by conjunctions, or occur in a series, either consistently use numerals or consistently spell them out. Although either method is acceptable, using numerals is often clearer—and certainly easier.

EXAMPLE   For the company picnic we need **twenty-five** pounds of fried chicken, **fifteen** pounds of potato salad, **one hundred twenty-five** cans of soda, **eighty-five** paper plates, **two hundred thirty** napkins, and **eighty-five** sets of plastic utensils.

OR

For the company picnic we need **25** pounds of fried chicken, **15** pounds of potato salad, **125** cans of soda, **85** paper plates, **230** napkins, and **85** sets of plastic utensils.

PRACTICE   Correct any errors in the use of numbers in the following sentences.

1. *Twenty thousand* ~~20,000~~ fans attended the Metallica concert at the stadium, and *twenty* ~~20~~ of them were ejected for various offenses.

2. One never knows when all 5 members of Jim's jazz band will show up; it could be at nine o'clock or at twelve forty-five.

3. For the retirement party, Charlie brought 15 pastries, Woz brought 1 Clark Bar, Barbara brought one hundred fifteen pounds of fresh tuna, and Carlton brought 3 chocolate cheesecakes.

4. The inauguration ceremony on January twentieth, two thousand and nine, was historically unique.

5. On the first day of the 2009 baseball season, sixty thousand people in Petco Park watched San Diego lose to the Dodgers by a score of 4 to 1.

Section Three Review

1. Underline or place in italics the **titles** of works that are published separately, such as books, plays, and films.

2. Use quotation marks to enclose the **titles** of works that are parts of other works, such as songs, poems, and short stories.

3. **Capitalize** the personal pronoun *I*.

4. **Capitalize** the first letter of every sentence.

5. **Capitalize** the first letter of each word in a title except *a, an, the,* coordinating conjunctions, and prepositions.

6. **Capitalize** all proper nouns and adjectives derived from proper nouns.

7. **Do not capitalize** names of academic subjects unless they refer to an ethnic or national origin or are the names of specific courses.

8. Spell out **numbers** that require no more than two words. Use numerals for numbers that require more than two words.

9. Always spell out a **number** at the beginning of a sentence.

10. In general, use **numerals** for dates, sections of books and plays, addresses, decimals, percents, fractions, exact amounts of money, scores, statistics, and time of day.

11. When **numbers** are compared, are joined by conjunctions, or occur in a series, either consistently use numerals or consistently spell them out.

Exercise 3A

The following sentences contain errors in the use of titles, capitalization, and numbers. Correct any errors you find.

1. The movie *f̶atal f̶ttraction* caused much discussion about how men treat women and women treat men.

2. The television series the sopranos was about a gang of mobsters in new jersey.

3. president bush decided to invade iraq not long after the twin towers of the world trade center in new york city were attacked by terrorists.

4. 30 people from st. barnaby's church gathered at 5 o'clock on the top of mount harrison to observe easter sunday.

5. When tony said "sex" instead of "6," his teacher said he had made a freudian slip.

6. The marxist strategy used by yale university helped its philosophy department defeat the english department of harvard university by a score of 15 to twelve.

7. On his way to rome on march fifteenth, forty-four B.C., brutus bought a cheap dagger for the equivalent of five dollars and ninety-five cents.

8. After he typed the memorandum on his apple computer, the secretary ordered three reams of copy paper, 250 file folders, four boxes of pencils, and 150 filters for the coffee machine.

9. The msg computer company donated two thousand three hundred forty dollars to homer and hortense college for computer programs to study the effect of a spam diet on discontented students.

10. leonard cohen recently appeared in london and sang 2 of my favorite songs, suzanne and bird on the wire.

11. when the late show with david letterman ended, a commercial for wit magazine followed.

12. One student in our shakespeare class told of an article in people magazine titled the bard, his mother, and freud.

Exercise 3A

continued

13. bruce smiled as he told the class the significance of willy loman's two heavy valises in the play death of a salesman.

14. Every day at the chicago art institute, over 150 people ask guards about the secret meaning of the pitchfork in grant wood's painting american gothic.

15. after professor thomas explained the poem do not go gentle into that good night to his literature 202 class, he bought 2 bottles of cutty sark scotch on the way home.

Exercise 3B

Compose sentences of your own according to the instructions.

1. Write a sentence that includes the author and title of a book.

During his vacation, Rafael read Jane Smiley's novel

A Thousand Acres.

2. Write a sentence that describes a song you like and the musician who wrote it or performs it.

3. Tell what movie you last saw in a theater and how much you paid to see it.

4. Write a sentence that tells what school you attend and what classes you are taking.

5. Write a sentence that tells the number of people in your family, the number of years you have gone to school, the number of classes you are taking, and the approximate number of students at your school.

6. Write a sentence that mentions a magazine you have read lately. If possible, include the title of an article.

7. In a sentence, describe your favorite television program.

continued

8. Tell where you would go on your ideal vacation. Be specific about the name of the place and its geographical location.

_____

_____

9. Write a sentence that includes your age and address. (Feel free to lie about either one.)

_____

_____

10. Write a sentence that names a musician or musical group that you like and a tape or compact disc that you like.

_____

_____

11. Write a sentence that includes the name of a local newspaper, its approximate circulation, and the average number of pages during the week.

_____

_____

12. Write a sentence that includes a work of art that you know about and the name of the artist. If you need to, make up the name of a work of art and its artist.

_____

_____

13. Write a sentence that includes the score of the last baseball, football, or basketball game you were aware of. If you are not a sports fan, make up a score.

_____

_____

continued

14. Write a sentence that tells what time you get up on Mondays, what time your first class starts, what time you have lunch, and what time you usually have dinner.

_____

_____

Exercise 3C

In the following paragraph, correct any errors in the use of capitalization, numbers, or titles.

1. Computer technology has transformed the M̶ovie/I̶ndustry, creating visual effects that are often stunning in their realism, but the story lines of these new movies are not much different from those of ~~40~~ *forty* years ago. **2.** Consider, for example, "Jurassic Park" of the 1990s and "Mysterious Island" of the 1950s. **3.** Both movies involve a group of about 5 people who are trapped on an Island inhabited by huge, dangerous animals that do not exist anywhere else. **4.** The animals in Jurassic Park, of course, are Dinosaurs; in Mysterious Island they are a gigantic bee, crab, and bird. **5.** As the magazine article <u>Monsters And Madness</u> points out, the plots in both movies are about the same. **6.** Two other movies that are not so different from each other are Mimic of nineteen ninety-seven and Them of the late nineteen fifties. **7.** Mimic involves cockroaches that have been genetically altered by a Scientist working in the Eastern part of <u>New York</u>. **8.** They live in old subway tunnels of new york city and have mutated until they are able to mimic the size and appearance of Humans. **9.** 100s of them are feasting on captured humans and are threatening to establish new colonies in the Spring, but luckily they are destroyed by fire and explosives. **10.** According to a review in newsweek, the plot of "Them" from the 1950s is very similar. **11.** In it ants have been mutated by radiation from Atomic testing. **12.** The giant Queen Ant and a consort of over 25 males have flown into the sewer tunnels under "Los Angeles" and have started a colony that threatens Civilization. **13.** They are destroyed the same way the cockroaches in <u>Mimic</u> are, with fire and explosives. **14.** Finally, the movie Independence Day, which came out on the fourth of july a few years ago, is similar in many ways to Invaders From Mars from the 1950s. **15.** As the los angeles times newspaper points out in an article titled save us from the aliens, both movies involve Aliens from Outer Space intent upon taking over the Planet. **16.** In addition, the 2 movies feature similar bug-headed enemies with no apparent sympathy or concern for Humanity. **17.** And in both movies representatives of the <u>Military</u> are called upon to save the day. **18.** Obviously, computer technology has made the movies of today exciting, but plots themselves have not changed much in the past 40 years.

Sentence Practice: Sentence Variety

Writing is challenging. As we have pointed out a number of times already, writing is a process that requires constant and countless choices. Much head scratching and crossing out go on between the beginning and the end of composing a paragraph. Each sentence can be framed in numerous ways, each version changing—subtly or dramatically—the relationships among the ideas.

Sometimes a short sentence is best. Look at the one that begins this paragraph and the one that begins the paragraph above. At other times you will need longer sentences to get just the right meaning and feeling. Sentence combining exercises give you an opportunity to practice how to express ideas in various ways by encouraging you to move words, phrases, and clauses around to achieve different effects.

When you construct a sentence, you should be aware not only of how it expresses your ideas but also of how it affects the other sentences in the paragraph. Consider the following paragraph as an example. It is the opening paragraph of Rachel Carson's book *The Edge of the Sea.*

> The edge of the sea is a strange and beautiful place. All through the long history of the earth it has been an area of unrest where waves have broken heavily against the land, where the tides have pressed forward over the continents, receded, and then returned. For no two successive days is the shoreline precisely the same. Not only do the tides advance and retreat in their eternal rhythms, but the level of the sea itself is never at rest. It rises or falls as the glaciers melt or grow, as the floor of the deep ocean basins shifts under its increasing load of sediments, or as the earth's crust along the continental margins warps up or down in adjustment to strain and tension. Today a little more land may belong to the sea, tomorrow a little less. Always the edge of the sea remains an elusive and indefinable boundary.

As you can see, Rachel Carson opens her paragraph with a short, simple sentence. Then she writes a sentence that is much longer and more complicated because it begins to explain the general ideas in the first one. It even seems to capture the rhythm of the sea against the land. She follows that one with another short, simple sentence. As the paragraph continues, she varies the length and complexity of her sentences according to what she needs to say. Notice how she ends the paragraph with another simple statement that matches her opening sentence.

Sentence Combining Exercises

In the following sentence combining exercises, you will practice writing sentences so that some are short and concise and others are lengthier and more complex.

⟲⟲ **EXAMPLE**   Combine the following sentences into either two or three sentences. Experiment with which sounds best.

a. There was a feud.
b. It began simply enough.
c. The Smiths' youngest son refused to marry the Millers' favorite daughter.
d. Mrs. Miller fed Grandfather Smith some potato salad.
e. The potato salad was tainted.
f. They were at the annual Presidents' Day picnic.
g. Nothing was the same after that.

The feud began simply enough. When the Smiths' youngest son refused to marry the Millers' favorite daughter, Mrs. Miller fed Grandfather Smith some tainted potato salad at the annual Presidents' Day picnic. Nothing was the same after that.

1. Combine the following sentences into three sentences.

a. There was a choice.
b. It was not difficult to make.
c. Jake was not the one who had robbed the stage.
d. Jake knew that the townspeople were convinced he was guilty.
e. The townspeople planned to lynch him if they caught him.
f. Jake had to steal a horse.
g. Jake had to leave town now.

_____

_____

_____

_____

continued

2. Combine the following sentences into three sentences.

   a. The male stickleback fish must be quite shy.
   b. He usually has a silver-colored belly.
   c. He is brown to green everywhere else.
   d. During mating season, his belly turns bright red.
   e. Perhaps he is trying to attract a mate.
   f. Perhaps he is blushing.

_____

_____

_____

_____

3. Combine the following sentences into four or five sentences:

   a. It was the championship day of the College World Series.
   b. Coach Barrigan of the Baltimore Lenores team received some good news.
   c. The best pitcher of the other team, the Hilo Alohas, was in the hospital.
   d. He had a viral infection.
   e. Their catcher was in jail.
   f. Good sportsmanship is important.
   g. Coach Barrigan agreed to refrain from his greatest pleasure.
   h. He would not chew tobacco during the game.

_____

_____

_____

_____

_____

Sentence Combining Exercises

continued

4. Combine the following sentences into two or three sentences.

    a. Some dictators are called benevolent.
    b. They do good things for the people.
    c. Napoleon Bonaparte was considered benevolent.
    d. Under Napoleon, industry expanded.
    e. Universities flourished.
    f. The civil law system was improved.
    g. The judicial system was reorganized.
    h. The Bank of France was established.
    i. Most dictators, however, are not benevolent.

_____

_____

_____

_____

_____

5. Combine the following sentences into four sentences:

    a. An astounding number of Americans died in the Civil War.
    b. More died than in all other wars combined.
    c. At first the northerners thought the war would be short.
    d. They called it the "Ninety Day War."
    e. No one believed it could last four bloody years.
    f. As many as 700,000 died in the war.
    g. That was more than double the number killed in World War II.

_____

_____

_____

_____

_____

Sentence Combining Exercises

continued

6. Combine the following sentences into three or four sentences.

    a. Forms of pizza have been around for hundreds of years.
    b. The pizza as we know it today did not come about until 1889.
    c. A tavern owner in Naples, Italy, was asked to concoct a dish to honor the visit of the Queen of Italy.
    d. His dish represented the colors of the Italian flag.
    e. Those colors are red, white, and green.
    f. The ingredients were tomatoes, mozzarella cheese, and basil.

\
\
\
\
\

7. Combine the following sentences into three sentences.

    a. In 1946 the United States conducted several atomic bomb tests.
    b. The tests took place on Bikini Atoll in the Marshall Islands.
    c. At the same time, the French introduced a new bathing suit.
    d. The bathing suit was skimpy.
    e. The bathing suit suggested an uninhibited state of nature.
    f. The bathing suit seemed to have the impact of an atomic bomb.
    g. It was quickly named the "bikini."

Sentence Combining Exercises

continued

8. Combine the following sentences into three sentences.

    a. The house was almost silent.
    b. A couple sat at a table.
    c. The table was in the kitchen.
    d. They were talking softly.
    e. They were talking about their children.
    f. The children were sleeping.
    g. The children were in their rooms upstairs.
    h. A clock was on a wall.
    i. The wall was filled with brightly colored crayon drawings.
    j. The clock had looked down on almost twenty years of family meals.
    k. The clock ticked quietly.

_____

_____

_____

_____

9. Combine the following sentences into three sentences.

    a. The first piece of Tupperware was a bathroom tumbler.
    b. It was made of polyethylene.
    c. It was made by Earl Tupper.
    d. Earl Tupper was a Du Pont chemist.
    e. He made it in 1945.
    f. The tumblers were popular.
    g. Next he made bowls.
    h. The bowls were in a variety of sizes.
    i. They had a revolutionary new seal.
    j. Flexing of the bowl's tight-fitting lid caused air to be expelled.
    k. The expelling of the air formed a vacuum.
    l. The vacuum caused outside air pressure to reinforce the seal.

_____

_____

_____

_____

Sentence Combining Exercises

continued

10. Combine the following sentences into three or four sentences.

    a. Today's "hot dog" really is named after a dog.
    b. The popular sausage was first developed in the 1850s.
    c. It was developed in Frankfurt, Germany.
    d. Some people called it a "frankfurter," after the city.
    e. Others called it a "dachshund sausage."
    f. It had a dachshund-like shape.
    g. In 1906 a New York cartoonist was drawing a vendor.
    h. The vendor was selling "hot dachshund sausages."
    i. The vendor was at a baseball game.
    j. The cartoonist abbreviated the term to "hot dog."
    k. The name stuck.

_____

_____

_____

_____

_____

_____

Essay and Paragraph Practice: Comparing and Contrasting

Assignment

Comparing or contrasting two topics is an activity that you participate in nearly every day. When you recognize that two people have much in common, you have observed similarities between them. When you decide to take one route rather than another, you have noticed differences between the two routes. Even something as simple as buying one toothpaste rather than another involves some sort of comparison and contrast. In fact, recognizing similarities and differences affects every part of our lives. How could you know if you were looking at a tree or a bush if you were not able to see their differences as well as their similarities?

Much college writing involves comparing or contrasting two topics. You may be asked to compare (show similarities between) the results of two lab experiments in a biology class or to contrast (show differences between) the religious beliefs of two cultures in an anthropology class. In addition, in many classes you may be asked to write papers or reports or to take essay exams in which you show both the similarities and the differences between two related topics.

Exercises 1C, 2C, and 3C in this chapter are comparison/contrast paragraphs. Exercise 1C compares holidays in the United States to holidays in Mexico; Exercise 2C compares King Lear in *The Tragedy of King Lear* to Willy Loman in *Death of a Salesman*; and Exercise 3C compares several movies of the 1990s to those of the 1950s. Note that each of these paragraphs opens with a topic sentence that makes a statement about similarities or differences.

Your assignment is to write an essay or a paragraph (whichever your instructor assigns) that compares and/or contrasts two related topics. Develop your paper from the ideas that follow.

Prewriting to Generate Ideas

Prewriting Application: Finding Your Topic

As you read the following topics, remember that the one that looks the easiest may not result in the best paper for you. Use the techniques of freewriting, brainstorming, and/or clustering to develop your reactions to several of these ideas before you choose one of them. Look for the topic idea that interests you the most, the one to which you have an emotional or personal reaction.

1. Compare and/or contrast your city or neighborhood with one you used to live in.

2. Compare and/or contrast a place as it is today with the way it was when you were a child.

3. Compare and/or contrast what you expected college to be like before you enrolled in your first class with what you found it to be like later on.

4. If you are returning to school after several years' absence, compare and/or contrast your last school experience with your current one.

5. Compare and/or contrast the characteristics of someone you know with a stereotype. For example, if you know an athlete or a police officer, compare and/or contrast that person's actual personality with the stereotype people have of athletes or police officers.

6. Compare and/or contrast your latest vacation or trip with your vision of the ideal vacation or trip.

7. Compare and/or contrast two sports, two athletes, or two teams.

8. Compare and/or contrast the person you are today with the person you were several years ago.

9. Compare and/or contrast any two places, persons, or events that you remember well.

10. If you have a background in two cultures, compare and/or contrast a few specific characteristics of both cultures.

Choosing and Narrowing the Topic

Once you have settled on several possible topics, consider these points as you make your final selection.

- Choose the more limited topic rather than the more general one.

- Choose the topic about which you could discuss several, not just one or two, similarities or differences.

- Choose the topic about which you have the most experience or knowledge.

- Choose the topic in which you have the most personal interest. Avoid topics about which you do not really care.

Writing a Thesis Statement or Topic Sentence

If your assignment is to write a single paragraph, you will open it with a topic sentence. If you are writing a complete essay, you will need a thesis statement at the end of your introductory paragraph. In either case, you will need a clear statement of the topic and central idea of your paper.

Prewriting Application: Working with Topic Sentences

Identify the topic sentences in Exercises 1C (page 293), 2C (page 305), and 3C (page 318). Then identify the topic and the central point in each topic sentence. Finally, state whether the topic sentence is introducing a paragraph that will examine similarities or differences.

Prewriting Application: Evaluating Thesis Statements and Topic Sentences

Write "No" before each sentence that would not make an effective thesis statement or topic sentence for a comparison or contrast paper. Write "Yes" before each sentence that *would* make an effective one. Determine whether each effective sentence is introducing a comparison paper or a contrast paper. Using ideas of your own, rewrite each ineffective sentence into one that might work.

_____ **1.** I had not seen my hometown of Monroe, South Dakota, for over fifteen years, so when I visited it last summer I was amazed at how little it had changed.

_____

_____

_____ **2.** My father and mother love to watch the Kentucky Derby.

_____

_____

_____ **3.** Many holidays that are common to both Mexico and the United States are celebrated in very different ways.

_____

_____

_____ **4.** Our society is much worse in this day and age than it used to be.

_____

_____

_____ 5. This year's San Diego Padres is a better team than last year's in several key areas.

_____

_____

_____ 6. *Roxanne*, a 1980s movie starring Steve Martin, contains many similarities to the play *Cyrano de Bergerac*.

_____

_____

_____ 7. About the only thing that snowboarders and skiers have in common is that they share the same mountain.

_____

_____

_____ 8. While walking down the Las Vegas Strip last year, I was amazed at how bright and colorful everything was, even at two o'clock in the morning.

_____

_____

_____ 9. Although both the San Diego Zoo and the Wild Animal Park feature exotic animals, the two places are not at all similar.

_____

_____

_____ 10. Many things have happened to me in the past few years to make me a more tolerant person.

_____

_____

Prewriting Application: Talking to Others

Form a group of three or four people and discuss the topics you have chosen. Your goal here is to help each other clarify the differences or similarities that you are writing about. Explain your points as clearly as you can. As you listen to the others in your group, use the following questions to help them clarify their ideas.

1. Is the paper focusing on similarities or on differences?

2. Exactly what similarities or differences will be examined in the paper? Can you list them?

3. Which similarities or differences need to be explained more clearly or fully?

4. Which points are the most significant or most interesting? Why?

5. Which similarity or difference should the paper open with? Which should it close with?

Organizing Similarities and Differences

Point-by-Point Order

One of the most effective ways to present your ideas when you compare or contrast two topics is called a **point-by-point** organization. Using this method, you cover one similarity or difference at a time. For example, if you were contrasting snowboarders and skiers, one of the differences might be the general age level of each group. The first part of your paper would then contrast the ages of most snowboarders with the ages of most skiers. Another difference might be the clothing worn by the two groups. So you would next contrast the clothing of snowboarders with the clothing of skiers. You might then contrast the physical activity itself, explaining what snowboarders do on the snow that is different from what skiers do. Whatever points you cover, you take them one at a time, point by point. An outline of this method for a single paragraph would look like this:

Point by Point—Single Paragraph

Topic Sentence:	About the only thing that snowboarders and skiers have in common is that they share the same mountain.

I. Ages

    A.   Snowboarders

    B.   Skiers

II. Clothing

    A.   Snowboarders

    B.   Skiers

III. Physical Activity

    A.   Snowboarders

    B.   Skiers

Concluding Sentence

Point by Point—Essay

If you are writing a complete essay, the point-by-point pattern changes only in that you devote a separate paragraph to each point. Develop each paragraph with details and examples to illustrate the differences or similarities you are discussing.

Introductory Paragraph

Introductory sentences

ending with a

thesis statement

Thesis Statement: About the only thing that snowboarders and skiers have in common is that they share the same mountain.

1st Body Paragraph

I. *Topic sentence* about the difference in ages

    A.   Snowboarders

                Examples

    B.   Skiers

                Examples

2nd Body Paragraph

II. *Topic sentence* about the difference in clothing

    A.   Snowboarders

                Examples

    B.   Skiers

                Examples

3rd Body Paragraph

III. *Topic sentence* about the difference in technique

    A.   Snowboarders

                Examples

    B.   Skiers

                Examples

Concluding Paragraph

Concluding sentences
bringing the essay
to a close

Subject-by-Subject Order

Another method of organization presents the topics **subject by subject.** Using this method, you cover each point of one topic first and then each point of the second topic. Be careful with this organization. Because the points are presented separately rather than together, your paper might end up reading like two separate descriptions rather than like a comparison or contrast of the two topics. To make the comparison or contrast clear, cover the same points in the same order, like this:

Subject by Subject—Single Paragraph

Topic Sentence:	About the only thing that snowboarders and skiers have in common is that they share the same mountain.
I. Snowboarders	
A.	Ages
B.	Clothing
C.	Technique
II. Skiers	
A.	Ages
B.	Clothing
C.	Technique
Concluding Sentence	

Subject by Subject—Essay

The following example illustrates a paper with two body paragraphs—one for each subject. Depending on the complexity of your topic or assigned length of your paper, you may need to write more than one body paragraph per subject.

Introductory Paragraph

Introductory sentences
ending with a
thesis statement
Thesis Statement: About the only thing that snowboarders and skiers have in common is that they share the same mountain.

1st Body Paragraph

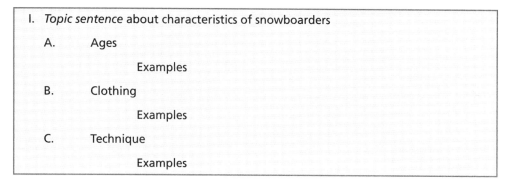

I. *Topic sentence* about characteristics of snowboarders

    A.   Ages

                Examples

    B.   Clothing

                Examples

    C.   Technique

                Examples

2nd Body Paragraph

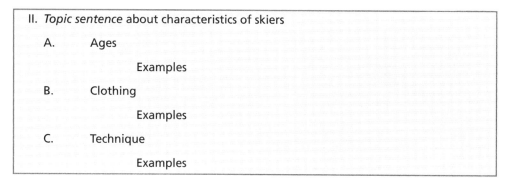

II. *Topic sentence* about characteristics of skiers

    A.   Ages

                Examples

    B.   Clothing

                Examples

    C.   Technique

                Examples

Concluding Paragraph

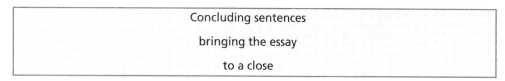

Concluding sentences

bringing the essay

to a close

Prewriting Application: Organization of the Comparison/Contrast Paragraph

Examine Exercise 1C (page 293), Exercise 2C (page 305), and Exercise 3C (page 318). Outline the paragraph in each exercise to determine its point-by-point or subject-by-subject organization.

Writing the Paper

Now write the rough draft of your paper. Pay particular attention to transitions as you write. If you are using a point-by-point organization, use a clear transition to introduce each point of comparison or contrast. For subject-by-subject organizations, write a clear transition as you move from the first subject of your paper to the second. In addition, as you write the second half of a subject-by-subject paper, use transitional words and phrases that refer to the first half of the paper in order to emphasize the similarities or differences.

Writing Application: Identifying Transitional Words, Phrases, and Sentences

Examine Exercises 1C (page 293), 2C (page 305), and 3C (page 318).

1. Identify the organizational pattern of each as point-by-point or subject-by-subject.

2. Identify transitions that introduce each point of comparison or contrast in a point-by-point paper or that move from one subject to another in a subject-by-subject paper.

3. In the subject-by-subject paper, identify transitions in the second half of the paper that emphasize the comparison or contrast by referring to the subject of the first half.

4. Identify any other transitions that serve to connect ideas between sentences.

Rewriting and Improving the Paper

1. Revise your sentences so they include specific and concrete details. As much as possible, use actual names of people and places, and refer to specific details whenever possible.

2. Add or revise transitions wherever doing so would help clarify movement from one idea to another.

3. Improve your preliminary thesis statement (if you are writing an essay) or your preliminary topic sentence (if you are writing a single paragraph) so that it more accurately states the central point of your paper.

4. Examine your draft for sentence variety. If many of your sentences tend to be of the same length, try varying their length and their structure by combining sentences using the techniques you have studied in the Sentence Practice sections of this text.

Rewriting Application: Responding to Paragraph Writing

Read the following paragraph. Then respond to the questions following it.

> ### *Romeo and Juliet*—Then and Now
>
> The 1968 movie version of William Shakespeare's play *Romeo and Juliet* contrasts with the updated version of 1996 in a number of ways. First, the 1968 director had the characters battle each other with swords. That is the way they fought back then, but today's youth couldn't really relate to that kind of situation. In the 1996 version the director wanted to

show a weapon that the audience had seen on TV shows and in other movies. Swords were replaced with shiny, artistic-looking handguns. Another contrast between the '68 version and the '96 one is the style of costumes. The '68 designers kept the clothing as it would have looked during Shakespeare's time, making the male actors wear puffy-sleeved shirts, tights, and little beanie hats. The women had to endure much worse attire, such as long, heavy dresses. The designers in the updated version knew that today's youth wouldn't sit through a movie about guys wearing tights or women wearing clothes that hid everything. Instead, they had the men wear shirts that were colorful, comfortable, and modern. They also wore basic black and dark blue pants. I felt I could take the characters more seriously in normal clothes than in the old English attire. Although both versions did keep the original words of the play, I am glad that the new version changed the music of the earlier one. For instance, the boring love song "A Time for Us" was replaced by a touching, romantic tune called "Kissing You." The new music helped me follow the plot a little better. When I watched the old version, there wasn't very much background music at all. I really had to follow what was going on by watching the actors, and even then the movie was hard to follow. In conclusion, I think the director of the '96 version did a wonderful job making *Romeo and Juliet* into a movie that appeals to the young people of today.

1. Identify the topic sentence. State its topic and central idea. Is it an effective topic sentence? Can you tell whether the paper will focus on similarities or differences?

2. Is this a point-by-point or subject-by-subject organization? How many points of contrast are covered in this paper? Identify them.

3. Identify the transitional sentences that introduce each major section of the paragraph. What other transitions are used between sentences?

4. Consider the organization of the paragraph. Would you change the order of the contrasts? Explain why or why not.

5. Consider the sentence variety. What sentences would you combine to improve the paragraph?

Rewriting Application: Responding to Essay Writing

Read the following essay. Then respond to the questions at the end of it.

Guamuchil

I was born in Guamuchil, Mexico, which is a small town near the Gulf of California. It is about six hundred miles south of the border in the state of Sinaloa. I have wonderful memories of growing up there, and I have wanted to visit it for many years. Therefore, I was really excited my husband and I decided to return to my hometown in 1994. Unfortunately, I found many changes there.

The very first difference I saw was the bridge that we crossed to enter the city from north to south. It used to be an attractive green bridge that crossed a wide flowing river. It had brightly painted rails that protected sidewalks on each side of it. In contrast to what I had described to my husband, the bridge now looked old and rundown. The paint on the rails was peeling off, and in some places the rails were crushed into the sidewalk because they had been hit by cars and never fixed. Even the river that I used to see every time I went across the bridge was almost gone. A very small stream was all that we could see.

Another thing that I had told my husband was that, even though the city was small, it had good streets and was well kept. I had even mentioned that many new stores with large, clean parking lots were being built when I had left. Unfortunately, the streets and stores now were very different. From the entrance of the city to the middle of it, we kept finding streets where the pavement was cracked and broken. In some streets as well as in parking lots, there were many big holes. And the stores were even worse. They looked run-down, and many of them were out of business. I was very unhappy at the sight.

Finally, when I lived in Guamuchil, it was a lively place, but now all that had changed. When I was young, I knew that we were not the richest town in the state, but the houses, shops, and cars remained well painted at all times, so the overall appearance of the city was presentable. However, when I visited it in 1994, everybody seemed to have lost hope for a better future, and they did not have the will or perhaps the money to fix the things they owned or to maintain a lively city instead of an old, run-down town.

I have not been back to Guamuchil since 1994, but I think I will visit it again soon. I know it will not be the way it was when I was young, but it is still my hometown, and I will never forget that.

1. Identify the thesis statement. State its topic and central idea. Is it an effective thesis statement? Can you tell whether the paper will focus on similarities or differences?

2. Identify each topic sentence. State its topic and central idea. Does each topic sentence clearly introduce one specific similarity or difference?

3. What transitional words introduce each new body paragraph?

4. Does the essay use a point-by-point or a subject-by-subject organization? Would you change the order of the paragraphs? Why or why not?

5. Is each similarity or difference explained clearly and fully? If you would improve any, explain how you would do so.

Proofreading

When proofreading your paper, watch for the following errors:

Sentence fragments, comma splices, and fused sentences

Misplaced modifiers and dangling modifiers

Errors in subject–verb agreement

Errors in pronoun case, pronoun–antecedent agreement, and pronoun reference

Errors in comma use

Errors in the use of periods, question marks, exclamation points, colons, semicolons, and quotation marks

Errors in capitalization, titles, and numbers

Misspelled words

Prepare a clean final draft, following the format your instructor has requested.

Chapter 5 Practice Test

I. Review of Chapters Two, Three, and Four

A. Correct any fragments, fused sentences, or comma splices in the following sentences. Do nothing if the sentence is correct.

1. A very good reason not to pay my income taxes.

2. The Somali bandits would not surrender the ship, therefore, the negotiators decided to sink it.

3. As Guinevere winked at Sir Lancelot.

4. Leaving the harbor, Aeneas looked for Dido she was standing on the cliff.

5. The Detroit Lions' fan stood in line at the ticket booth, he wondered why no one was in front of him or behind him.

B. Correct any dangling or misplaced modifiers in the following sentences. Do nothing if the sentence is correct.

6. After going off the vitamin supplements, the baseball player's uniform was too large for him to wear.

continued

7. Beginning to feel fatigued, the twenty-four pack of beer was removed from her backpack by Hillary.

_____

_____

8. The Irish lassie holding the small dog with the shamrock tattoo on the right shoulder ordered a pint of Guinness.

_____

_____

9. It was already 6:05, so Wyatt was only able to grab one pistol.

_____

_____

10. Staring at the two paths, the one less traveled seemed to be the best choice.

_____

_____

C. Correct any subject–verb agreement errors in the following sentences. Do nothing if the sentence is correct.

11. Each of the skiers in Salt Lake City want to win a gold medal.

12. Do the coach or the captain of the team know where the volleyballs are?

13. A pack of timber wolves have been seen running through Yellowstone this year.

14. There was a broken refrigerator, a cast iron bathtub, and a washing machine in the back of his pickup.

15. Twenty years of fighting and wandering were a long time for Odysseus to be away from Penelope.

D. Correct any pronoun use errors in the following sentences. Do nothing if the sentence is correct.

16. Someone on one of the upper floors was playing a song by the Rolling Stones on his or her saxophone.

continued

17. Cosmo stared at the oyster next to the rice roll, but he couldn't bring himself to eat it.

18. In Barcelona, people kept staring at Penelope Cruz and I.

19. I wondered if it was her who asked for asparagus with her Spam.

20. My brother was surprised when I told him that you are supposed to pull to the side of the road when you hear a siren.

II. Chapter Five

A. Add commas to the following sentences where necessary. Do nothing if the sentence is correct.

21. The hot bright sun was high in the sky but Icarus did not notice.

22. After visiting Disneyland in Anaheim California President Obama and his daughters headed for Disney World in Orlando Florida.

23. Barbara did you decide to use the Flannery O'Connor story or do you prefer the Eudora Welty one?

24. At the annual neighborhood garage sale Jon bought a rusty wheelbarrow a velvet portrait of Elvis Presley a tub of wallpaper paste and a pair of wooden snow skis.

25. Although it had been cold all winter the snow that fell in Murrieta California on November 26 2005 surprised everyone.

26. Before the beginning of the play Tennessee found some glass figurines and placed them on the stage.

27. Laertes poisoned the point of his sword; however it was accidentally switched with Hamlet's sword which was not poisoned.

28. Ebenezer Scrooge who was a miserly old man was surprised to see Jacob Marley his dead partner.

29. Stella said "Stan get that wacky woman out of my house."

30. Oprah wanted to feature the author's book on her show but he rudely refused.

Chapter 5 Practice Test

continued

B. Add periods, exclamation points, question marks, quotation marks, semicolons, colons, and apostrophes (or *'s*) where necessary. Do not add or delete any commas.

31. Ptolemy wondered if the earth really was at the center of the universe

32. As the Confederates lined up twenty-five feet from two hundred Yankees, Jed asked Ebenezer, Aint this rather crazy

33. These supplies are absolutely necessary four cans of Spam, a pound of cayenne pepper, eight cloves of garlic, two pounds of onions, and a case of Alka-Seltzer

34. Never again yelled Batman as he leapt from the skyscraper

35. All of his friends planned to take the whale-watching tour however, Pinocchio didnt want to go with them

36. The dam had a small hole in it the little Dutch boy put his finger in it

37. The idea that our behavior is determined by environment has been largely disproved, stated psychiatrist Steven Pinker

38. Willys sons were neither as successful nor as well-liked as Charleys son

39. Dante asked, Are you sure you know how to get out of here

40. Jackson Pollock was unable to paint between the lines fortunately, no one seemed to mind

C. In the following sentences correct any errors in the use of titles, capitalization, and numbers. Do not add or delete any commas. Do nothing if the sentence is correct.

41. The film elegy, starring ben kingsley and penelope cruz, is based on a novel by phillip roth.

42. sir lawrence olivier starred in and directed shakespeare's play henry v to raise the morale of the british people during world war ii.

43. almost 500 people stood outside an ohio penitentiary on january twenty-first, two thousand nine, to protest capital punishment.

44. 785 people asked for their money back after attending the concert by the chula vista philharmonic kazoo band last friday.

continued

45. Peter Sprague, who performs on the compact disc blurring the edges, is a member of the san diego jazz society.

46. At last night's showing of the classic horror film invasion of the body snatchers, professor hohman ate a jumbo hershey's chocolate bar.

47. By the end of the revolutionary war, only his mother still loved benedict arnold.

48. After doing his history and psychology homework, Bill started his english assignment, which was to write an analysis of billy collins's poem shoveling snow with buddha.

49. When he arrived in los angeles from the war in iraq, musef was admitted as a junior to ucla.

50. It was two twenty-five P.M. when Arlo entered the sweet tooth candy company and stole thirty-three pieces of saltwater taffy, three hundred ten jelly beans, and 6 large chunks of dark chocolate.

Choosing the Right Words and Spelling Them Correctly

English is a diverse language. It has borrowed words from hundreds of different sources. *Moccasin,* for instance, is Native American in origin; *patio* comes from Spanish; *colonel* and *lieutenant* entered English from Norman French; and *thermonuclear* is both Greek and Latin. All of this diversity makes English a complex and interesting language, but it also makes it quite difficult sometimes.

As you know, we have three words that sound just like *to* and three words that sound just like *there.* In fact, English is full of words that sound alike or that have such similar meanings that they are often mistaken for one another. A careful writer learns to make distinctions among these words.

Failing to make correct word choices or to spell words correctly can cause a number of problems. Most importantly, you may fail to make your ideas clear, or you may confuse your reader. In addition, you may lose the confidence of your reader if your writing contains misspelled or poorly chosen words. Sometimes, you can even embarrass yourself.

For instance, here is a fellow who wants to meet either a fish or the bottom of a shoe:

EXAMPLE   When I went to college, I did not know a **sole.**

This person has writing mixed up with the building trade:

EXAMPLE   I began to take my talent for writing for **granite,** but I lacked the ability to organize my thoughts in a coherent **manor.**

And here the early American settlers enjoy a means of transportation that hadn't yet been invented:

EXAMPLE   The pioneers appeared to prefer the open **planes** to the dense forests.

Most misspellings and incorrect word choices, however, are not as humorous or embarrassing as these. Instead, they are simple errors in word choice that are usually caused by carelessness and a lack of attention to detail.

Use Your Dictionary

This chapter will cover errors in word choice and spelling caused by irregular verbs and by words that are commonly confused. It will also present several of the basic "rules" of spelling. However, if you are not sure of a particular spelling (the difference between *effect* and *affect,* for instance), consult your dictionary. A dictionary shows how to spell, pronounce, and use words. A dictionary gives you the definitions of words, shows you the principal parts of verbs, and tells you whether or not a word is appropriate for formal writing. In addition, most dictionaries contain other useful information, such as biographical and geographical data.

Irregular Verbs

Because verbs in the English language change their spelling in a variety of ways to express different verb tenses, spelling them correctly can sometimes be a challenge. To use verbs correctly, you need to know the basic verb forms. These forms are known as the **three principal parts of the verb: the present, the past, and the past participle.**

You use the present to form both the present and future tenses, the past to form the past tense, and the past participle (with *have, has, had*) to form the perfect tenses.

Most verbs, the **regular verbs,** form the past and past participle by adding *d* or *ed* to the present. For example, the three principal parts of *create* are *create* (present), *created* (past), and *created* (past participle). The three principal parts of *talk* are *talk, talked,* and *talked.*

However, about two hundred verbs form the past and past participle in different ways. These verbs are called the **irregular verbs.** They are some of the oldest and most important verbs in English, such as *eat* or *fight* or *buy*—basic human actions. Because these words are so common, you should know their principal parts. Here is a list of the principal parts of most irregular verbs.

Present	*Past*	*Past Participle*
am, are, is	was, were	been
beat	beat	beaten
become	became	become
begin	began	begun
bend	bent	bent
bet	bet	bet
bite	bit	bitten
bleed	bled	bled
blow	blew	blown
break	broke	broken
bring	brought	brought
build	built	built
burst	burst	burst
buy	bought	bought
catch	caught	caught
choose	chose	chosen
come	came	come
cost	cost	cost
cut	cut	cut
dig	dug	dug

Present	*Past*	*Past Participle*
do, does	did	done
draw	drew	drawn
drink	drank	drunk
drive	drove	driven
eat	ate	eaten
fall	fell	fallen
feed	fed	fed
feel	felt	felt
fight	fought	fought
find	found	found
fly	flew	flown
forget	forgot	forgotten or forgot
freeze	froze	frozen
get	got	got or gotten
give	gave	given
go, goes	went	gone
grow	grew	grown
hang	hung	hung
hang (to execute)	hanged	hanged
have, has	had	had
hear	heard	heard
hide	hid	hidden
hit	hit	hit
hold	held	held
hurt	hurt	hurt
keep	kept	kept
know	knew	known
lay (to place or put)	laid	laid
lead	led	led
leave	left	left
lend	lent	lent
let	let	let
lie (to recline)	lay	lain
light	lit	lit
lose	lost	lost
make	made	made
mean	meant	meant
meet	met	met

Present	*Past*	*Past Participle*
pay	paid	paid
prove	proved	proved or proven
put	put	put
quit	quit	quit
read	read	read
ride	rode	ridden
ring	rang	rung
rise	rose	risen
run	ran	run
say	said	said
see	saw	seen
sell	sold	sold
send	sent	sent
set	set	set
shake	shook	shaken
shine	shone or shined	shone or shined
shoot	shot	shot
show	showed	shown
shrink	shrank	shrunk
shut	shut	shut
sing	sang	sung
sink	sank	sunk
sit	sat	sat
sleep	slept	slept
slide	slid	slid
speak	spoke	spoken
speed	sped	sped
spend	spent	spent
spin	spun	spun
stand	stood	stood
steal	stole	stolen
stick	stuck	stuck
sting	stung	stung
strike	struck	struck
swear	swore	sworn
sweep	swept	swept
swim	swam	swum
swing	swung	swung

Present	*Past*	*Past Participle*
take	took	taken
teach	taught	taught
tear	tore	torn
tell	told	told
think	thought	thought
throw	threw	thrown
wake	woke or waked	woken or waked
wear	wore	worn
weave	wove	woven
weep	wept	wept
win	won	won
wind	wound	wound
wring	wrung	wrung
write	wrote	written

Special Problems with Irregular Verbs

Lie–Lay

1. The irregular verb *lie* means "to recline." It never takes a direct object. The principal parts of this verb are *lie, lay,* and *lain.*

EXAMPLES

On Saturdays, I **lie** in bed until at least 11:00.

Last Saturday, I **lay** in bed until almost 1:00.

Today, I **have lain** in bed too long.

2. The verb *lay* means "to place or put." It takes a direct object. Its principal parts are *lay, laid,* and *laid.*

EXAMPLES

As Paul enters the house, he always **lays** his keys on the table.

Yesterday Paul **laid** his keys on the television set.

After he **had laid** the flowers on the kitchen table, Mr. Best kissed his wife.

Sit–Set

1. The verb *sit* means "to be seated." It never takes a direct object. Its principal parts are *sit, sat,* and *sat.*

EXAMPLES

At the movies, Juan usually **sits** in the back row.

Last week Juan **sat** in the middle of the theater.

2. The verb *set* means "to place or put." It takes a direct object. Its principal parts are *set, set,* and *set.*

◎◎ EXAMPLES   At night Floyd always **sets** a glass of water by his bed.

Cora **set** her books on the librarian's desk.

Rise–Raise

1. The verb *rise* means "to stand" or "to attain a greater height." It never takes a direct object. Its principal parts are *rise, rose,* and *risen.*

◎◎ EXAMPLES   I like it when the sun **rises** over the mountains on a clear day.

All of the people **rose** every time the queen entered the room.

2. The verb *raise* is a regular verb. It means "to elevate." It takes a direct object. Its principal parts are *raise, raised,* and *raised.*

◎◎ EXAMPLES   Every morning a Boy Scout **raises** the flag in front of the school.

Christopher always politely **raised** his hand whenever he had a question.

Verbs with *U* in the Past Participle

Because these verbs sound odd, some people tend to use the past form when they should be using the past participle. Here are the ones that are most often confused.

drink	drank	**drunk:**	So far I **have drunk** eight glasses of water today.
swim	swam	**swum:**	Petra **has swum** thirty-five laps today.
shrink	shrank	**shrunk:**	The grocer wondered why his profits **had shrunk.**
sing	sang	**sung:**	Often Carmine **has sung** the National Anthem before hockey games.

◎◎ PRACTICE   Underline the correct verb form in the parentheses.

1. In the daytime, Michelle's pet rat just (lays <u>lies</u>) in the corner of his cage and sleeps.

2. Esmeralda has (drank drunk) two quarts of lemonade and a gallon of Mountain Dew, but she says she feels fine.

3. Byron bragged that he had (swam swum) all the way even with a bad foot.

4. Maverick (sat set) a $100 poker chip in the middle of the table.

5. Homer had (ate eaten) all of the Spam parfait before he (digged dug) into the marshmallow delight.

6. Jackie was (lying laying) under the old oak tree when someone tied a yellow ribbon around it.

7. The suitors asked Penelope why her knitting had (shrank shrunk).

8. The rat terrier (drank drunk) from its water bowl and then (lay laid) down in the sun.

9. Norah Jones had (sang sung) so exquisitely that David Letterman just sat there as the audience (raised rose) to a standing ovation.

10. The map that (lead led) to the treasure had (laid lain) undiscovered in Harold's attic for thirty years.

Section One Review

1. The **three principal parts of a verb** are **present, past,** and **past participle.**

2. **Regular verbs** form the past and past participle by adding *d* or *ed* to the present.

3. **Irregular** verbs form the past and past participle in a variety of other ways. See the lists on pages 344–347.

4. Irregular verbs that often cause confusion are *lie/lay, sit/set, rise/raise,* and verbs with *u* in the past participle.

Exercise 1A

Underline the correct form of the verb in the parentheses.

1. Participating on the swim team, Naomi figures she has (swam <u>swum</u>) thousands of miles.

2. Aaron (throwed threw) the cell phone into his backpack when he (saw seen) the principal approaching.

3. At 9:00 A.M. on Friday, a huge bubble descended from the sky and (busted burst) in the busiest intersection of Temecula.

4. What pictures are (drawed drawn) on the plaque aboard the *Pioneer 10* spacecraft?

5. After the banquet, goblets, bones, vegetable fragments, and a few togas (lay laid) all over the imported rugs.

6. The boys (sitting setting) at the back of the classroom did not know what to do when Quetzalcoatl appeared in the room.

7. Quasimodo realized that, as he was talking to the woman, he had not (rang rung) the bells.

8. Everyone knew something was wrong the day the sun (raised rose) in the west.

9. Caesar crossed the Rubicon River and then realized that his favorite toga had (shrank shrunk).

10. After floating for a few minutes, the paper kite finally (sank sunk) into the pond.

11. Mr. Valenzuela thought that he had (lain laid) his key on the desk in his office.

12. Once Siddhartha had (threw thrown) aside the need to understand, he (began begun) to experience enlightenment.

13. After swimming across the river, Tarzan (wrang wrung) out his zebra skin and (hanged hung) it across the limb of a tree.

14. Delores (set sat) down the food that she had (brung brought) in honor of Mexico's Independence Day.

15. After the bride and groom had (shook shaken) the hand of each guest, they were ready for the reception to be over.

Exercise 1B

In the blanks, write the correct form of the verb indicated.

1. Clete looked down and saw that a ten-dollar bill _____*lay*_____ by his right shoe. (lie)

2. Ares thought Mars looked familiar when they _____ down together on Mt. Olympus. (sit)

3. Hercules was _____ several tasks to complete. (give)

4. Amelia Earhart had _____ halfway across the Pacific with no problems whatsoever. (fly)

5. Ulysses and his men made sure that the giant had _____ all of the caskets of wine before they began their escape. (drink)

6. Once gas prices had _____ to four dollars per gallon, many people canceled their vacations. (rise)

7. The exhausted man saw that, once more, the stone _____ at the bottom of the hill. (lie)

8. Bruce had _____ nearly the entire glass of buttermilk before Anne told him it was spoiled. (drink)

9. When Theo saw Vincent's painting, he knew his brother had _____ the night sky in a very different way. (see)

10. Jasmine had _____ home to apologize to her father, but he would not speak to her. (come)

11. Has Quasimodo _____ the bells yet? (ring)

12. Once he had _____ enough money, Simon built a new hall for the Grape Stompers Square Dance Club. (raise)

13. Antigone was angry because her brother's body had been _____ out on the battlefield for days without being buried. (lie)

14. Everyone laughed when Steve claimed he had _____ from Long Beach to Catalina Island. (swim)

15. After drinking the potion, Alice noticed that she had _____ to the size of a rabbit. (shrink)

Exercise 1C

Check the following paragraph for correct verb forms. Circle any incorrect verb forms and write the correct forms above them.

1. I agree with the American writer Henry David Thoreau, who has *written* ~~wrote~~ that most people lead lives of "quiet desperation," always looking for happiness in the wrong places. **2.** For instance, last night I seen several television commercials that show what many Americans value. **3.** A beer commercial shown a sexy scene of a man and woman in a bar, as if a good beer would bring sex and romance. **4.** I actually have friends who have drank a certain brand of beer because they think they are more attractive when they drink it. **5.** Another commercial advertised Princess Cruises. **6.** It showed the sun raising in the east as happy people laid around the pool of a huge ship. **7.** These examples may seem silly, but I have knowed many people who think a beer or a cruise or a cell phone would make them happy. **8.** Thoreau would probably have bust out laughing at these ideas. **9.** He felt that people throughout history have spended way too much time working to get things that they thought would make them happy. **10.** He seen that when people finally got these things, they were still unhappy and discontented. **11.** Not long ago the ten-year-old son of a friend of mine begged her to buy him a pair of sports shoes that costed over $120. **12.** When my friend told him that she could not afford such expensive shoes, he set down and cried. **13.** He had came to believe that he had to have the shoes to be liked. **14.** I agree with the English writer William Wordsworth, who wrote, "Getting and spending we lay waste our powers." **15.** Both Wordsworth and Thoreau knew that if we spend our time looking for happiness in things and possessions, we will miss the real happiness that is laying right in front of us, and we will always be "desperate." **16.** In my life I choose to believe that what I have bought or wore or ate is not as important as whether I have appreciated nature and my fellow human beings. **17.** Henry David Thoreau and William Wordsworth would agree with me.

Commonly Confused Words

Most word choice errors are made either because two words sound alike or look alike or because their meanings are so similar that they are mistakenly used in place of each other. Here are some of the most commonly confused sets of words.

A/an/and

A is used before words that begin with **consonant sounds.** It is an article, a type of **adjective.**

🌀 **EXAMPLES**   a porcupine, **a** bat, a sword, a good boy

An is used before words that begin with **vowel sounds.** It is also an article.

🌀 **EXAMPLES**   an apple, **an** honor, **an** unusual cloud formation

And is a **coordinating conjunction** used to join words, phrases, or clauses.

🌀 **EXAMPLE**   Homer **and** Hortense

Accept/except

Accept means "to take or receive what is offered or given." It is a **verb.**

🌀 **EXAMPLE**   Severino gladly **accepted** the reward for the money he had returned.

Except means "excluded" or "but." It is a **preposition.**

🌀 **EXAMPLE**   Flowers were in everyone's room **except** Sonia's.

Advice/advise

Advice means "an opinion about what to do or how to handle a situation." It is a **noun.**

🌀 **EXAMPLE**   The counselor gave Phillipa **advice** about how to apply for graduate school.

Advise means "to give advice" or "to counsel." It is a **verb.**

🌀 **EXAMPLE**   The judge **advised** the defense attorney to control his temper.

Affect/effect

Affect means "to influence" or "to produce a change in." It is a **verb.**

EXAMPLE   The continued destruction of the ozone layer will **affect** future weather patterns drastically.

Effect is "a result" or "something brought about by a cause." It is a **noun.**

EXAMPLE   The decorator liked the **effect** of the newly painted room.

NOTE: *Effect* can be used as a verb when it means "to bring about" or "to cause."

EXAMPLE   The reward **effected** a change in the lion's behavior.

All ready/already

All ready means "everyone or everything is prepared or ready."

EXAMPLE   After a strenuous game of softball, we were **all ready** for a cold root beer.

Already means "by or before a specific or implied time."

EXAMPLE   By the time he had climbed the first flight of stairs, Bob was **already** out of breath.

All right/alright

All right means "satisfactory" or "unhurt."

EXAMPLE   After she fell from her horse, Hannah smiled and said she was **all right.**

Alright is a nonstandard spelling of *all right*. It is not widely used in formal writing. Do not use it in college papers.

Among/between

Among means "in the company of" or "included with." Use it when discussing <u>three or more</u> things or ideas. It is a **preposition.**

EXAMPLE   **Among** the demands of the workers was drinkable coffee.

Between means "in or through the space that separates two things." Use it only when you are discussing <u>two things or ideas</u>. It is a **preposition.**

EXAMPLE   Betty could not choose **between** Sid and Slim.

Amount/number

Use *amount* to refer to things that are usually not separated, such as milk, oil, salt, or flour.

◎◎ EXAMPLE   The **amount** of sugar the recipe calls for is two cups.

Use *number* to refer to things that are usually separated or counted individually, such as people, books, cats, or apples.

◎◎ EXAMPLE   The large **number** of people in the small room made the air stuffy.

Anxious/eager

Anxious means "apprehensive, uneasy, worried." It is an **adjective.**

◎◎ EXAMPLE   The lawyer was **anxious** about the jury's verdict.

Eager means "keen desire or enthusiasm in pursuit of something." It is also an **adjective.**

◎◎ EXAMPLE   The children were **eager** for summer vacation to begin.

Are/our

Are is a **linking verb** or a **helping verb.**

◎◎ EXAMPLES   We **are** late for dinner.

We **are** leaving soon.

Our is a **possessive pronoun.**

◎◎ EXAMPLE   **Our** dinner was delicious.

Brake/break

Brake is the device that stops or slows a vehicle. It may be used as a **noun** or a **verb.**

◎◎ EXAMPLES   The service station attendant told Molly that her **brakes** were dangerously worn.

Arlo **braked** just in time to avoid going over the cliff.

Break can also be used as a **noun** or a **verb.** As a **verb,** it means "to cause to come apart by force."

◎ EXAMPLE   Every time Humphrey walks through a room, he **breaks** something.

As a noun, *break* means "an interruption of an action or a thing."

◎ EXAMPLES   When there was a **break** in the storm, we continued the game.

The worker fixed the **break** in the water pipe.

Choose/chose

Choose means "select." It is a **present tense verb.**

◎ EXAMPLE   Every Friday afternoon, the children **choose** a movie to watch in the evening.

Chose means "selected." It is the **past tense** of *choose*.

◎ EXAMPLE   Last Friday, the children **chose** Pocahontas.

Complement/compliment

A *complement* is "that which completes or brings to perfection." It is a **noun** or a **verb.**

◎ EXAMPLES   The bright yellow tie was a handsome **complement** to Pierre's new suit.

The bright yellow tie **complemented** Pierre's new suit.

A *compliment* is "an expression of praise, respect, or courtesy." It is a **noun** or a **verb.**

◎ EXAMPLES   Whenever Mr. Trujillo receives a **compliment** for his beautiful sculptures, he smiles and blushes.

Whenever his wife **compliments** Mr. Trujillo for his beautiful sculptures, he smiles and blushes.

Conscience/conscious

Conscience is "a knowledge or sense of right and wrong." It is a **noun.**

◎ EXAMPLE   Javier said that his **conscience** kept him from looking at Lucy's paper during the physics examination.

Conscious can mean either "aware" or "awake." It is an **adjective.**

◎ EXAMPLE   As he walked through the dark woods, Frank was **conscious** of the animals all around him.

Disinterested/uninterested

Disinterested means "neutral" or "impartial." It is an **adjective.**

EXAMPLE   A judge must remain **disinterested** as he considers a case before him.

Uninterested means "not interested." It is an **adjective.**

EXAMPLE   Shirley was profoundly **uninterested** in the subject of the lecture.

PRACTICE   Underline the correct word in the parentheses.

1. The hikers were so (<u>eager</u> anxious) to get to the trail that they forgot to

   get (<u>advice</u> advise) about the local weather.

2. Norman Bates suffered from a guilty (conscious conscience) whenever he

   saw (a an) empty rocking chair.

3. Dido could never (except accept) that Aeneas had had such a dramatic

   (effect affect) on her.

4. The group of children argued (between among) themselves over who

   should (break brake) the news about Piggy.

5. (A An) ideal jury should be composed of twelve (uninterested

   disinterested) people.

6. The best (advice advise) I can give you will have no (affect effect) on the

   outcome whatsoever.

7. Not only was the movie (disinteresting uninteresting), but we had (already

   all ready) seen it last summer.

8. Even though she was ill, Abbie told her father she felt (alright all right)

   because she was (eager anxious) to go to Disneyland.

9. The (number amount) of persons in the king's party seemed important to

   Oedipus.

10. Serena (complimented complemented) the chef for how well his béarnaise

sauce (complimented complemented) his wild mushroom risotto cakes.

11. The Bobolinks knew that (are our) chances of winning were small if we

did not give our center a (break brake).

12. Jose Luis had to (chose choose) between (braking breaking) for the cat in

the road or swerving into oncoming traffic.

Fewer/less

Use *fewer* to discuss items that can be counted separately, such as trees,
automobiles, or pencils. It is an **adjective.**

⊚⊚ EXAMPLE   When the cutters had finished, there were many **fewer** trees in the grove.

Use *less* to refer to amounts that are not usually separated, such as water, dirt,
sand, or gasoline. It is an **adjective.**

⊚⊚ EXAMPLE   Because of the drought, there is **less** water in the lake this year.

Lead/led

As a **noun,** *lead* is a heavy metal or a part of a pencil. As a **verb,** it is the
present tense of the verb *to lead,* meaning "to guide" or "to show the way."

⊚⊚ EXAMPLES   The diver used weights made of **lead** to keep him from floating to the surface.

Every summer Mr. Archer **leads** his scout troop on a long backpacking trip.

Led is the past or past participle form of the **verb** *to lead.*

⊚⊚ EXAMPLE   Last summer, Mr. Archer **led** his scout troop on a backpacking trip.

Loose/lose

Loose means "not confined or restrained, free, unbound." It is an **adjective.**

⊚⊚ EXAMPLE   Mr. Castro was chasing a cow that had gotten **loose** and was trampling
his garden.

Lose means "to become unable to find" or "to mislay." It is a **verb.**

⊚⊚ EXAMPLE   I was afraid I would **lose** my contact lenses if I went swimming with them.

Passed/past

Passed is the past or past participle form of the **verb** *to pass*, which means "to go or move forward, through, or out."

EXAMPLE   As I drove to school, I **passed** a serious traffic accident.

Past as an **adjective** means "gone by, ended, over." As a **noun**, it means "the time that has gone by." As a **preposition**, it means "beyond."

EXAMPLES   His **past** mistakes will not bar him from further indiscretions.

In the **past,** I have always been in favor of opening doors for women.

Horst waved as he drove **past** Jill's house.

Personal/personnel

Personal means "private" or "individual." It is an **adjective.**

EXAMPLE   Helen feels her political ideas are her **personal** business.

Personnel means "persons employed in any work or enterprise." It is a **noun.**

EXAMPLE   The sign on the bulletin board directed all **personnel** to report to the auditorium for a meeting.

Precede/proceed

Precede means "to go before." It is a **verb.**

EXAMPLE   The Great Depression **preceded** World War II.

Proceed means "to advance or go on." It is a **verb.**

EXAMPLE   After a short pause, Mrs. Quintan **proceeded** with her inventory.

Principal/principle

As an **adjective,** *principal* means "first in rank or importance." As a **noun,** it usually means "the head of a school."

EXAMPLES   Kevin's **principal** concern was the safety of his children.

At the assembly the **principal** discussed drug abuse with the students and teachers.

A *principle* is a "fundamental truth, law, or doctrine." It is a **noun.**

EXAMPLE   One of my **principles** is that you never get something for nothing.

Quit/quite/quiet

Quit means "to stop doing something." It is a **verb.**

EXAMPLE   George **quit** smoking a year ago.

Quite means "completely" or "really." It is an **adverb.**

EXAMPLE   It was **quite** hot during the whole month of August.

Quiet means "silent." It is usually used as an **adjective,** but it can be used as a **noun.**

EXAMPLES   The **quiet** student in the third row rarely said a word.

In the **quiet** of the evening, Hank strummed his guitar.

Than/then

Use *than* to make comparisons. It is a **conjunction.**

EXAMPLE   It is cloudier today **than** it was yesterday.

Then means "at that time" or "soon afterwards" or "next." It is an **adverb.**

EXAMPLE   Audrey mowed the backyard, and **then** she drank a large iced tea.

Their/there/they're

Their is a **possessive pronoun** meaning "belonging to them."

EXAMPLE   All of the people in the room suddenly started clinking the ice in **their** drinks.

There is an **adverb** meaning "in that place."

EXAMPLE   "Let's park the car **there**," proclaimed Fern.

They're is a contraction for *they are.*

EXAMPLE   "**They're** back," said the little girl ominously.

Threw/through

Threw is the past tense form of the **verb** *to throw.*

EXAMPLE   Hector **threw** the spear with godlike accuracy.

Through is a **preposition** meaning "in one side and out the other side of."

EXAMPLE   The ship sailed **through** the Bermuda Triangle without peril.

To/too/two

To is a **preposition** meaning "in the direction of."

EXAMPLE Jeremy went **to** his rustic cabin by the babbling brook for a poetic weekend.

Too is an **adverb** meaning "also" or "more than enough."

EXAMPLES Cecily was at the spree **too**.

The senator found that the burden of public adulation was **too** heavy.

Two is the number after *one*.

EXAMPLE Bill has **two** daughters and one cat and too many televisions, so he wants to go to Jeremy's rustic cabin too.

We're/were/where

We're is a contraction for *we are*.

EXAMPLE We're almost there.

Were is a **linking verb** or a **helping verb** in the past tense.

EXAMPLES We **were** late for dinner.

Our hosts **were** eating dessert when we arrived.

Where indicates **place.**

EXAMPLES **Where** is the key to the cellar?

He showed them **where** he had buried the money.

Your/you're

Your is a **possessive pronoun** meaning "belonging to you."

EXAMPLE "**Your** insights have contributed greatly to my sense of well-being," said the toady.

You're is a contraction for *you are*.

EXAMPLE "**You're** just saying that because **you're** so nice," replied the other toady.

🌀 PRACTICE   Underline the correct words in the parentheses.

1. The (number amount) of players on the team is decreasing because of (to too two) many injuries, so the managers announced that (there they're their) probably going to cancel the next game.

2. (There Their) have been (less fewer) visitors to Old Faithful this year (then than) in any of the past ten years.

3. The (principle principal) asked me about (you're your) decision to transfer next year.

4. When he walked (passed past) the pond, Mr. Mallard (through threw) bread crumbs to the ducks.

5. As the tour guide (lead led) the visitors deep into Mammoth Cave, she warned them to stay on the marked path because they could easily (loose lose) (there their they're) way.

6. For (personal personnel) reasons Margaret has decided to sell her papillon and toy poodle, even though (there their they're) both friendly, loving dogs.

7. The gentle questioning by Socrates (lead led) many people to new (principals principles) by which they could live their lives.

8. After just (to too two) days on *Facebook*, the hermit decided that (to too two) many people wanted (to too two) be his friend.

9. William wondered why the (number amount) of people in the audience was (fewer less) (then than) when the play had begun.

10. All the commercials that (preceded proceeded) the movie almost caused Bruce Banner to (loose lose) his patience.

11. It was (quiet quit quite) early when I woke up, so I was (quiet quit quite) as I made the coffee.

12. The *American Idol* finalists (where were we're) not sure (where were we're) to stand when (a an and) angry parent stormed the stage.

Section Two Review

Be careful when you use the following words:

a/an/and

accept/except

advice/advise

affect/effect

all ready/already

all right/alright

among/between

amount/number

anxious/eager

are/our

brake/break

choose/chose

complement/compliment

conscience/conscious

disinterested/uninterested

fewer/less

lead/led

loose/lose

passed/past

personal/personnel

precede/proceed

principal/principle

quit/quite/quiet

than/then

their/there/they're

threw/through

to/too/two

we're/were/where

your/you're

Exercise 2A

Underline the correct word in the parentheses.

1. The prospects for victory are much greater now (then <u>than</u>) they were just five minutes ago.

2. The new hybrids use (fewer less) gallons of gas and rarely (break brake) down.

3. Cerberus, the three-headed dog, was (anxious eager) to see (their they're there) supply of Spam.

4. (Proceeding Preceding) the bull fight in Pamplona, Spain, Ernest ran down the street (among between) dozens of bulls.

5. Mrs. Mallard had (quite quit quiet) a difficult time (accepting excepting) the fact that her husband was still alive.

6. When Dr. Frankenstein was (through threw), he wondered what (effect affect) the new brain would have on his experiment.

7. In an attempt (to too two) ease her guilty (conscience conscious), Pam finally admitted she had taken Andrea's chocolate bar.

8. Barry was so (uninterested disinterested) in sports that he did not care when Michael Phelps visited (are our) school.

9. The local post office did not know what to do with the large (amount number) of letters addressed to Kris Kringle.

10. It is perfectly (alright all right) if you eat more casserole (then than) (your you're) sister does.

11. The space shuttle was (all ready already) for lift off when one of the crew asked if anyone had brought a map.

12. Charlie (complimented complemented) his son for accurately explaining the concept of inertia.

13. Ulysses was afraid that if he stayed away (to too two) long, he would (lose loose) his wife and home.

14. Jack Aubrey's men went to (their there they're) battle stations when they saw the ship that they (were where we're) approaching.

15. The word *hypotenuse* proved (to too two) be (to too two) difficult for either of the (to too two) contestants (to too two) spell.

Exercise 2B

Correct any word choice errors in the following sentences.

1. Mr. Fernandez felt honored as he ~~excepted~~ *accepted* his award for heroism.

2. We had all ready canceled summer school when are principle decided to cut everyone's pay.

3. When Ishmael became conscience of all the people staring at him, he wondered if his tale seemed to outlandish to be true.

4. It's alright with me if you put you're plutonium in the back seat.

5. Mr. Frost did not know which path to chose, so he asked his friend for advise.

6. Lewis and Clark thanked the native people who had lead them threw the mountains.

7. When they drove passed the demonstrators, Jack started to loose his temper.

8. The McDonalds anxiously looked forward to there upcoming trip to the Bahamas.

9. Ginsberg's "Howl" was more significant then most other poetry of the fifties.

10. Hester complemented Pearl on the amount of A's she had received.

11. My daughters where disinterested in trying to name the presidents on Mount Rushmore.

12. A long tale of woe and bad luck proceeded Arlo's request too borrow $500.

13. You're Spam recipe will make a tasty dessert for are company's personal.

14. Victor Frankl stood between the three guards and wondered if he should finally make a brake for freedom.

15. Huck's conscious bothered him when he realized how his story had effected Jim.

Exercise 2C

Edit the following paragraph for word use. Correct any word choice errors in the paragraph.

1. Many students and administrators at Beach City College want to prevent skinheads and
neo-Nazis from presenting ~~they're~~ *their* disgusting views, but the reasons they give are not strong
enough to violate the ~~principal~~ *principle* of free speech. **2.** Many administrators say that it is quit dangerous
to let these people on campus. **3.** There advise is to bar them from speaking. **4.** However, when
members of the student council discussed the matter between themselves, they past a resolution
in support of free speech. **5.** According to them, if the administrators are afraid the audience will
brake the law by attacking the speakers, than they should hire security personal for the
speech. **6.** Another reason administrators are not anxious to have these speakers on campus is
that most students are disinterested in there racist views. **7.** I, for one, am happy that most students
will chose to ignore these speakers, but my conscious tells me that we still have to let them
speak. **8.** Less than ten people may show up to listen, but we must not loose sight of the fact that
are Constitution supports all free speech, not just popular speech. **9.** Finally, a large amount of
students have objected to these speakers because racist ideas have lead to violence and even war
in the passed. **10.** I have to admit that these racist ideas make me feel ill, but we need to except
the principal that we can't listen only too the people with whom we agree. **11.** Threw my studies
in political science, I have learned that the best way to fight the affect of dangerous ideas is to
respond with worthy ideas. **12.** When the founders of are country where writing the
Constitution, they did not say that only certain groups had the right of free speech. **13.** To
protect are own free speech, we have to protect the speech of all people, even speech that is
quiet abhorrent to us and are beliefs.

Spelling Rules

Spelling words correctly should be simple. After all, if you can say a word, it would just seem to make sense that you should be able to spell it. Why, then, is accurate spelling such a problem for some people? Well, as anyone who has ever written anything in English knows, one of the problems is that the same sound is spelled different ways in different situations. For instance, the long *e* sound may be spelled *ea,* as in *mean; ee,* as in *seem; ei,* as in *receive; ie,* as in *niece;* or *e-consonant-e,* as in *precede.* On the other hand, many words in English use similar spellings but have totally different pronunciations, as in *rough, bough, though, through,* and *cough.* As if these problems weren't enough, there are times when consonants are doubled (*rob* becomes *robbed*), times when consonants are not doubled (*robe* becomes *robed*), times when a final *e* is dropped (*move* becomes *moving*), and times when the final *e* is not dropped (*move* becomes *movement*). Unfortunately, these are just a few of the variations that occur in the spelling of English words—so perhaps it is understandable that accurate spelling poses a problem for many people.

In this section, you will study various rules of spelling that will help you through specific spelling situations. However, before we examine the specific rules of spelling, consider these points to improve your spelling in any writing activity.

Techniques to Improve Your Spelling

1. <u>Buy and use a dictionary.</u> Small, inexpensive paperback dictionaries are available in nearly every bookstore or supermarket. Keep one next to you as you write and get used to using it.

2. <u>Pay attention to your own reactions as you write.</u> If you are not confident of the spelling of a word, assume you have probably misspelled it and use your dictionary to check it.

3. <u>Don't rely too much on spelling checkers.</u> Although spelling checkers are excellent tools that you should use, don't assume they will solve all of your spelling problems, because they won't. They are particularly useless when you confuse the kinds of words covered in the previous section, such as *their, there,* and *they're.*

4. <u>Pronounce words carefully and accurately.</u> Some misspellings are the result of poor pronunciation. Examine the following misspelled words. Pronounce and spell them correctly. Extend the list with examples of other words you have heard mispronounced.

Incorrect	Correct	Incorrect	Correct
athelete	_____	perfer	_____
discription	_____	perscription	_____
enviroment	_____	probally	_____
heigth	_____	realator	_____
libary	_____	suprise	_____
nucular	_____	unusal	_____
paticular	_____	usally	_____

5. <u>Use memory tricks.</u> You can memorize the spelling of many words by using some memory techniques.

There is **a rat** in *separate.*

The first **ll**'s are parallel in *parallel.*

Dessert *has two **ss**'s because everyone wants two desserts.*

6. <u>Read more often.</u> The most effective way to become a better speller (and, for that matter, a better writer and thinker) is to read on a regular basis. If you do not read novels, perhaps now is the time to start. Ask your instructor to recommend some good books, newspapers, and magazines.

7. <u>Learn the rules of spelling.</u> The following explanations should help you improve your spelling. However, note that each of these "rules" contains numerous exceptions. You must use a dictionary if you have any doubt about the spelling of a word.

Using *ie* or *ei*

You have probably heard this bit of simple verse:

> Use *i* before *e*
> Except after *c*
> Or when sounded like *ay*
> As in *neighbor* or *weigh.*

Although there are exceptions to this rule, it works in most cases.

ⓢⓢ EXAMPLES

IE	EI (after C)	EI (sounded like Ay)
grief	deceive	sleigh
niece	ceiling	eight
belief	receipt	weigh
achieve	perceive	neighbor

Exceptions:

ⓢⓢ EXAMPLES

ancient	conscience	foreign	neither	science	stein
caffeine	deity	height	protein	seize	their
codeine	either	leisure	proficient	society	weird

ⓢⓢ PRACTICE

Supply the correct *ie/ei* spellings in the following sentences.

1. A silver sh*ie*ld fell to the floor and landed on the b*ei*ge carpet.

2. At her retirement party, Ann rec___ved many tributes from her fr___nds.

3. Michelangelo looked at the c__ling and wondered how much paint would be suffic__nt.

4. Robert stopped his sl__gh by some snowy woods and breathed a qu__t sigh of rel__f.

5. N__ther Sancho Panza nor Dulcinea bel__ved the w__rd story about dragons and windmills.

Keeping or Changing a Final -*y*

When you add letters to a word ending in -*y*, change the *y* to *i* if it is preceded by a consonant. If it is preceded by a vowel, do not change the -*y*. A major exception: If you are adding -*ing*, never change the y.

◎◎ EXAMPLES

Preceded by a Consonant				*Preceded by Vowel*			
study	+ ed	=	studied	delay	+ ed	=	delayed
pretty	+ est	=	prettiest	buy	+ er	=	buyer
happy	+ ness	=	happiness	employ	+ ment	=	employment

Exceptions:

study	+ ing	=	studying	say	+ d	=	said
worry	+ ing	=	worrying	pay	+ d	=	paid

◎◎ PRACTICE   Add the suffix in parentheses to each of the following words.

1. study   (ed)   *studied*

           (es)   *studies*

           (ing)   *studying*

2. angry   (est)   ———

           (er)   ———

           (ly)   ———

3. portray   (ed)   ———

           (s)   ———

           (ing)   ———

           (al)   ———

4. silly   (ness)   ———

           (er)   ———

           (est)   ———

5. employ   (er)   ———

           (ed)   ———

           (able)   ———

Keeping or Dropping a Silent Final -e

When a word ends in a silent -e, drop the -e when you add an ending that begins with a vowel. Keep the -e when you add an ending that begins with a consonant.

EXAMPLES

Before a Vowel						*Before a Consonant*				
move	+	ing	=	moving		hope	+	less	=	hopeless
advise	+	able	=	advisable		move	+	ment	=	movement
pure	+	ity	=	purity		safe	+	ly	=	safely

Exceptions:

EXAMPLES

courage	+	ous	=	courageous		judge	+	ment	=	judgment
change	+	able	=	changeable		argue	+	ment	=	argument
notice	+	able	=	noticeable		true	+	ly	=	truly

PRACTICE Add the ending shown to each word, keeping or dropping the final -e when necessary.

1. require + ment = *requirement*

2. require + ing = _____

3. inspire + ing = _____

4. love + able = _____

5. love + ly = _____

6. manage + ing = _____

7. manage + ment = _____

8. complete + ly = _____

9. judge + ment = _____

10. notice + able = _____

Doubling the Final Consonant

In a single-syllable word that ends in one consonant preceded by one vowel (as in *drop*), double the final consonant when you add an ending that starts with a vowel. If a word has two or more syllables, the same rule applies *only if the emphasis is on the final syllable*.

EXAMPLES

One Syllable	Two or More Syllables *(emphasis on final syllable)*
drop + ing = dropping	expel + ing = expelling
slap + ed = slapped	occur + ence = occurrence
thin + est = thinnest	begin + er = beginner

PRACTICE

Add the indicated endings to the following words. Double the final consonants where necessary.

1. brag   +   ing   =   _bragging_

2. wild   +   est   =   _____

3. refer   +   ed   =   _____

4. proceed   +   ing   =   _____

5. dim   +   er   =   _____

6. clean   +   er   =   _____

7. commit   +   ed   =   _____

8. forget   +   able   =   _____

9. happen   +   ing   =   _____

10. compel   +   ed   =   _____

Using Prefixes

A **prefix** is one or more syllables added at the start of a word to change its meaning. **Do not change any letters of the root word when you add a prefix to it.** (The **root** is the part of the word that carries its central idea.)

EXAMPLES

prefix	+	root	=	new word
im	+	possible	=	impossible
mis	+	spell	=	misspell
il	+	legal	=	illegal
un	+	necessary	=	unnecessary

PRACTICE

Circle the correct spellings.

1. dissappoint (disappoint)

2. unatural   unnatural

3. dissatisfied   disatisfied

4. illegible   ilegible

5. mistrial   misstrial

6. imoral   immoral

7. mispell   misspell

8. ireversible   irreversible

9. ilicit   illicit

10. unethical   unnethical

Forming Plurals

1. Add -*s* to make most nouns plural. Add -*es* if the noun ends in *ch, sh, ss,* or *x.*

⊚ EXAMPLES

Add -s		*Add -es*	
street	streets	church	churches
dog	dogs	bush	bushes
problem	problems	hiss	hisses
issue	issues	box	boxes

2. If the noun ends in *o,* add *-s* if the *o* is preceded by a vowel. Add *-es* if it is preceded by a consonant.

⊚ EXAMPLES

Add -s					*Add -es*				
stereo	+	s	=	stereos	hero	+	es	=	heroes
radio	+	s	=	radios	potato	+	es	=	potatoes

Exceptions: *pianos, sopranos, solos, autos, memos*

3. Some nouns that end in *-f* or *-fe* form the plural by changing the ending to *-ve* before the *s.*

⊚ EXAMPLES

half	+	s	=	halves
wife	+	s	=	wives
leaf	+	s	=	leaves

4. Some words form plurals by changing spelling.

⊚ EXAMPLES

woman	=	women
goose	=	geese
foot	=	feet
child	=	children

5. Many words borrowed from other languages also form plurals by changing spelling.

⊚ EXAMPLES

alumnus	=	alumni
alumna	=	alumnae
analysis	=	analyses
basis	=	bases
medium	=	media
crisis	=	crises
criterion	=	criteria
memorandum	=	memoranda
phenomenon	=	phenomena

◎◎ PRACTICE   Write the plural forms of the following words.

      1. tax   *taxes*

      2. monkey

      3. echo

      4. knife

      5. match

      6. month

      7. kiss

      8. stereo

      9. candy

      10. phenomenon

Commonly Misspelled Words

Many words that are commonly misspelled do not relate to any particular spelling rule. In such cases, you need to be willing to use a dictionary to check the correct spelling.

◎◎ PRACTICE   Correct each of the misspelled words below. Use a dictionary when you are unsure of the correct spelling.

    1. accross   *across*   **4.** behavor

    2. alot   **5.** brillient

    3. athelete   **6.** buisness

7. carefuly   ——————

8. carreer   ——————

9. competion   ——————

10. definate   ——————

11. desparate   ——————

12. develope   ——————

13. diffrent   ——————

14. dinning   ——————

15. discribe   ——————

16. dosen't   ——————

17. embarass   ——————

18. enviroment   ——————

19. exagerate   ——————

20. Febuary   ——————

21. fasinate   ——————

22. goverment   ——————

23. grammer   ——————

24. heigth   ——————

25. imediate   ——————

26. intrest   ——————

27. knowlege   ——————

28. mathmatics   ——————

29. neccessary   ——————

30. ocassion   ——————

31. oppinion   ——————

32. oportunity   ——————

33. orginal   ——————

34. particlar   ——————

35. potatoe   ——————

36. preform   ——————

37. prehaps   ——————

38. probally   ——————

39. ridiclous   ——————

40. seperate   ——————

41. simular   ——————

42. sincerly   ——————

43. studing   ——————

44. suprise   ——————

45. temperture   ——————

46. Thrusday   ——————

47. unusal   ——————

48. writting   ——————

Section Three Review

1. Using *ie* or *ei:*

    > Use *i* before *e*
    >
    > Except after *c*
    >
    > Or when sounded like *ay*
    >
    > As in *neighbor* or *weigh.*

2. Keeping or Changing a Final *-y:*

    - Change the *-y* to *-i* when the *y* follows a consonant.

    - Do not change the *-y* to *-i* if the *y* follows a vowel.

    - Do not change the *-y-* to *-i* if you are adding *-ing.*

3. Keeping or Dropping a Silent Final *-e:*

    - In general, drop the final *-e* before an ending that begins with a vowel.

    - In general, keep the final *-e* before an ending that begins with a consonant.

4. Doubling the Final Consonant:

    - In a one-syllable word, double the final consonant only if a single vowel precedes the final consonant.

    - In a word of more than one syllable, apply the above rule only if the last syllable is accented.

5. Using Prefixes:

    - A prefix is one or more syllables added at the start of a word to change its meaning. Do not change any letters of the root word when you add a prefix to it.

6. Forming Plurals:

    - Add *-s* to make most nouns plural. Add *-es* if the noun ends in *ch, sh, ss,* or *x.*

    - If a noun ends in *o,* add *-s* if the *o* is preceded by a vowel. Add *-es* if the *o* is preceded by a consonant.

    - Some nouns that end in *-f* or *-fe* form the plural by changing the ending to *-ve* before the *s.*

    - Some words, especially words borrowed from other languages, form plurals by changing spelling.

7. Using Your Dictionary:

    - Whenever you're in doubt about the spelling of a word, consult your dictionary.

Exercise 3A

Correct any spelling errors in the following sentences by crossing out the incorrectly spelled word and writing the correct spelling above it.

1. Jerry's ~~neice~~ *niece* was sure that too much ~~studing~~ *studying* would ruin her social life.

2. Arnold was disatisfied when he was served cold potatos and runny eggs.

3. Serena could not beleive that she had mispelled such an easy word.

4. Henry refused to join any political movments because he disliked arguements of any kind.

5. Two weeks after Jenna had enlistted in the Marine Corps, she finally admited that she had made a serious mistake.

6. Two chimnies on our street collapsed during the dissastrous earthquake.

7. Orotund has tryed all of the methods advertised to cause a person to lose wieght.

8. Because so many of Yolanda's activities are ilegal, she rarly talks about them.

9. The flaws of today's heros are almost always quite noticable.

10. Minerva's knowlege was limited when it came to astrophysics, but her intrest was great.

11. The extinction of the dinosaurs probally occured as the result of a meteor strike.

12. In an extremly harsh but wise decision, Solomon declared the infant would be cut into two halfs.

13. The team was dissappointed when it heard about Manny's suspension, and its preformance suffered.

14. Do you truely believe that there is a goverment conspiracy to hide the truth of John F. Kennedy's assasination?

15. A sense of excitment filled the room as the paleontologists prepared to reveal their valueable new discovery.

Exercise 3B

Correct any spelling errors in the following sentences by crossing out the incorrectly spelled word and writing the correct spelling above it. If a sentence is correct, do nothing to it.

1. When the police arrived Maxwell ~~discribed~~ *described* the person who had stolen his two ~~radioes~~ *radios*.

2. Brent's consceince began to bother him when he realized that he should have left the last doughnut for Steve.

3. Everyone was stunned when the popular athelete was convicted of commiting a bank robbery.

4. Her husband's use of ilicit drugs bothered Amanda more than his falsifying of sales tax reciepts.

5. Bruce had always been a dutyful son, but latly his behavor had become quite questionable.

6. Would war be unecessary if the leaders of both countrys spent the weekend together at Disneyland?

7. Both of the monkies seemed as if they were standing in judgement of their peers.

8. Even though people were throwing tomatos and eggs, the couragous performer continued to sing.

9. Harold had always wanted to collect butterflys, but he definately did not like the idea of killing them.

10. Monica always says that alot of a person's problems can be resolved with a little tolerence and patience.

11. When the senator publically announced that he was quiting, everyone in the audeince gaspped.

12. After makeing the winning three-point shot, Kobe shared his receipe for success.

13. Lawrence stared at the ceiling, unable to believe how fierce the grief was that he felt ever since his neighbor had committed that weird, heinous act.

14. In Andrea's opion, warm tempertures and clear skys are usally preferable to cold wind and snow.

15. Javier controled his desire to interfere and offerred encouragment and support instead.

Exercise 3C

Correct any spelling errors in the following sentences by crossing out the incorrectly spelled word and writing the correct spelling above it. If a sentence is correct, do nothing to it.

1. Although I ~~beleive~~ *believe* that the beaches in my hometown of Sun City are some of the most beautiful on this coast, I also know that they have some ~~definate~~ *definite* problems that need to be corrected. **2.** For example, on any given weekend, it is extremly difficult to find a parking place anywhere near the beach after 9:30 A.M., no matter how carefuly one looks. **3.** Of course, begining in early summer, any beach in southern California is crowded on the weekends, but it's ridiclous when people who live in the area can't find any place to park at all. **4.** Just last weekend, after studing all morning, I drove down Pacific Coast Highway from Vista Way to Solana Beach Boulevard without manageing to find even one open parking space. **5.** I was truely dissappointed; all I saw was mile after mile of parked cars. **6.** Another problem with our beaches is the litter. **7.** A few years ago, I could take an evening stroll accross the sand and enjoy the lingerring warmth of the day. **8.** Today, however, there is a noticable difference. **9.** People cannot take liesurely walks on the beach these days without worring about where they are stepping. **10.** Thier next step might unnearth a discarded beer can or peices of broken radios or the sandy halfs of someone's sandwich. **11.** The final problem that bothers me is the behavor of lifeguards emploied by the city. **12.** I'm very worryed that our lifeguards are more intrested in flirting with the opposite sex than in watching bathers in the ocean. **13.** For instance, when I was at the beach last weekend, the lifeguard near us spent probally half of the morning talking to cute girls. **14.** I was releived that there were no emergencys because I saw him look at the water only three or four times. **15.** Although these problems are not the only ones we have in Sun City, they need to be solved before our once beautiful, safe beaches become too unpleasant to visit.

Sentence Practice:
Effective and Meaningful Sentences

These final sentence combining exercises are presented without specific directions. There will be a number of possible combinations for each group. Experiment to discover the most effective way to combine the sentences, supplying transitional words where necessary. You may also want to change the order in which the ideas are presented.

Sentence Combining Exercises

🌀 **EXAMPLE**
    a. The first marathon was run in 1896.
    b. It was run at the Olympic Games in Athens, Greece.
    c. The marathon was founded to honor the Greek soldier Pheidippides.
    d. He is supposed to have run from the town of Marathon to Athens in 409 B.C.E.
    e. The distance is 22 miles, 1470 yards.
    f. He ran to bring the news of the victory of the Greeks over the Persians.
    g. In 1924 the distance was standardized to 26 miles, 385 yards.

The first marathon was run at the Olympic Games in Athens, Greece, in 1896. The marathon was founded to honor the Greek soldier Pheidippides, who, in 409 B.C.E., is supposed to have run from the town of Marathon to Athens, a distance of 22 miles, 1470 yards, to bring the news of the victory of the Greeks over the Persians. In 1924 the distance was standardized to 26 miles, 385 yards.

1. Combine the following sentences.

    a. Four states do not call themselves "states."
    b. They are Kentucky, Massachusetts, Pennsylvania, and Virginia.
    c. They call themselves "commonwealths."
    d. "Commonwealth" is a term used in early English royal land charters.

Sentence Combining Exercises

continued

2. Combine the following sentences.

    a. Some people feel boxing should be outlawed.
    b. Boxing is a violent sport.
    c. Two people try to knock each other unconscious.
    d. One boxer hits the other boxer in the face.
    e. The brain of the boxer who is hit slams against the inside of his skull.
    f. He has a concussion.
    g. He is knocked out.

_____

_____

_____

_____

_____

3. Combine the following sentences.

    a. Many people believe the Indian population in the New World was destroyed through years of warfare with the settlers.
    b. In reality it was decimated by diseases.
    c. These were diseases such as smallpox, measles, cholera, and influenza.
    d. By the year 1600, 80 percent of the Aztecs and Incas had died from such diseases.
    e. By 1640, the Iroquois confederation in North America had lost nearly half of its people to similar diseases.
    f. They died because they lacked any racial immunity to these diseases.

_____

_____

_____

_____

_____

_____

Sentence Combining Exercises

continued

4. Combine the following sentences.

    a. There is a custom of hanging holly in the house at Christmas.

    b. Old Germanic races of Europe used to hang evergreen plants indoors in winter.

    c. The plants were a refuge for the spirits of the forest.

    d. Holly was considered a symbol of survival by pre-Christian Romans.

    e. The Romans used it as a decoration during their Saturnalia festival at the end of December.

    f. Christians began to celebrate Christmas at the end of December.

    g. Many of the old customs like hanging holly were preserved.

5. Combine the following sentences.

    a. The Battle of Hastings took place in 1066.

    b. It is said to be the most important event in the history of the English language.

    c. The Norman French defeated the English.

    d. It is known as the Norman Conquest.

    e. The Normans spoke French.

    f. French became the dominant language in England for a while.

Sentence Combining Exercises

continued

6. Combine the following sentences.

    a. The English commoners tended the animals in the fields.
    b. The words for animals before we eat them are "cow," "pig," "deer," and "lamb."
    c. These are original English words.
    d. The Norman French nobility ate the meat of the animals the English tended in the fields.
    e. The words for animals when we eat them are "steak," "pork," "venison," and "mutton."
    f. These words came from French.

_____

_____

_____

_____

7. Combine the following sentences.

    a. The first president of the United States was John Hanson.
    b. It was not George Washington.
    c. Washington was the first president once the U.S. Constitution was adopted.
    d. The U.S. Constitution was adopted in 1789.
    e. The United States had existed as a sovereign nation for thirteen years before that time.
    f. In 1781, John Hanson was elected by Congress.
    g. He was elected as the President of the United States under the Articles of Confederation.
    h. He served for one year.
    i. Six other presidents followed him before the U.S. Constitution was established.

_____

_____

_____

_____

_____

Sentence Combining Exercises

continued

8. Combine the following sentences.

   a. An optometrist tested 275 major league baseball players.
   b. He found that having cross-dominant eyesight can help a person hit a baseball better.
   c. Cross-dominant eyesight refers to seeing better with the left eye if a person is right-handed and vice versa.
   d. Only about 20 percent of the general population has cross-dominant eyesight.
   e. Over 50 percent of the baseball players that he examined have it.

   _____

   _____

   _____

   _____

   _____

9. Combine the following sentences.

   a. The name of the "pup tent" supposedly originated during the Civil War.
   b. General Sherman's backwoodsmen were being inspected by General Grant.
   c. The backwoodsmen objected to too much discipline.
   d. Grant walked by their tents.
   e. The soldiers got down on all fours.
   f. They barked and howled like hound dogs.
   g. The little tents used by soldiers began to be called "pup tents."

   _____

   _____

   _____

   _____

Sentence Combining Exercises

continued

10. Combine the following sentences.

    a. George Hancock was a Chicago Board of Trade reporter.
    b. He is credited with devising the official forerunner of softball.
    c. It was Thanksgiving Day, 1887.
    d. He wanted to liven things up.
    e. He was at the Farragut Boat Club.
    f. He started a game.
    g. He used a battered boxing glove as a ball.
    h. He used a broomstick as a bat.
    i. His game has been called Indoor–Outdoor.
    j. It has been called Kitten Ball.
    k. It has been called Playground Ball.
    l. It has been called Diamond Ball.
    m. It has been called Mush Ball.
    n. It was 1932.
    o. It received its present name of softball.

SECTION

5

Essay and Paragraph Practice: Expressing an Opinion

Assignment

You have now written narrative and descriptive papers (in Chapters One and Two) and several expository papers (in Chapters Three, Four, and Five). Your final writing assignment will be to state and support an **opinion.** As in earlier chapters, Exercises 1C, 2C, and 3C in this chapter have been designed as paragraph models of this assignment. Exercise 1C argues that Thoreau is correct in his belief that people look for happiness in the wrong places; Exercise 2C expresses the opinion that the principle of free speech protects even racist speakers; and Exercise 3C claims that the beaches in Sun City have problems that need correction.

Note that each of these paragraphs includes a topic sentence that expresses an opinion supported by details and examples drawn from the writer's personal knowledge or experience. For instance, the paragraph in Exercise 1C presents examples to support Thoreau's opinion that people look for happiness in the wrong places. These examples suggest that many people think that the clothes they wear, the beer they drink, or even the shampoo they use can affect how happy they are. Your assignment is to write a paper in which you express an opinion that you support with examples and details drawn from your own experiences or observations.

Prewriting to Generate Ideas

Prewriting Application: Finding Your Topic

Use prewriting techniques to develop your thoughts about one of the following topics or a topic suggested by your instructor. Before you choose a topic, prewrite to develop a list of possible reasons and examples that you can use to support your opinion. Don't choose a topic if you do not have examples with which you can support it.

1. Choose a proverb and show why it is or is not good advice. Consider these:

   Don't count your chickens before they hatch.

   The early bird gets the worm.

   Look before you leap.

390

If at first you don't succeed, try, try again.

If you can't beat 'em, join 'em.

Money can't buy happiness.

2. Support an opinion about the condition of your neighborhood, your college campus, your home, or some other place with which you are familiar.

3. Some people compete in nearly everything they do, whether it be participating in sports, working on the job, or studying in college classes. Other people find competition distracting and even offensive. Write a paragraph in which you support your opinion about competition.

4. Do you eat in fast-food restaurants? Write a paragraph in which you support your opinion about eating in such places.

5. Should parents spank children? Write a paper in which you support your opinion for or against such discipline.

6. Should high school students work at part-time jobs while going to school? Write a paper in which you support an opinion for or against their doing so.

7. Do you know couples who live together without marrying? Write a paper in which you support an opinion for or against such an arrangement.

8. Is peer pressure really a very serious problem for people today? Write a paper in which you support an opinion about the seriousness of peer pressure.

9. Is racism, sexism, homophobia, or religious intolerance still a common problem in our society? Write a paper in which you support your opinion one way or the other.

10. Do general education requirements benefit college students? Write a paper in which you support your opinion about such classes.

Choosing and Narrowing the Topic

Once you have settled on several possible topics, consider these points as you make your final selection.

■ Choose the more limited topic rather than the more general one.

■ Choose the topic about which you could discuss several, not just one or two, reasons in support of your opinion.

■ Choose the topic about which you have the most experience or knowledge.

■ Choose the topic in which you have the most personal interest. Avoid topics about which you don't really care.

Writing a Thesis Statement or Topic Sentence

If your assignment is to write a single paragraph, you will open it with a topic sentence. If you are writing a complete essay, you will need a thesis statement at the end of your introductory paragraph. In either case, you will need a clear statement of the topic and central idea of your paper.

Prewriting Application: Working with Topic Sentences

Identify the topic sentences in Exercises 1C (page 353), 2C (page 368), and 3C (page 382). What are the topic and the central point in each topic sentence?

Prewriting Application: Evaluating Thesis Statements and Topic Sentences

Write "No" before each sentence that would not make an effective thesis statement or topic sentence *for this assignment*. Write "Yes" before each sentence that would make an effective one. Using ideas of your own, rewrite each ineffective sentence into one that might work.

_____   **1.** The intersection of Whitewood and Los Alamos is one of the most dangerous traffic spots in our city.

_____

_____

_____   **2.** Sometimes the old proverb "If at first you don't succeed, try, try again" is the worst advice that one can give a person.

_____

_____

_____   **3.** Racism has existed in our country for many years.

_____

_____

_____   **4.** My father and mother are not married and never have been.

_____

_____

_____ **5.** Not everyone needs to be married to have a strong relationship and a happy family.

_____

_____

_____ **6.** Almost every young teenager could benefit from participating in competitive sports.

_____

_____

_____ **7.** Many high school students today work at part-time jobs.

_____

_____

_____ **8.** Body piercing can be a healthy, safe expression of one's individuality.

_____

_____

_____ **9.** There are several good reasons why a person should never drink any carbonated soft drinks.

_____

_____

_____ **10.** Most people's family values are going straight downhill.

_____

_____

Prewriting Application: Talking to Others

Form a group of three or four people and discuss the topics you have chosen. Your goal here is to help each other clarify your opinions and to determine if you have enough evidence to support them. Explain why you hold your opinion and what specific reasons and examples you will use to support it. As you listen to the others in your group, use the following questions to help them clarify their ideas.

1. Can the opinion be reasonably supported in a brief paper? Is its topic too general or broad?

2. What specific examples will the writer provide as support? Are they convincing?

3. What is the weakest reason or example? Why? Should it be made stronger or completely replaced?

4. Which reasons or examples are the strongest? Why?

5. Which reason or example should the paper open with? Which should it close with?

Organizing Opinion Papers

An **emphatic** organization, one that saves the strongest supporting material until last, is perhaps most common in opinion papers. If you have a list of three, four, or five good reasons in support of your opinion, consider arranging them so that you build up to the strongest, most convincing one.

Writing the Essay

If your assignment is to write a complete essay:

- Place your **thesis statement** (which should clearly state your opinion) at the end of the introductory paragraph.

- Write a separate **body paragraph** for each reason that supports your opinion.

- Open each body paragraph with a **topic sentence** that identifies the one reason the paragraph will discuss.

- Within each body paragraph, use specific **facts, examples,** and **details** to explain and support your reason.

Writing the Paragraph

If your assignment is to write a single paragraph:

- Open it with a **topic sentence** that clearly identifies your opinion.

- Use **clear transitions** to move from one reason in support of your opinion to the next.

- Use specific **facts, examples,** and **details** to explain and support your reasons.

Writing Application: Identifying Transitional Words, Phrases, and Sentences

Examine Exercises 1C (page 353), 2C (page 368), and 3C (page 382). Identify the transitions that introduce each new reason offered in support of the opinion. Then identify any other transitions that serve to connect ideas between sentences.

Rewriting and Improving the Paper

1. Revise your examples so they are specific and concrete. As much as possible, use actual names of people and places.

2. Add or revise transitions wherever doing so would help clarify movement from one idea to another.

3. Improve your preliminary thesis statement (if you are writing an essay) or your preliminary topic sentence (if you are writing a single paragraph) so that it more accurately states the central point of your paper.

4. Examine your draft for sentence variety. If many of your sentences tend to be of the same length, try varying their length and their structure by combining sentences using the techniques you have studied in the Sentence Practice sections of this text.

Rewriting Application: Responding to Paragraph Writing

Read the following paragraph. Then respond to the questions following it.

School Sports

Many of my relatives believe that playing sports in high school and college is a waste of time and energy, but I disagree. I believe that school sports can help a person stay out of trouble and can lead to bigger and better things. I know, for instance, that sports can help young people who are heading for trouble with the law. I have a close friend who grew up in a very hostile environment. His parents abused him, and he belonged to gangs ever since he was very young. He had been in and out of juvenile court several times when he discovered something special about himself. He discovered that he is a good athlete. He began to excel at baseball and football. He developed a love for both sports. After playing football at Escondido High School, he earned a full scholarship to the University of Nevada. Playing sports can also help people emotionally. For example, sports have helped me learn to control my anger. I am a very emotional person, and when I get angry I just want to hit someone—hard. Whenever I feel like that, I get out on the football field and get physical. By the end of a hard practice, I'm ready to go back and live my life. Football helps me when I'm stressed out or depressed, too. I can always count on my teammates to bring me back up when I'm down. Furthermore, playing sports encourages students to stay in school and motivates them to do well. I'm the kind of person who hates school, but through sports I have learned that the road to success includes an education. There have been many times when I have wanted to drop out of school, but always holding me back is my love for the game of football. I know that football is not always going to be there for me, but school sports have changed my life and have affected the lives of many others as well.

1. Identify the topic sentence. State its topic and central idea. Does it express a definite opinion?

2. How many supporting points are presented in this paper? Identify them.

3. Identify the transitional sentences that introduce each major supporting point. What other transitions are used between sentences?

4. Consider the organization of the paragraph. Would you change the order of the supporting material? Explain why or why not.

5. Consider the sentence variety. What sentences would you combine to improve the paragraph?

Rewriting Application: Responding to Essay Writing

Read the following essay. Then respond to the questions at the end of it.

City Life

Because my father was in the navy, our family moved many times when I was growing up. As a result, I have lived in many different sizes of cities and towns all across the United States, from a tiny farm town outside Sioux Falls, South Dakota, to San Diego, California, one of the largest cities in the United States. After all these moves, I have developed my own opinions about where I want to spend my life. I know that small-town life has its attractions for some people, but as far as I'm concerned large cities offer the kind of life I like to live.

One of the reasons I like living in large cities is that there is always so much to do. I can see plays and movies, attend cultural and sporting events, go shopping, or take walks in the park. For example, within a one-week period last month, I went with my parents to see <u>Phantom of the Opera,</u> I attended a Padres baseball game with some friends, I spent a day at the Del Mar Fair, and I went shopping at Horton Plaza Mall. I am sure I could not have had that kind of week in a small town. This weekend I plan to visit the San Diego Wild Animal Park, where condors have been saved from extinction and are now being released into the wild.

I also like large cities because I get the chance to meet people from so many different cultural and ethnic backgrounds. For instance, in one of my first college classes, I met a person from South Vietnam who has become one of my good friends. He and his family have been in the United States for ten years, and they have all sorts of terrifying stories to tell about how they fled their country to start a new life. I also have many Hispanic and African-American friends, a natural result of growing up in an area that has a large mix of people.

Finally, I enjoy large cities for a very practical reason. Because there are so many different kinds of companies and industries where I live, I can be relatively sure that I will always be able to find a job somewhere. My goal is to become a software designer, and a large city is exactly the kind of place where I will find many job opportunities. San Diego is the home of many high-tech companies, like Qualcomm, Peregrine, and Oracle. Whether I end up working for one of these companies or starting my own software business, a large city like San Diego is the place to be.

I suppose life in large cities is not for everybody, but it sure is for me. I cannot imagine spending my day watching the cows or listening to crows in some tiny rural town. Maybe someday I will want the peace and quiet of a place like that, but not today.

1. Identify the thesis statement. State its topic and central idea. Is it an effective thesis statement? Does it state a definite opinion?

2. Identify each topic sentence. State its topic and central idea. Does each topic sentence clearly state a reason in support of the thesis?

3. What transitional words introduce each new body paragraph?

4. Consider the organization of the body paragraphs. Would you change their order in any way? Why or why not?

5. Is each reason supported with specific facts, examples, and details? Identify where such specific support is used. Where would you improve the support?

Proofreading

When proofreading your paper, watch for the following errors:

Sentence fragments, comma splices, and fused sentences

Misplaced modifiers and dangling modifiers

Errors in subject–verb agreement

Errors in pronoun case, pronoun–antecedent agreement, or pronoun reference

Errors in comma use

Errors in the use of periods, question marks, exclamation points, colons, semicolons, and quotation marks

Errors in capitalization, titles, and numbers

Errors in the use of irregular verbs or in word choice

Misspelled words

Now prepare a clean final draft, following the format your instructor has asked for.

Chapter 6 Practice Test

I. Review of Chapters Three, Four, and Five

A. Correct any misplaced or dangling modifiers. Do nothing if the sentence is correct.

1. Skiing beyond the resort's boundaries, a deadly avalanche hurtled down the mountain.

   _____

   _____

2. Ms. Wray almost fainted when Mr. Kong asked her to dance.

   _____

3. Luis offered his soda to the student that he had kept in his cooler.

   _____

   _____

4. Rolling over the dirt road, a Honda Civic approached my horse with two flat tires and slowly came to a stop.

   _____

   _____

5. Exhausted by a day of hard labor, a hot shower and a good sleep seemed inviting.

   _____

   _____

B. Correct any subject–verb agreement or pronoun use errors in the following sentences. Do nothing if the sentence is correct.

6. The measles were common among children until a vaccine was developed.

7. Richard was looking forward to taking his wife out to dinner and a movie, but it was too expensive.

8. Each man, woman, and child in the stadium have a chance to win $1,000.

9. Bill and I tried to fix the computer by ourself, but a hammer was the only tool we knew how to use.

10. Anyone who rides a horse must be sure that you let it know who is in charge.

Chapter 6 Practice Test

continued

C. Add commas to the following sentences where necessary.

11. Outside the casino on the far edge of the Las Vegas Strip a fire truck roared to a stop and three people dressed in clown suits jumped from its cab.

12. After Patti had finished ordering supplies she started scheduling classes finding available classrooms and sending book orders out to the faculty.

13. Mr. Dungeness walked sideways all the way to 523 Jones Street Seawater Maine; unfortunately the tartar sauce had arrived at the same address in Clamdevon New York last week.

14. Jenna's pet bird a friendly African gray parrot calls her name whenever she walks by.

D. Add periods, question marks, exclamation points, quotation marks, semicolons, colons, and apostrophes (or 's) where necessary and correct any mistakes in the use of capitalization, titles, and numbers. Do not add or delete any commas.

15. Minerva, goddess of wisdom, was not invited to the party as a result, she refused to talk to these deities the god of war, the goddess of love, and the god of wine.

16. Dont you want to visit my Fathers farm asked Dylan.

17. Was it Oscar Wilde who said, The only way to get rid of a temptation is to yield to it.

18. The los angeles times reported that one hundred and twenty-six people experienced food poisoning at a diner last week.

19. The score was eighty-three to sixty-five in favor of the los angeles lakers when bruce decided he would rather read the reader's digest article titled how to be a good dad.

20. Aurora enjoyed her english class last spring, but her brothers psychology class sounded interesting too.

continued

II. Chapter Six

A. In the blanks, write the correct forms of the verbs indicated.

21. The little bear was distressed when it realized that someone had been _____ in its

    bed. (lie)

22. Hermes had _____ almost the entire race before anyone noticed the wings on his

    feet. (run)

23. The space shuttle commander asked her co-pilot if anyone had _____ the key to

    the restroom. (bring)

24. The students at the sorority party had _____ nearly fifteen kegs of apple cider

    before the dean arrived. (drink)

25. After Poseidon had _____ halfway around the world, he decided he'd rather be

    lord of the sky. (swim)

B. Correct any verb form errors in the following sentences. Do nothing if the sentence is correct.

26. Susan Boyle had sang for just a few moments when everyone started to pay attention.

27. After Othello saw the handkerchief, he wanted to lay down and take a nap.

28. The hawk setting at the top of the grape trellis watched the toy poodle cross the yard.

29. As she lay in her bed, Emily thought she heard the buzz of a fly.

30. After the heavy rain, the townspeople expected the river to bust through its banks.

C. Underline the correct word in the parentheses.

31. Although Bill had (lead led) the entire race, in the end Cyrano won by a nose.

32. The (principle principal) reason to stop at red lights is to avoid being killed.

continued

33. Natasha had no idea what (effect affect) the CD by Eminem would have on her mother.

34. Mahatma Gandhi once offered this good piece of (advise advice): "One must be the change one wishes to see in the world."

35. Once they had eaten, the three friends decided to divide the bill evenly (among between) themselves.

D. Correct any incorrect word choices in the following sentences. Do nothing if the sentence is correct.

36. When Bill reached El Camino Real, he took a moment to complement himself for walking so far.

37. After young Woz returned the Clark Bar to the candy counter, his conscious was clear.

38. This week's discussion will focus on the amount of angels that can dance on the head of a pin.

39. Archibald was already to recite his poem, but the audience had already left the church.

40. Does anyone know who is more powerful then a speeding locomotive?

E. Underline the correctly spelled words in the parentheses.

41. The two sisters and (their they're) friends were all (embarrassed embarassed) when Harold arrived at the Goth party wearing pink.

42. After (worring worrying) about the weather for days, Linnea finally decided to plant (tomatos tomatoes) and zucchini.

43. The team was (disappointed dissappointed) when the (atheletic athletic) director cancelled the game.

44. By the time it (occurred occured) to Richard to ask for help with his new poem, he was (completly completely) exhausted.

45. The biggest (suprise surprise) was the (requirement requirment) that we all wear formal dress.

Chapter 6 Practice Test

continued

F. Correct any spelling errors in the following sentences by crossing out the incorrectly spelled word and writing the correct spelling above it.

46. When asked how much wieght he had gained over the holidays, Steve bravly told the truth.

47. The goverment forms contained an amazing number of mispellings.

48. The brochure's discription of South Dakota's Badlands made Darwin's neice even more determined to spend her summer there.

49. Homer was refering to bread, not money, when he admitted he had stolen some dough.

50. Alejandra probally knew Mark Twain's real name, but she forgot it in her excitment at meeting Hal Holbrook.

I. Chapter One

A. Underline all subjects once and all verbs twice.

    1. Did Brad play the role of the eighty-year-old infant?

    2. Hera and Zeus remarried for the thousandth time.

    3. Kate Chopin wrote in the nineteenth century, yet she was not recognized as a great

       artist until the twentieth century.

    4. Deborah smiled gratefully when she received the acceptance letter from

       Plough shares literary journal.

    5. Before King Solomon stood two women, each claiming the baby.

B. In the space provided, indicate whether the underlined word is a noun (N), pronoun (Pro), verb (V), adjective (Adj), adverb (Adv), preposition (Prep), or conjunction (Conj).

    _____   **6.** London Bridge <u>eventually</u> deteriorated and fell into the river.

    _____   **7.** From his <u>secret</u> hiding place, Frank saw the last pods loaded onto the trucks.

    _____   **8.** Hamlet wanted to trick the King, <u>so</u> he acted crazy.

    _____   **9.** Vulcan <u>will</u> repair that damaged horseshoe for you.

    _____   **10.** <u>Everyone</u> knew that Lord Byron was born with clubfoot.

C. In the following sentences, place all prepositional phrases in parentheses.

    11. Some of the people sneered at Elvis's haircut.

    12. Stopping his horse by the woods on a snowy evening, the man sat and thought.

    13. Driving down Highway 51, Bobby Zimmerman felt like a rolling stone.

    14. President Obama led his dog onto the plane and sat beside it.

    15. Because of the budget, the governor changed to a cheaper cigar.

continued

II. Chapter Two

A. Correct all fragments, comma splices, and fused sentences. If the sentence is correct, do nothing to it.

16. The man embarrassed when his wig blew off.

_____

_____

17. Roxanne opened her eyes and noticed his nose, then she began to giggle.

_____

_____

18. Wondering where he was going, Faith watched as her husband walked into the forest.

_____

_____

19. The new mechanic kept asking for a left-handed screwdriver nobody had one.

_____

_____

20. Dimmesdale bought some new tee-shirts his chest had begun to itch.

_____

_____

21. As Van Gogh was looking up at the night sky.

_____

_____

22. The young girl idolized Spiderman, however, she wondered if he ate flies.

_____

_____

continued

23. Maya loves the beauty of nature sometimes it all seems like an illusion.

_____

_____

24. Sit down.

_____

_____

25. Holding the microphone as he sang "Satisfaction."

_____

_____

B. Compose simple, compound, complex, and compound-complex sentences according to the instructions.

26. Write a simple sentence that contains at least one prepositional phrase.

_____

_____

27. Write a compound sentence. Use a coordinating conjunction and appropriate punctuation to join the clauses.

_____

_____

28. Write a compound sentence. Use a transitional word or phrase and appropriate punctuation to join the clauses.

_____

_____

continued

29. Write a complex sentence. Use *if* as the subordinator.

_____

_____

30. Write a compound-complex sentence. Use the subordinator *after.*

_____

_____

III. Chapter Three

A. Correct any misplaced or dangling modifiers in the following sentences. If the sentence is correct, do nothing to it.

31. Determined to liberate India, Gandhi's success came through his philosophy of nonviolent resistance.

_____

_____

32. The woman entered the luxury hotel with two jaguars on a leash wearing scarlet high-heeled shoes.

_____

_____

33. Bored by the poor performance of the home team, the stadium quickly emptied.

_____

_____

34. Mr. Sprat's wife only preferred lean meat.

_____

_____

continued

35. Avoiding the heavy traffic on the main street, James Bond's route took him into a dark alley.

_____

_____

36. The drunken driver barely missed the child on the sidewalk who was swerving crazily down the street.

_____

_____

37. A woman speaking to the minister quietly began to weep.

_____

_____

38. Breathing a sigh of relief, the lost camper finally heard a familiar voice.

_____

_____

39. A black spider crawled onto the dog with a red hour-glass on its belly when it sat next to the woodpile.

_____

_____

40. Seeing the man who had been stalking her, her heart began to pound.

_____

_____

continued

B. Add phrases or clauses to the following sentences according to the instructions. Be sure to punctuate carefully.

41. Add a verbal phrase. Use the verb *run*.

Donna reached the summit a half hour before the others.

_____

_____

42. Add an adjective clause.

The man chased the BMW.

_____

_____

43. Add a present participial phrase to the beginning of this sentence. Use the verb *reach*.

The warriors prepared for battle.

_____

_____

44. Add an appositive phrase.

My brother-in-law left Atlanta and moved to San Diego.

_____

_____

45. Add an infinitive verbal phrase to this sentence. Use the verb *hang*.

After searching all day, Rosario found the perfect picture.

_____

_____

IV. Chapter Four

A. Correct any subject–verb agreement errors in the following sentences by crossing out the incorrect verb form and writing in the correct form above it. If the sentence is correct, do nothing to it.

46. Every rider on each of the thoroughbred horses have been carefully checked for weight.

47. A heavily armed team with rifles, pistols, machine guns, and other weapons are watching the house where the suspect lives.

48. Does the police officers or the ambulance driver know who caused the accident?

49. Every Friday at 3:00, a teacher with fifteen students arrive at my sugar-free ice cream store.

50. Somebody who still loves Janis Joplin and Jimi Hendrix have left a strange message on your voice mail.

51. Yesterday, fifty pounds of fresh fish were delivered to the homeless shelter.

52. Rice or baked potatoes serve as a good side dish for many meals.

53. Anyone who has heard one of Yo-Yo Ma's concerts know that he plays wonderfully.

54. Here is the tongue stud and piercing needle that you left at the party.

55. Every candidate for the three available positions hope to be chosen for an interview.

B. Correct any pronoun use errors in the following sentences by crossing out the incorrect pronoun and writing in the correct one above it. In some cases you may have to rewrite part of the sentence. If the sentence is correct, do nothing to it.

56. When a customer enters that drug store, you are greeted by people dressed like aspirins.

57. When we entered the French restaurant, Marie and myself agreed that we would each order snails.

58. Homer had left his chewing tobacco in his truck, but when he returned to the parking lot, he couldn't find it.

59. Both Deborah and Carlton have lovely voices, but Deborah practices her singing more often than him.

60. Karl said that he couldn't stand Bob Dylan and that he loved country music; this changed the wedding plans.

continued

61. The jazz orchestra from Memphis got on their bus and headed for Louisiana.

62. The new members of the math club wanted to solve the problem by themself.

63. Bruce proudly announced that the best bowlers in the league were Brent and him.

64. The coach told us to run ten laps and then turn out our lights by 8:00, which I really didn't want to do.

65. At the wedding reception, one of bridesmaids dropped their glove into the punch bowl.

V. Chapter Five

A. Add commas to the following sentences where necessary. If the sentence is correct, do nothing to it.

66. Yes I like blackened catfish and I like lots of grits with it.

67. The waiter served the soup lit the candles picked up the salad plates and tried to remain dignified as he spilled the wine into the diner's lap.

68. I was married on July 19 1969 and on July 20 1969 a man walked on the moon.

69. A dose of Beano for example is suggested as part of your pre-dinner preparations.

70. After writing a series of short choppy sentences Ernest decided to try to write some longer ones.

71. Once upon a time for example children dressed in costumes on Halloween night and then trusted that the treats they received were perfectly safe.

72. The African gray a soft-spoken friendly parrot can imitate hundreds of words and other sounds.

73. As Jack was taking photographs in Mammoth Lakes California Susan was indulging her innocent but secret delights.

continued

74. Arlene stood before the volunteers and announced "We need help cooking food cleaning walls washing clothes and babysitting the children."

75. Mother Teresa of course was a holy woman but even she was not perfect.

B. Add periods, exclamation points, question marks, semicolons, colons, quotation marks, or apostrophes (or 's) where necessary in the following sentences. If the sentence is correct, do nothing to it. Do not add or delete any commas.

76. Could the saxophonist Rahsaan Roland Kirk really hold a note for more than five minutes

77. President John Kennedy once said, Mankind must put an end to war, or war will put an end to mankind

78. Maxwells list included the following items a telephone in his shoe, a pen with invisible ink, and a secret agent trench coat.

79. Hasnt the sky fallen yet asked Henny Penny in a disappointed voice

80. Elvis asked Priscillas brother why he had stepped on his blue suede shoes

C. Correct any errors in the use of capitalization, titles, or numbers in the following sentences. If the sentence is correct, do nothing to it.

81. harper lee's book to kill a mockingbird, which is set in the south, is her only novel.

82. brian wilson attended a college that is 5 miles west of surf city avenue.

83. ms. hohman brought in 25 copies of cosmopolitan for her class called introduction to women's issues.

84. In our literature class we read the poem fern hill, which is one of dylan thomas's most popular poems.

85. a chicken dinner at the brown derby costs eighteen dollars and ninety-nine cents.

continued

VI. Chapter Six

A. In the following sentences correct any errors in the use of irregular verbs by crossing out the incorrect forms and writing in the correct ones above. If the sentence is correct, do nothing to it.

86. The raven setting on the desk kept saying the same thing over and over.

87. The priest had rang the church bell, but the people had not went into the church.

88. Cecil had never saw a blue heron before the one that had flew into his backyard.

89. By the end of the party, no one had ate any of the game hen stuffed with Spam that

Homer and Hortense had brung.

90. Paul lied in his bed thinking that he had swam all the way across the lake.

B. In the following sentences, correct any spelling errors caused by using the wrong word. Cross out any incorrect words and write the correct words above. If the sentence is correct, do nothing to it.

91. The affect of the news was that David ate to much ice cream after dinner.

92. The dean said he will not except you're insincere apology.

93. Each year less people visit the Queen Mary then the year before.

94. Last year two floral elephants lead the Rose Parade as it preceded down Colorado

Boulevard.

95. The amount of soldiers deserting in the Civil War bothered the officers who lead

the troops.

C. Correct any spelling errors in the following sentences by crossing out the incorrect spellings and writing the correct spellings above them.

96. Torvald was begining to see something diffrent about Nora's attitude.

97. Iago claimed that Desdemona had decieved him about the thiefs who had stolen the

handkerchief.

continued

    98. Alot of people using the Internet become victims of ilegal scams.

    99. James was embarassed by his grammer errors in his college application.

  100. When Bobby felt the temperture rise an unusal amount, he knew a hard rain was

       going to fall.

Appendix: Working with ESL Issues

If English is your second language, you know the confusion and frustration that can sometimes result when you try to apply the many different grammar rules and usage patterns of English. Of course, you are not alone. Anyone who has ever tried to speak or write a second language has encountered the same problem. This appendix is meant to review some of the more common issues that ESL writers face.

Count and Noncount Nouns

- **Count nouns** are nouns that exist as separate items that can be counted. They usually have singular and plural forms: *one bottle, two bottles; one thought, two thoughts; one teacher, two teachers.*

- **Noncount nouns** are nouns that cannot be counted and usually do not take plural forms. Here are some common noncount nouns:

EXAMPLES

Food and drink:	*meat, bacon, spinach, celery, water, milk, wine*
Nonfood material:	*equipment, furniture, luggage, rain, silver, gasoline*
Abstractions:	*anger, beauty, happiness, honesty, courage*

Note that **noncount nouns** stay in their singular form. It would be incorrect to say *bacons, furnitures, or courages.*

- Some nouns can be either **count** or **noncount,** depending on whether you use them as specific, countable items or as a substance or general concept.

EXAMPLES

Noncount:	The *fruit* on the table looks delicious.
Count:	Eat as many *fruits* and vegetables as you can each day.
Noncount:	Supposedly, nothing can travel faster than the speed of *light.*
Count:	The *lights* in the house were all on when we arrived home.

◉◎ PRACTICE   If the underlined word is a count noun, write its plural form in the blank. If it is a noncount noun, write *noncount* in the blank.

1. Alyssa's <u>happiness</u> was apparent as she drove into the driveway.   *noncount*

2. She held in her hand a <u>picture</u> of her two brothers.   _____

3. Enrique did not know the <u>name</u> of the world's largest island.   _____

4. Henry felt great <u>satisfaction</u> when he hit a grand slam

   home run.   _____

5. The emperor was angry when he realized the <u>laughter</u> was

   directed at his new suit of clothes.   _____

6. Cameron wondered which <u>planet</u> was the fourth

   from the sun.   _____

7. Quarters used to be made out of <u>silver</u>, but today copper

   makes up more than 90 percent of each quarter.   _____

8. When the state ran out of money, the federal <u>government</u>

   did not come to its rescue.   _____

9. Jacob's teacher was unimpressed when he identified the

   Dust Bowl as a popular football game held every <u>year</u> in January.   _____

10. Yesenia's <u>claustrophobia</u> prevented her from boarding

    the airplane.   _____

Articles with Count and Noncount Nouns

Indefinite Articles

- The **indefinite articles** are *a* and *an*. They are used with *singular count nouns* that are *general* or *nonspecific*. Usually, the noun is being introduced for the first time.

EXAMPLES   Yesterday I saw **a car** with two teenagers in it.

An apple fell from the tree and rolled into the pool.

In these sentences, *car* and *apple* are general count nouns that could refer to any car or any apple at all, so the articles *a* and *an* are used with them.

- Do not use indefinite articles with noncount nouns.

EXAMPLES

(Incorrect)	She suffers from an insomnia.
(Correct)	She suffers from insomnia.
(Incorrect)	Americans value a freedom and an independence.
(Correct)	Americans value freedom and independence.

PRACTICE   Correct the following sentences by crossing out any unnecessary use of *a* or *an* or by adding *a* or *an* where needed. If a sentence is correct, do nothing to it.

1. My sister gave me ᵃ radio to take to the beach.

2. Chantal suffered from an amnesia, so she could not remember her

   date of birth.

3. He is a vegetarian, so he doesn't eat a meat.

4. Monica's husband falls asleep in his chair whenever they watch movie.

5. A jealousy is what caused him to act so rudely.

Definite Articles

The word *the* is a **definite article.** It is used with *specific nouns*, both *count* and *noncount*. You can usually tell if a noun is specific by its context. In some cases, other words in a sentence make it clear that the noun refers to a specific thing or things. In other instances, the noun has been mentioned in a previous sentence, so the second reference to it is specific.

EXAMPLES

I bumped into *the table* in the hallway.	(This singular count noun refers to a *specific* table, the one in the hallway.)
A car and a motorcycle roared down the street. *The car* sounded as if it had no muffler.	(This singular count noun refers to a *specific* car, the one in the previous sentence.)
The men who robbed the bank looked young.	(This plural count noun refers to *specific* men, the ones who robbed the bank.)
The courage that he demonstrated impressed me.	(This noncount noun refers to the *specific* courage of one man.)

PRACTICE

Correct the following sentences by crossing out any unnecessary use of *the* or by adding *the* where needed. If a sentence is correct, do nothing to it.

1. I do not like ^*the* man who lives next door.

2. The tolerance is a quality admired many people.

3. Irene was surprised at disappointment that she felt.

4. The psychiatrist in the next office specializes in treating the insomnia.

5. My car does not use the gasoline in its diesel engine.

Articles with Proper Nouns

- Use *the* with plural proper nouns (*the United States, the Smiths*).

- Do not use *the* with most singular proper nouns (*John, San Diego, Germany*). There are, however, many exceptions.

- Use *the* with some singular proper nouns, including names of oceans, seas, and rivers (*the Mississippi River, the Atlantic Ocean*), names using *of* (*the Republic of China, the University of Colorado*), and names of large regions, deserts, and peninsulas (*the Mideast, the Sahara Desert, the Iberian Peninsula*).

No Articles

Noncount nouns and plural nouns are often used without an article to make general statements. (Remember that *all* singular count nouns require an article, whether they are specific or general.)

⊗⊗ EXAMPLE   *Racism* and *prejudice* should worry *parents* and *teachers.*

In this sentence, the noncount nouns *racism* and *prejudice* as well as the plural count nouns *parents* and *teachers* do not use articles because they are general, referring to *any* racism or prejudice and *any* parent or teacher.

⊗⊗ PRACTICE   In the spaces provided, write the appropriate article (*a, an,* or *the*) wherever one is needed. If no article is needed, leave the space blank.

1. Jerry had never seen __*a*__ giraffe before he traveled to _____ Africa.

2. Cerberus is the name of _____ dog that won _____ Most Beautiful Pet contest.

3. His decision to tell _____ truth about his theft required _____ courage.

4. When Bill sees _____ homeless person, he always offers to buy him _____ meal.

5. _____ person who owns _____ red Honda that I hit is shouting at me.

6. _____ resentment was _____ only personal characteristic that Marie would not give up.

7. When she was robbed for _____ third time, Dora decided to buy _____ security system.

8. _____ chief of police could not believe what _____ rookie officer had just said.

9. Last year I decided to take _____ vacation to _____ Philippines.

10. Marissa eats _____ doughnuts every day because they give her a sense of _____ happiness.

Subjects

■ English, unlike some other languages, requires a *stated* subject in nearly every sentence. (Commands are an exception. See Chapter 1.) Subjects are required in all subordinate clauses as well as in all main clauses.

EXAMPLES

(incorrect)	Is hot in Las Vegas in August.
(correct)	*It* is hot in Las Vegas in August.
(incorrect)	My brother yelled with delight when hit a home run.
(correct)	My brother yelled with delight when *he* hit a home run.

■ Although some languages immediately follow a subject with a pronoun that refers to the subject, it is incorrect to do so in English.

EXAMPLES

| (incorrect) | The cashier *she* gave me the wrong amount of change. |
| (correct) | The cashier gave me the wrong amount of change. |

■ If a subject follows the verb, a "dummy" subject is used before the verb.

EXAMPLES

| (incorrect) | Are some suspicious men at the door. |
| (correct) | *There* are some suspicious men at the door. |

PRACTICE Correct any errors in the following sentences by crossing out subjects that are not needed or by adding subjects that are missing.

1. ^*There* Were no lights on in the house when we arrived home.

2. Prometheus he was chained to a rock.

3. Sohini wanted to return to India because missed her family.

4. Although we were all hungry, the fish it was too spoiled to eat.

5. My brother told me is raining in Reno tonight.

6. When Ichiro looked at his paycheck, decided to ask for a raise.

7. My cousin's parents they were very rude to me last night.

8. Is too hot to wear a long-sleeved shirt today.

9. After the party it had ended, everyone left Ensenada and drove home.

10. Don Quixote attacked the windmill so that could win the love of Dulcinea.

Helping Verbs and Main Verbs

Choosing the right combination of helping verbs and main verbs can be difficult if English is your second language. To make the correct choices, you must first understand a few things about main verbs and helping verbs. (See Chapter 1 for a more thorough discussion of this topic.)

- If the verb consists of one word, it is a main verb (MV).

◎◎ EXAMPLE

       MV
The old waiter **stared** at the table.

- If the verb consists of two or more words, the last word of the verb is the main verb (MV). The earlier words are helping verbs (HV).

◎◎ EXAMPLES

      HV MV
The old waiter **is staring** at the table.

      HV   MV
The old waiter **must leave** soon.

Helping Verbs

There are only twenty-three helping verbs in English, so it is not difficult to become familiar with them. Nine of the helping verbs are called *modals*. They are always helping verbs. The other fourteen words sometimes function as helping verbs and sometimes as main verbs. Here are the twenty-three helping verbs:

Modals:	can	will	shall	may
	could	would	should	might
				must

Forms of do:	do, does, did
Forms of have:	have, has, had
Forms of be:	am, is, are, was, were, be, being, been

Main Verbs

To use helping verbs and main verbs correctly, you need to know the forms that main verbs can take. All main verbs use five forms (except for *be*, which uses eight).

Base Form	-S Form	Past Tense	Past Participle	Present Participle
walk	walks	walked	walked	walking
call	calls	called	called	calling
eat	eats	ate	eaten	eating
give	gives	gave	given	giving
ring	rings	rang	rung	ringing

Notice that the past tense and the past participle of *call* and *walk* are spelled the same way, by adding *-ed*. They are called regular verbs. However, the past tense and past participle of *eat* and *ring* change spelling dramatically. These are irregular verbs. If you are unsure how to spell any form of a verb, use your dictionary. The spelling of each form is listed there.

Combining Helping Verbs and Main Verbs

When combining helping verbs and main verbs, pay careful attention to the verb forms that you use.

- **Modal + base form.** After one of the nine modals (*can, could, will, would, shall, should, may, might, must*), use the base form of a verb.

EXAMPLES

(incorrect)	He **will leaving** soon.
(correct)	He **will leave** soon.

- **Do, does, did + base form.** When forms of *do* are used as helping verbs, use the base form after them.

EXAMPLES

(incorrect)	**Did** your daughter **asked** you for a present?
(correct)	**Did** your daughter **ask** you for a present?

- **Have, has, or had + past participle.** Use the past participle form after *have, has,* or *had*. Check a dictionary if you are not sure how to spell the past participle.

EXAMPLES

(incorrect)	The monkey **has eating** all of the fruit.
(correct)	The monkey **has eaten** all of the fruit.
(incorrect)	We **had walk** ten miles before noon.
(correct)	We **had walked** ten miles before noon.

■ **Forms of be + present participle.** To show continuous action, use the present participle (the *-ing* form) after a form of *be* (*am, is, are, was, were, be, been*).

⊚⊚ **EXAMPLES**   (incorrect)   I reading the book.

(correct)   I am reading the book.

■ **Forms of be + past participle.** To express passive voice (the subject receives the action rather than performs it), use a form of *be* followed by the past participle form.

⊚⊚ **EXAMPLES**   (incorrect)   The football **was threw** by the quarterback.

(correct)   The football **was thrown** by the quarterback.

⊚⊚ **PRACTICE**   Correct any errors in the use of helping verbs and main verbs.

1. After breakfast, my uncle will ~~reading~~ *read* the paper.

2. He had trained hard, but he did not ran fast enough to win the marathon.

3. The man who was standing at the corner has taking that woman's purse.

4. The suspect said the bag of money was gave to him by someone else.

5. Did your son walked all the way home?

6. Benjamin's son does not wants any of his good advice.

7. Everyone who meets that man is frighten by his violent behavior.

8. My neighbor Zaira has work hard all her life to support her children.

9. Please be quiet because I am concentrate on my homework.

10. If you want to be released, you must telling who took the money.

Two-Word Verbs

Many verbs in English consist of a verb with a preposition. Together, the verb and its paired word create an *idiom*, which has a meaning you cannot know simply by learning the meaning of the verb or its paired word. For example, both *up* and *out* can be used with the verb *stay*, but they have very different meanings. *To stay up* means to remain awake. *To stay out* means to remain out of the house or out of a discussion.

When a verb is joined to a preposition introducing a prepositional phrase, the two words will not usually be separated.

⊚⊚ EXAMPLES   (correct)   Danny and Jenna *argued* about the proposed law.

   (incorrect)   Danny and Jenna *argued* the proposed law about.

However, sometimes a verb is joined to a word *not* introducing a prepositional phrase, even though the word itself seems to be a preposition. (The words *off, on, up, down,* and *out* commonly do not introduce prepositional phrases after a verb.) In such cases, the verb and its paired word are sometimes separated.

⊚⊚ EXAMPLES   (correct)   Hector decided to *try on* the blue tuxedo before he left.

   (correct)   Hector decided to *try* the blue tuxedo *on* before he left.

Here are some common two-word verbs:

approve of	Her mother did not *approve of* the gown she chose for her prom.
ask out	Fabiana hoped that Nick would not *ask* her *out*.
call off	When it started to rain, we *called off* the game.
call on	Because he was in the neighborhood, Farbod decided to *call on* his aunt.
come across	While shopping at Macy's, we *came across* my biology instructor.
drop by	Lester does not appreciate it when people *drop by* (or *in*) unexpectedly.
drop off	Will you *drop* me *off* at the dentist's office?
figure out	After much discussion, we finally *figured out* what to do.
find out	Did you ever *find out* where he lives?
interfere with	It is not wise to *interfere with* a police officer on duty.
look after	Will Rachel *look after* our cockatiel while we are gone?
look over	Irene wanted to *look* the place *over* before they rented it.
look up	Please *look up* his phone number in your address book.
make up	Waldo loves to *make up* stories about his childhood.
object to	Does anyone here *object to* the smell of cigarette smoke?
pick out	Shauna was unable to *pick out* the man who robbed her.
reason with	It is difficult to *reason with* an angry two-year-old.
show up	We were all surprised when the mayor *showed up* at the party.
think over	Give me a few minutes while I *think* it *over*.

try on	The shoes looked too small, but he *tried* them *on* anyway.
turn up	Cathy was certain the lost hamster would *turn up* somewhere.
wait for	Isabel listened to music while she *waited for* the train.
wait on	The server who *waited on* us asked if we had enjoyed the food.

◉◉ PRACTICE   Create sentences of your own using the following two-word verbs. Use the sentences above as models. If you are uncertain of the meaning of a verb, consult a dictionary.

1. turn up   *If my lost keys don't turn up soon, we'll have to call a cab.*

2. figure out _____

_____

3. look after _____

_____

4. call off _____

_____

5. reason with _____

_____

6. approve of _____

_____

7. drop by _____

_____

8. make up

_____

_____

9. try on

_____

_____

10. object to

_____

_____

Adjectives in the Correct Order

Adjectives usually precede the nouns that they modify. When one or more adjectives precede a noun, follow these guidelines.

- In a series of adjectives, place determiners first. (Determiners consist of articles, possessives, limiting and quantity words, and numerals.) Examples of determiners: _the_ old car, _Jim's_ empty wallet, _her_ sad face, _this_ heavy box, _some_ scattered coins, _three_ dead trees.

- If one of the modifiers is usually a noun, place it directly before the word it modifies: _the boring basketball game, the rusty trash can._

- Evaluative adjectives (_beautiful, interesting, courageous_) usually come before descriptive adjectives (_small, round, red, wooden_): _the beautiful red rose, an interesting wooden cabinet._

- Descriptive adjectives indicating size usually appear before other descriptive adjectives (but they appear after evaluative adjectives): _my huge leather sofa, a strange little old man._

In general, avoid long strings of adjectives. More than two or three adjectives in a row will usually sound awkward to the native English speaker.

◎◎ PRACTICE   Arrange the following groups of adjectives in the correct order.

1. (blue, the, ugly) car

   _____

2. (leather, torn, his) jacket

   _____

3. (hairy, three, huge) horses

   _____

4. (Chinese, an, expensive) restaurant

   _____

5. (plastic, this, plain) stapler

   _____

6. (favorite, father's, family, my) tradition

   _____

7. (recent, a, art, modern) exhibit

   _____

8. (red, vinyl, old, that) floor

   _____

9. (dishonest, car, used, some) salespersons

   _____

10. (blue, five, beach, these, enormous) balls

   _____

Answers to Practices

Chapter One

Page 3:

2. Harebrained, name, salon, city
3. Pandora, box, hand
4. Humpty, men, wall, problem
5. Barack Obama, speech, inauguration

Page 4:

2. Hades, Persephone, marriage
3. spring, Persephone, coast, Greece
4. husband, breezes, Aegean Sea
5. autumn, clothes, home, underworld
6. Alice, amazement, cat, grin
7. Love, tolerance, characteristics, racism, prejudice
8. success, experiment, shock, Benjamin Franklin
9. candle, light, condition, room
10. Hafiz, poet, century, wit, humor, eroticism, reverence, sacred

Pages 5–6:

2. nouns: piggy, market
   pronouns: Each, us, which
3. nouns: *Minnow,* harbor, tour
   pronouns: it
4. nouns: P. T. Barnum, suckers
   pronouns: you, what
5. nouns: Bambi, father, admiration, antlers
   pronouns: his, he
6. nouns: explanation, fractals
   pronouns: anyone, her
7. nouns: Super Bowl, advertisements, brother
   pronouns: its, my, them
8. nouns: veterans, Korea, Vietnam, Iraq, injuries
   pronouns: Many, those, who
9. nouns: collection, books, Herman Melville, Nathaniel Hawthorne
   pronouns: My, anything
10. nouns: poetry, Emily Dickinson, description, hummingbird
    pronouns: almost, who, her

Page 6:

Answers will vary. Here are some possible ones.

2. <u>Homer</u> will share <u>his</u> Spam with <u>his</u> <u>sister</u>.
3. <u>Jack</u> <u>Nicholson</u> asked <u>me</u> to be quiet while <u>Kobe</u> shot <u>his</u> free throw.
4. <u>Emily</u> liked the <u>brownies</u> that <u>I</u> bought at the <u>fair</u>.
5. <u>Herman</u> searched <u>his</u> backpack to find a <u>bandage</u> because <u>his</u> <u>daughter</u> had cut <u>her</u> foot.

Page 7:

2. burned
3. wear
4. searched
5. talked

Page 8:

2. is
3. felt
4. seem
5. are

Page 9:

2. verb: wanted
   tense: past
3. verb: will sit
   tense: future
4. verb: killed
   tense: past
5. verb: plays
   tense: present

Page 11:

2. MV
3. HV
4. HV
5. MV
6. MV

7. HV
8. HV
9. MV
10. HV

Pages 11–12:

A.

2. HV: have
   MV: caused
3. HV: was
   MV: swinging

4. HV: Will
   MV: try
5. HV: should have
   MV: offered

B. Answers will vary. Here are some possible ones.

7. Jesse James <u>grabbed</u> the engraved revolver and <u>handed</u> it to his brother.
8. Penelope <u>had</u> <u>waited</u> patiently for Odysseus for twenty years.

9. <u>Has</u> Shakespeare <u>written</u> the tragedy that I <u>paid</u> him for?
10. Lady Godiva <u>should</u> not <u>have</u> <u>ridden</u> her horse when she <u>was</u> not <u>wearing</u> any clothes.

Page 13:

2. HV : could
   MV: defeat
   Verbal: Playing
3. HV: will
   MV: describe
   Verbal: To illustrate

4. HV: had
   MV: taken
   Verbal: attending
5. HV: might
   MV: agree
   Verbal: stirring, to give

Page 13:

2. HV: were
   MV: discussing
   Verbal: to alleviate
3. HV: Does
   MV: want
   Verbal: to marry
4. MV: has
5. HV: must have
   MV: seen
   Verbal: rising
6. HV: has
   MV: agreed
   Verbal: To please, to play

7. HV: should have
   MV: accepted
   Verbal: To tell
8. HV: was
   MV: awarded
   Verbal: Impressing
9. HV: has been
   MV: trying
   Verbal: to find
10. HV: Does
    MV: recognize
    Verbal: attacking

Page 14:

2. S: prison
   MV: sits
3. S: prisoners
   HV: would
   MV: drown

4. S: men
   HV: were
   MV: shot
5. S: Alcatraz
   HV: was
   MV: closed

Page 15:

2. S: prunes
   HV: were
   MV: offered

3. S: game
   HV: did
   MV: attract

4. S: store
   HV: was
   MV: praised

5. S: men
   MV: faced

Page 16:

2. S: dish, spoon
   MV: ran

3. S: John Glenn, assistants
   MV: prepared, ate

4. S: Eighteenth Amendment
   HV: was
   MV: ratified
   S: it
   HV: was
   MV: repealed

5. S: Barack Obama
   HV: was
   MV: inaugurated
   S: people
   MV: felt

Page 17:

2. S: President Franklin D. Roosevelt
   MV: was

3. S: Colonel Mustard
   HV: could have
   MV: hidden

4. S: elephant
   MV: is

5. S: You (understood)
   MV: Forget

Pages 17–18:

2. subject: Sonny
   verb: could have treated

3. subject: Neil Armstrong
   verb: might have hesitated

4. subject: glue
   verb: is certified

5. subject: person
   verb: Will close

6. subject: Godzilla
   verb: was looking

7. subject: You (understood)
   verb: Tell

8. subject: daughter
   verb: loves
   subject: I
   verb: would prefer

9. subject: people
   verb: must have been

10. subject: Little Mermaid
    verbs: looked, winked

Pages 18–19:

Answers will vary. Here are some possible ones.

2. *S   MV*
   The doctor left the building
   MV
   and called a taxi.

3. *S   HV   MV*
   His car was running well last night.

4. *HV   S   MV*
   Did she find the missing briefcase?

5. *MV*
   Leave the restaurant now.

6. *MV   S*
   Here stands the last redwood tree.

7. *S   S*
   The man from Peru and his son
   MV
   flew to Los Angeles.

8. *S   HV   MV*
   The old man was sneezing violently
   S   MV
   until he passed the meadow.

9. *S   HV   MV*
   A thief had broken into my house in
   S
   the middle of the day, but no one
   HV   MV
   had paid any attention.

10. *S   MV*
    People often eat at Pepe's Cafe
    S   MV
    although the food is not very good.

Page 26:

2. *Hot* and *crispy* modify *fries*.

3. *Usually* modifies *has*, and *tuna* modifies *sandwich*.

4. *Tedious* modifies *movie*, and *mercifully* modifies *short*.

5. *Tiny* modifies *animals*, and *continually* modifies *ran*.

Page 27:

A.

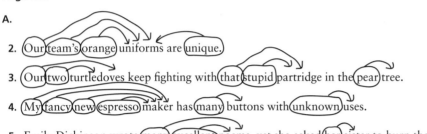

2. Our team's orange uniforms are unique.

3. Our two turtledoves keep fighting with that stupid partridge in the pear tree.

4. My fancy new espresso maker has many buttons with unknown uses.

5. Emily Dickinson wrote many excellent poems, yet she asked her sister to burn them.

B. Answers will vary. Here are some possible ones.

7. An *old* aardvark wandered into our *back* yard and looked for ants.

8. The *old* hermit lived in a *log* cabin in the woods.

9. The *mangy* dog in the street avoided the car and the *speeding* truck.

10. Officials tried to blame the mess on the *many* birds that lived near the *dirty* pond.

Page 29:

A.

2. The happy couple always said that they were extremely lucky.

3. The black widow sometimes gleefully destroys her mate.

4. As Ichabod Crane rode swiftly down the lane, he was already beginning to worry about the headless horseman.

5. Dido was excruciatingly sad as she stood on the rather sheer cliff.

B. Answers will vary. Here are some possible ones.

7. The frightened school children *barely* escaped from the Twin Towers.

8. Elmo *quickly* ran to the garbage can and looked for the puppet.

9. The dune buggy missed the cactus but smashed *violently* into the tree.

10. The ship escaped many perils, but it *never* reached its destination.

Page 31:

1. quieter, quietest
2. slower, slowest
3. prettier, prettiest
4. more deceitful, most deceitful
5. more rapidly, most rapidly
6. easier, easiest
7. more convenient, most convenient
8. farther, farthest
9. more slowly, most slowly
10. more effective, most effective

Pages 32–33:

1. My sister considers Will Smith a **better** actor **than** Sean Penn.
2. The **worst** mistake he made was deciding to buy the **most expensive** car on the lot.
3. Although Abraham Lincoln was one of our greatest presidents, some say he was the **ugliest** one.
4. Karl Marx was **very** intelligent, although his theory of economics did not work very **well.**
5. Of the two, who is the **more** famous, Marie Antoinette or Anne Boleyn?
6. Russell Crowe, who is from Australia, is the **best** actor on the screen today.
7. Marlon Brando felt **bad** when he forgot his lines during rehearsal.
8. The Trojans were **better** prepared than the Greeks, but the Greeks were **trickier.**
9. The eggplant frosting tasted **worse** to Bill **than** the Brussels sprouts pie.
10. Sofia always drives **safely,** even when she has to get somewhere as **quickly** as possible.

Pages 39–40:

A.

2. subject: Kate Winslet
   verb: won
   conjunctions: and
3. subject: fans
   verb: were
   subject: she
   verb: did receive
   conjunction: for
4. subject: Sam
   verb: did like
   subject: he
   verb: did care
   conjunction: nor
5. subject: sink
   verb: would drain
   subject: we
   verb: called
   conjunction: so

B.

7. but, yet
8. and
9. for
10. so

Page 41:

2. Without, from
3. During, on
4. near, for
5. behind, at

Pages 42–43:

A.

2. Prep   Obj
   (from a popular drinking song)
3. Prep   Obj
   (of Fort McHenry)
   Prep Obj
   (in 1814)
4. Prep   Obj
   (by the sight)
   Prep   Obj
   (of the American flag)
   Prep   Obj
   (over the fort)
5. Prep   Obj
   (During the attack)
   Prep   Obj
   (of "The Star-Spangled Banner")
   Prep   Obj
   (on the back)
   Prep   Obj
   (of an envelope)

6. Prep   Obj
   (with a tune)
   Prep   Obj
   (in many taverns)
7. Prep Obj
   (in Heaven)
   Prep   Obj
   (by John Stafford Smith)
   Prep Obj
   (in 1780)
8. Prep Obj Obj Obj   Obj
   (about wine, song, love, and revelry)
9. Prep   Obj
   (at official ceremonies)
   Prep   Obj
   (for many years)
10. Prep   Obj
    (In spite of its popularity)
    Prep   Obj
    (until March 3, 1931)

Page 52:

1. The farmer waited in front of the bank.
2. The **old** farmer waited in front of the bank.
3. The old farmer **in overalls** waited in front of the bank.
4. The old farmer in **faded** overalls waited in front of the bank.
5. The old farmer in faded overalls waited **patiently** in front of the bank.

Chapter Two

Pages 81–82:

2. MC
3. MC
4. N
5. SC
6. MC

7. SC
8. MC
9. SC
10. N

Page 82:

2. SC
3. PP
4. PP
5. SC
6. SC

7. PP
8. PP
9. SC
10. PP

Pages 82–83:

2. Lewis Carroll created the word *chortle*, (which) is a combination of two other words.

3. After the battle in the lake, Beowulf returned to the hall.

4. Puck gave the potion to Titania, (who) was sleeping.

5. (If) you really loved me, you would give your chocolate to me.

6. A reformed slave trader wrote "Amazing Grace," (which) is played at police officers' funerals.

7. He retook the oath of office (because) the Chief Justice had misplaced one of the words.

8. Sylvia, (whose) clothes were totally inappropriate, was embarrassed.

9. Fergal was all smiles (after) he read *Ulysses* for the third time.

10. Gettysburg was the place (where) the most important battle was fought.

Page 84:

2. (Whenever) Homer wants a snack, he fries a thick slab of Spam.

3. Narcissus stared into the stream (because) he was in love.

4. (Although) the old man's wings were dirty and broken, everyone believed he was an angel.

5. James Barrie was inspired to write *Peter Pan* by a family (after) he told stories of Peter to the children of a friend.

Page 84:

Answers will vary. Here are some possible ones:

2. After the war was over, Robert E. Lee was appointed president of a college.
3. Cyrus eats twice a week at a Thai restaurant although he has never really enjoyed Thai food.
4. Homer asked for a bag for his black-eyed peas so that he could surprise Hortense with them.
5. Because he was a deluded fool, the emperor walked naked into the village.

Page 85:

2. A cello player (whom) the owner knew led the house band.

3. The next player hired was a pianist (who) was the wife of the cellist.

4. Rum Adagio, (which) is my favorite drink, is always served in a bright red glass.

5. A Persian cat (that) everyone calls Ludwig begs for treats on the bar.

Page 86:

Answers will vary. Here are some possible ones.

1. Ludwig, who is picky, has her own special dish by the backdoor.
2. The eagle flew into the trees that surrounded the house.
3. No one at the Monterey Bay Aquarium, which is famous for its sea exhibits, had ever met Poseidon.
4. The Belly Up, where I met my wife, is a popular music venue in San Diego County.
5. Many people who have very good intentions make resolutions for the next year on New Year's Eve.

Pages 86–87:

1. <u>After the club closes</u>, the musicians play their own compositions. (Adv)

2. <u>Because the new President values good music</u>, Yo-Yo Ma played at his inauguration.

3. Enrique often dreamed about his grandparents, <u>who lived in Chihuahua, Mexico</u>.

4. <u>When the double rainbow appeared in the sky</u>, Finnegan grabbed my mother and kissed her.

5. A dog <u>that had long ears and a goofy laugh</u> kept following me around the amusement park.

Page 87:

Answers will vary. Here are some possible ones.

2. <u>After the fireworks exploded in the family room,</u> the building burst into flames and burned to the ground. (Adv)
3. The monk <u>who had objected to all the noise</u> sat in a lotus position and took three deep breaths. (Adj)
4. Prometheus warmed his hands by the fire <u>after he had spent most of the day outdoors</u>. (Adv)
5. <u>As soon as Larry King introduced them</u>, Bill Gates and Steve Jobs began to argue. (Adv)

Pages 94–95:

Answers will vary. Here are some possible ones.

2. In the morning I could smell the bacon cooking.
3. There goes the newest jet fighter.
4. Sign the peace treaty quickly.
5. Roberta and Carlos went to the mall and bought some new clothes.

Pages 96:

Answers will vary. Here are some possible ones.

2. General Washington stood in the boat; I was one of the rowers.
3. It was a long, hard row; therefore, I was quite tired.
4. Califia was shy, yet she wanted to join the other women.
5. I was sick of Bradley's strange eating habits; therefore, I quit sitting with him at meals.

Page 97:

2. compound:	S: Sumerians	V: needed	
	S: they	V: made	
3. simple:	S: pictures	V: were	
4. compound:	S: tablets	V: were baked	
	S: thousands	V: have lasted	
5. compound:	S: pictures	V: were created	
	S: type	V: is called	
6. simple:	S: pictures	V: came	
7. simple:	S: Egyptians	V: recorded	
8. compound:	S: material	V: was	
	S: it	V: came	
9. simple:	S: inventor	V: made	
10. compound:	S: books	V: were written	
	S: knowledge	V: did reach	

Pages 98–99:

Answers will vary. Here are some possible ones.

2. Tomaso liked it best when the sun set behind his ranch.
3. His Ford Mustang, which he has owned since 1965, is a classic.
4. Although it was raining, he headed for the beach.
5. We finally arrived in San Diego, where I had spent much of my youth.

Page 100:

Answers will vary. Here are some possible ones.

2. John will join us at the play, or he will see us at dinner after he has visited his mother.
3. The man whom you asked me about has just walked in; however, he is not alone.
4. If the trees falls on the house, we will be injured, but I am not worried because it has not fallen yet.
5. The Padres will win the pennant, and then they will go to the World Series because their pitching is so strong.

Page 101:

2. compound:	S: versions	V: are
	S: stories	V: do give
3. complex:	S: slippers	V: appeared
	S: version	V: was translated
4. simple:	S: shoes	V: were made
5. compound-complex:	S: story	V: used
	S: word	V: was
	S: that	V: meant
	S: that	V: meant
6. complex:	S: Charles Perrault	V: was
	S: who	V: translated
7. simple:	S: versions	V: depict
8. compound:	S: Cinderella	V: is helped
	S: versions	V: use
9. compound-complex:	S: mother	V: is
	S: she	V: appears
	S: she	V: takes
10. compound:	S: cows, goats	V: assist
	S: mice	V: come

Pages 111–112:

Answers will vary. Here are some possible ones.

2. *fragment:* The vampire who had fallen in love with a mortal.
   possible correction: The vampire who had fallen in love with a mortal did not know what to do next.
3. *fragment:* Even though the state budget was finally approved.
   possible correction: No one was smiling, even though the state budget was finally approved.
4. *fragment:* To mark the way out of the forest.
   possible correction: Hansel and Gretel dropped bread crumbs to mark the way out of the forest.
5. *fragment:* After they had given up almost all hope of rescue.
   possible correction: After they had given up almost all hope of rescue, Gilligan spotted a ship.
6. *fragment:* Because the rapids and waterfall were approaching.
   possible correction: Davy tried to stop his canoe because the rapids and waterfall were approaching.

7. *fragments:* Until he failed to define *Quetzalcoatl*. Thinking it was some kind of snake.

   possible correction: Ricardo was winning the contest until he failed to define *Quetzalcoatl*, thinking it was some kind of snake.

8. *fragment:* That appears in the myths of many cultures.

   possible correction: The trickster is an important character that appears in the myths of many cultures.

9. *fragment:* To see the stars that were hidden by the city lights.

   possible correction: He wanted to see the stars that were hidden by the city lights.

10. *fragment:* When you come to a fork in the road.

    possible correction: When you come to a fork in the road, Yogi said to take it.

Pages 115–116:

Answers may vary. Here are some possible ones.

2. F   The huge blimp was attempting to dock in New Jersey when suddenly it burst into flames.

3. C

4. CS   Chuck Berry was playing "Hail, Hail, Rock and Roll" on the radio; meanwhile, Gomer and Homer finished the catfish and hushpuppies.

5. F   Dia de los Santos Inocentes is similar to April Fool's Day, but it is celebrated on December 28.

6. CS   Hue had not heard of the Trung sisters; as a result, her grandmother was deeply embarrassed.

7. F   Pluto kept feeding Cerberus chocolate turtles; even though Cerberus knew they were not good for him, he ate them anyway.

8. C

9. F   Andrea's memoir was a national success; in fact, it won two major literary awards.

10. CS   When Mr. Nosferatu came over for dinner last night, he kept staring at my fiancee's neck.

Chapter Three

Pages 153–154:

2. Using questionable statistics, he claimed that half of all bank robberies happened on Friday.

3. Swimming silently under the ship, Nessie avoided the monster hunters.

4. We listened to "American Pie," the Don McLean song written after the death of Buddy Holly.

5. Robinson, standing alone on the beach, stared at the footprint in the sand.

6. The pink Cadillac parked by the curb in New York intrigued Andy.

7. Stunned by Mr. Spock's phaser, the Klingon fell to the deck of the ship.

8. Colonel Chamberlain's troops repulsed the rebels trying to out-flank the Yankees at the Battle of Gettysburg

9. Staring at the Grecian urn, Keats considered the nature of truth and beauty.

10. Comets, named after the Greek word for "long hair," are always exciting sights.

Page 155:

2. Placing the letter in an obvious spot, Mr. Poe knew that no one would find it.

3. Luckily, William Tell knew the correct way to aim a crossbow.

4. Bitten by a radioactive spider, Peter Parker dreamed about houseflies.

5. The wretched man looked at the only sentence to contain 823 words without a period.

6. *Les Miserables,* written by Victor Hugo, is the only French book with such an extended sentence.

7. Yelling loudly, the Rebels charged up the hill toward the Yankees.

8. Frightened by the bright light, Gollum returned to the darkness of the cave.

9. Goya picked up his candle hat and wondered which candle to light first.

10. The Black Knight stood on the tall building and pondered his promise to save the city.

Page 164:

2. *Beowulf,* which is an Old English epic poem, was written about 1000 A.D.

3. Anyone who even thinks about stealing my fried okra will seriously regret it.

4. Hurling, which is a sport played primarily in Ireland, is being considered for future Olympics.

5. Maurice Ravel, who was a famous French composer, wrote *Bolero,* which became one of the most popular concert pieces of the twentieth century.

6. The frustrated contestant could not name the planet that was third from the sun.

7. Maurice Ravel asked Toots Thielemans, who is a famous harmonica player, to perform *Bolero* for the crowd.

8. The women who were arguing about the baby decided to ask Solomon for advice.

9. The plane that Chelsea had jumped from was circling 13,500 feet above Chula Vista, where she went to high school.

10. Wolf Moonglow, who was an exceptionally hirsute man, was telling us about the time when he first began to study lycanthropy.

Pages 165–166:

2. Gothic cathedrals are often ornamented with gargoyles, grotesque sculptures of evil spirits.

3. Hera and Zeus, two powerful gods, often quarreled about his wandering eyes.

4. Harry Houdini, a famous American escape artist and magician, spent many years exposing fraudulent mediums and mind readers.

5. The one-armed (man), Richard Kimble's elusive enemy, was recently seen playing the slot machines in Las Vegas.

6. (Patrick Stewart), the former Captain Picard of the *U.S.S. Enterprise*, has also starred as Captain Ahab of the *Pequod*.

7. Whenever Elmo shows up, (Cole,) my only grandson, becomes all smiles.

8. D. H. Lawrence always kept in touch with (John Thomas,) a close childhood friend.

9. Miles Davis's (Kind of Blue,) perhaps the most famous jazz album, has just been re-issued in a box that contains a tee shirt showing Miles.

10. Bill Liscomb was a pioneer in (hang gliding,) a popular sport among the Peter Pan crowd.

Pages 166–167:

Answers will vary. Here are some possible ones.

2. Amelia Earhart, <u>a famous aviator</u>, vanished while flying over the Pacific Ocean.
3. Bruce Springsteen, <u>who is Bob's favorite singer</u>, put on a great half-time show at the 2009 Super Bowl.
4. Wile E. Coyote, <u>my favorite cartoon character</u>, carefully constructed the trap.
5. Angelina, <u>a well-known actress</u>, asked Brad to change the diapers of their latest child.
6. Spike Lee's film told a story about the Buffalo Soldiers of World War II, a <u>term for African-American soldiers dating back to the Civil War</u>.
7. Ewan McGregor, <u>who was born in Crieff, Scotland</u>, might have groaned when he first read the stilted lines of Obi-Wan Kenobi.
8. Artists <u>who lived during the Renaissance</u> often depicted the gods and goddesses of ancient Rome in marble.
9. In *The Odyssey*, Homer also describes the voyage of Odysseus's son, <u>Telemachus</u>.
10. Mount Vesuvius, <u>which killed thousands of people when it erupted</u>, still smolders over the ruins of Pompeii.

Page 176–177:

2. The poet standing at the curb <u>dejectedly</u> stared at the rejection letter in his hand.
   The poet standing at the curb stared dejectedly at the rejection letter in his hand. (Other answers are possible.)
3. Correct
4. The sinister-looking man who had been sitting in the corner <u>silently</u> got up and left the room.
   The sinister-looking man who had been sitting silently in the corner got up and left the room.
   (Other answers are possible.)
5. By the time he had <u>almost</u> fallen ten thousand feet, the skydiver was wondering if he should open his chute.
   By the time he had fallen almost ten thousand feet, the skydiver was wondering if he should open his chute.
6. Peyton Farquhar <u>nearly</u> crept to the edge of the trees before he saw the Union soldiers.
   Peyton Farquhar crept nearly to the edge of the trees before he saw the Union soldiers.
7. Because she had eaten a large lunch, Aracela <u>just</u> decided to order a small dinner salad.
   Because she had eaten a large lunch, Aracela decided to order just a small dinner salad.
8. Because she was worried about her health, Shawna asked Fernando <u>frequently</u> to take her to the gym.
   Because she was worried about her health, Shawna frequently asked Fernando to take her to the gym. (Other answers are possible.)
9. The world-famous prevaricator would <u>only</u> invite the gullible to his dinner.
   The world-famous prevaricator would invite only the gullible to his dinner.
10. Susan Boyle <u>almost</u> surprised everyone in the building when she started to sing.
    Susan Boyle surprised almost everyone in the building when she started to sing.

Pages 178–179:

2. Marco Polo presented the golden chest to the Pope <u>filled with exotic spices</u>.
   Marco Polo presented the golden chest filled with exotic spices to the Pope.

3. Artemis shot the arrow at the frightened stag <u>using her strong bow</u>.
Using her strong bow Artemis shot the arrow at the frightened stag.
(Other answers are possible.)

4. The astronauts on Mars were monitored by personnel at NASA <u>who were sitting in a space rover on the surface of the planet</u>.
The astronauts on Mars who were maneuvering a space rover over the red soil were monitored by personnel at NASA.

5. My German shepherd lunged at the skunk, <u>which sleeps at the foot of my bed</u>, when it entered our garage.
My German shepherd, <u>which sleeps at the foot of my bed</u>, lunged at the skunk when it entered our garage.

6. *Full Metal Jacket* has become a classic film about the Vietnam War <u>directed by Stanley Kubrick</u>.
Directed by Stanley Kubrick, *Full Metal Jacket* has become a classic film about the Vietnam War.
(Other answers are possible.)

7. Homer daydreamed about Hortense <u>chewing on his plug of tobacco</u>.
Homer, chewing on his plug of tobacco, daydreamed about Hortense.
(Other answers are possible.)

8. The space aliens stared at the herd of sheep <u>with cone-shaped heads and large oval eyes</u> before they fired their weapons.
The space aliens with cone-shaped heads and large oval eyes stared at the herd of sheep before they fired their weapons.

9. My mother loved the film *Milk*, but my uncle did not, <u>praising its honest handling of the life of a brave man</u>.
My mother, praising its honest handling of the life of a brave man, loved the film *Milk*, but my uncle did not.
(Other answers are possible.)

10. The Lewis and Clark expedition finally arrived at the Pacific Ocean, <u>which had been gone for months</u>.
The Lewis and Clark expedition, which had been gone for months, finally arrived at the Pacific Ocean.

Page 180:

2. D
3. C
4. D
5. D

Pages 182–183:

2. <u>Disappointed by his 3,098th failure,</u> the rock of Sisyphus rolled back down the hill.
Disappointed by his 3,098th failure, Sisyphus watched the rock roll back down the hill.
(Other correct answers are possible.)

3. <u>After telling the lie,</u> Pinocchio's nose began to grow.
After Pinocchio told the lie, his nose began to grow.
(Other correct answers are possible.)

4. Correct

5. <u>Examining their hearts,</u> the lives of the newly dead were judged by Osiris.
Examining their hearts, Osiris judged the lives of the newly dead.
(Other correct answers are possible.)

6. <u>Concerned about her students' dangling modifiers,</u> Leanne's new lesson plan began to take shape.
Concerned about her students' dangling modifiers, Leanne developed a new lesson plan.
(Other answers are possible.)

7. <u>To balance the stone at the top of the hill,</u> it was secured with duct tape by Sisyphus.
To balance the stone at the top of the hill, Sisyphus secured it with duct tape.
(Other answers are possible.)

8. <u>Huffing and puffing as hard as he could,</u> the house of bricks would not blow down.
Huffing and puffing as hard as he could, the Big Bad Wolf could not blow down the house of bricks.
(Other correct answers are possible.)

9. <u>Startled by the sudden explosion</u>, the summer sky was filled with cranes and egrets.
   Startled by the sudden explosion, cranes and egrets filled the summer sky.
   (Other correct answers are possible.)

10. <u>To ask for more food,</u> the bowl was lifted into the air.
    To ask for more food, Oliver lifted the bowl into the air.
    (Other correct answers are possible.)

Chapter Four

Pages 218–219:

2. The toy **poodles escape** from the yard nearly every day.

3. My **friend** often **visits** me at school.

4. The text **messages have** made everything even worse.

5. His **explanation** always **confuses** the entire class.

Pages 220–221:

2. The rooster adopted by our neighbor's children (<u>crows</u> crow) at dawn every day.
   (S above "crows")

3. Every firefighter and police officer in the city (<u>has</u> have) brought an item to the auction.
   (S above "firefighter", S above "officer")

4. A plate of possum pie and a bowl of collard greens (sounds <u>sound</u>) like a great way to start the day.
   (S above "plate", S above "bowl")

5. Some of the bike riders from the southern towns (<u>wear</u> wears) brightly colored scarves to the convention.
   (S above "Some")

6. Each glass bottle and plastic container (<u>was</u> were) recovered from the trash and recycled.
   (S above "bottle", S above "container")

7. Somebody from one of our local schools (<u>has</u> have) won the prestigious Peacock scholarship.
   (S above "Somebody")

8. The movie's soundtrack and pacing (appeals <u>appeal</u>) to me more than its plot and characterization.
   (S above "soundtrack", S above "pacing")

9. A squirrel with two cats chasing it (<u>was</u> were) running down the street.
   (S above "squirrel")

10. Most of the earth's surface (<u>is</u> are) covered by water.
    (S above "Most")

Page 222:

2. A family of porcupines (<u>has</u> have) taken up residence in my cellar.
   (S above "family")

3. Rory is one of the dogs that (plays <u>play</u>) Frisbee so well.
   (S above "Rory", S above "dogs")

4. Neither Angelina nor Jennifer (<u>knows</u> know) that Madonna plans to adopt a child.
   (S above "Angelina", S above "Jennifer", S above "Madonna")

5. His pet albino porcupine or his three striped iguanas (<u>seem</u> seems) to take all of Al's attention.
   (S above "porcupine", S above "iguanas")

6. That crowd of people at the end of the pier (<u>belongs</u> belong) to the Polar Bear Club.
   (S above "crowd")

            S   S

7. Henry is the only citizen in Concord who (<u>refuses</u> refuse) to pay taxes.

                      S   S

8. (<u>Has</u> Have) the eggplant casserole or the vegetarian omelet been added to tomorrow's menu?

                  S   S

9. The speeches that Senator Cassius makes (<u>impress</u> impresses) the people each time.

            S   S

10. Esperanza is one of the triathletes who (does <u>do</u>) not know how to swim.

Pages 223–224:

            S

2. Fifteen inches of rain (fall <u>falls</u>) in Murrieta every winter.

            S

3. The topic at today's meeting (<u>is</u> are) the six chickens I keep in my backyard.

            S

4. The news of Demeter's missing daughter (<u>has</u> have) cast a shadow across the land.

            S

5. Gymnastics (<u>does</u> do) not interest Antonio nearly as much as competitive ice fishing.

                                                      S

6. After deliberating for three days, the jury in the Mallory trial (<u>has</u> have) not yet reached a verdict.

            S

7. Five ounces of gold (<u>sells</u> sell) for nearly $5,000 today.

                                        S   S

8. Here, alive and well-fed, (is <u>are</u>) the two-headed horned toad and the legless lizard from the pet store down the street.

                      S

9. Esther's favorite hobby (<u>requires</u> require) paperclips and pots of glue.

            S

10. Ten miles of unpaved road (<u>lies</u> lie) between my house and the beach.

Page 230:

2. Most people are naturally uncomfortable when **they** are in a new environment.

3. A new student should try to arrive at the campus early, especially if **he or she** wants to find a parking place.

4. When my daughter left home for her first class, **I** could see she was worried.

5. After the first week or so, **one** (or **a person**) gets used to the new routine.

Page 232:

2. Everybody at the prison was angry when **he** (or **she**, if a woman's prison) **was** required to lie flat on the ground.

3. When parents read a story by the Brothers Grimm, **they** might scare **their** children.

4. correct

5. Neither Galileo nor Copernicus could keep **his** eyes focused on the ground.

6. Someone with gray hair wants to read **his** (or **her**) poetry at the department meeting.

7. correct

8. When a tourist visits Yosemite, **he or she** should not approach the bison.

9. correct

10. An immigrant from another country is often surprised when **he or she sees** the size of a typical restaurant serving in the United States.

Pages 235:

Answers will vary. Here are some possible ones.

2. When Abbott told Costello the names of the baseball players, Costello became very confused.

3. During the trip Michelle Obama spent time with Queen Elizabeth, and the Queen did not act very friendly.

4. When Gary introduced his in-laws to his parents, he hoped his parents would not reveal his secret.

5. The famous archer shot an arrow through the apple on his son's head, and then he sold the apple on eBay.

Page 236:

Answers will vary. Here are some possible ones.

2. The king shepherd barked all night when our neighbors were having a party, so I called the police.

3. There were many pieces of glass on the kitchen floor, but Ibrahim had not broken any of the dishes.

4. Rafiki was looking forward to watching the Padres play the Angels, but the game was rained out.

5. Our plans were ruined when it rained all day Friday and then cleared up on Saturday.

Page 238:

2. Lorenzo, a misanthrope, prefers to spend his days by **himself.**

3. Homer and Hortense sent a dehydrated Spam omelet to **us** for Christmas.

4. Whenever Fergal and **I** have time, we meet for lunch at the Market Street Café.

5. After three gigs in a row, Pam and Eric finally had a weekend to **themselves.**

Page 238:

2. Brent wondered if Frances and **he** would make it to Hawaii this year.

3. My accountant **made the government suspicious when** he filled in my tax return in pencil and took a large deduction for jelly doughnuts. (Other correct answers are possible.)

4. Jose Luis apologized to his brother, but **his brother** was still angry. (Other correct answers are possible.)

5. correct

6. I could test my model boat in the pool, but **the pool** is not clean. (Other correct answers are possible.)

7. I have always enjoyed the genius of Picasso, **whose paintings** I saw two of at the museum. (Other correct answers are possible.)

8. John and Yoko spent some time by **themselves** after their famous "bed-in" in Amsterdam.

9. Bean **broke his nose when he** stuck a peppermint stick in it. (Other correct answers are possible.)

10. Charlotte Brontë told Emily that Anne's new novel was not as well-written as **Emily's.** (Other correct answers are possible.)

Page 245:

2. obj	**7.** obj
3. sub	**8.** obj
4. obj	**9.** sub
5. obj	**10.** obj
6. sub	

Page 247:

2. me	**7.** him
3. her	**8.** she
4. he	**9.** she
5. me	**10.** he
6. she	

Page 248:

2. who

3. whom

4. whoever

5. whomever

Page 248:

2. me

3. he

4. she

5. me

Page 249:

2. me

3. he

4. her

5. I

Pages 249–250:

2. I

3. its, it's

4. she

5. whomever

6. him

7. him

8. her

9. whom

10. she

Chapter Five

Page 279:

2. The jetliner crash-landed in the Hudson River, but everyone was rescued.

3. correct

4. The archeologist left for northern New Mexico, for he wanted to see the Pre-Puebloan ruins.

5. He wanted to record his findings, so he brought his camera equipment along.

Page 280:

2. My red-beans-and-rice dish contains red beans, a ham hock, cayenne pepper, tomato sauce, and many other secret ingredients found only in New Orleans.

3. Martin finished the ninety-five items, grabbed a hammer, and nailed them to the church door.

4. The realistic, convincing performance by Mickey Roark in *The Wrestler* was amazing.

5. The Super Bowl crowd was ecstatic, for Bruce Springsteen had put on a scintillating performance.

6. The dirty, unkempt man stumbled into camp, and the first thing he wanted was a Popsicle.

7. correct

8. You may embrace a geocentric view of the universe if you wish, or you may accept the heliocentric model.

9. Sam called Bill, loaded his pickup with fishing gear, went by Starbucks, and headed for the lake.

10. The courageous, proud Cherokee Chief Tsali surrendered to save the rest of his people in the Smoky Mountains.

Page 282:

2. On board the Santa Maria in 1492, Columbus and his crew were relieved to find that the world is not flat.

3. Saving for six months, Bill Gates was able to buy an iPhone 3G.

4. While they were completing the transaction for the iPhone, the Apple salesperson asked Gates for a picture identification.

5. Yes, Freud named some of his psychological observations after people in Greek myths.

6. Approaching the crash site, Matt Scudder slowed to a stop.

7. As the artist looked up at the ceiling, he hoped the Pope would like it.

8. After scrupulously examining the body, Dr. Scarpetta decided the larvae had been laid at 8:00 yesterday.

9. In order to create a romantic atmosphere, Juliet played Louis Armstrong's "A Kiss to Build a Dream On" for Romeo.

10. To find the Holy Grail, Perceval spent years wandering throughout Europe and Great Britain.

Page 283:

2. Wynton Marsalis, on the other hand, knows more about jazz than any other living person I know.

3. Marsalis went to Juilliard School of Music and plays trumpet; moreover, he plays both classical and jazz trumpet excellently.

4. Wynton, incidentally, has a father who plays jazz piano, a brother who plays saxophone, and another brother who plays percussion.

5. John Hancock detested signing his name; for instance, he hesitated to sign one of the famous documents of history.

Pages 284–285:

2. The use of steroids by baseball players, which is in the news almost every day, threatens to damage the reputation of the sport.

3. Claudius, who was the brother of the murdered King Hamlet, met an ironic death.

4. correct

5. The *Titanic*, which was supposed to be one of the safest ships ever built, sank on its maiden voyage.

Page 285:

2. correct

3. Rosa Parks, determined not to sit at the back of the bus, was instrumental in beginning the civil rights movement.

4. Dustin Hoffman, playing Willy Loman in *Death of a Salesman*, revealed the complexity of Arthur Miller's famous character.

5. Bill's daughter, frightened by his condition, called 911.

Page 286:

2. Persephone stared at the pomegranate, the only fruit in sight.

3. Eros, the son of the goddess Aphrodite, plays all sorts of tricks on mortals.

4. One of the Roman versions of Eros is Cupid, the angelic-looking creature with a bow and arrow.

5. The hummingbirds at my house, an extremely picky group, refuse to drink at my feeder.

Pages 287:

2. The package that was mailed on Friday, September 13, 1875, from Transylvania, Ohio, never made it to Carlsbad, California.

3. Hellboy's girlfriend smiled and said, "Red is the color of my true love's hair."

4. The multicolored togas arrived at The Debauchery, 415 Cicero Street, Rome, Arkansas, on the day before Saturnalia began.

5. Throw the ball, Peyton.

Page 288:

2. A misanthrope, who is a person who dislikes other people, is usually not well liked.

3. *The Tell-Tale Tart*, a novel by Dulcinea Baker, will soon be a movie.

4. Mallory, how many actors have played James Bond?

5. This year Easter occurs on April 12, 2009, which is the first Sunday after the first full moon after the vernal equinox.

6. The missing coprolite was found on August 10, 1954, in Rome, Georgia.

7. Clint Eastwood, accepting his latest Oscar, wore a gun belt with a six-shooter in it.

8. "The spiders have arrived," said Harker, "and I'm ready."

9. Mark Misanthrope, for instance, has not one single friend.

10. Clark, please tell Scarlett, who is a sensitive Southern belle, that you apologize for using the word *damn*.

Pages 295–296:

2. Have you fed Cerberus?

3. The *Titanic* is sinking!

4. The pitcher asked his catcher if he should throw a curve.

5. Has Penelope been underground for six months yet?

6. What is a quark?

7. Help me!

8. Michael received his Ph.D. from Arizona State University.

9. Why did they leave the game so early?

10. After five days the fish wondered if it had worn out its welcome.

Page 297:

2. The aspiring star did the following to prepare for his audition: got disturbing tattoos all over his body, dyed his hair extravagant colors, and learned two chords on the guitar.

3. We seem to be running out of super heroes; however, I am sure more will magically appear when needed.

4. correct

5. Brad hated one thing about fatherhood more than any other: changing his baby's dirty diapers.

Pages 298–299:

2. Batman was afraid of losing his significant other to the district attorney; moreover, he had lately developed a fear of heights.

3. Who was it who said, "Give me Spam, okra, hushpuppies, and rhubarb pie, or give me nothing"?

4. My favorite Mae West quotation is this one: "When I'm good, I'm very good, but when I'm bad, I'm better."

5. Coltrane looked at Davis and said, "Tell me a few of my favorite things."

6. "Where should I hide the letter?" asked Edgar.

7. Was it Mark Twain who said, "I believe that our Heavenly Father invented man because he was disappointed in the monkey"?

8. Ironman screamed, "Get me some rust preventative!"

9. Humpty fell off the wall and broke; he could not understand why all the king's men were calling for Super Glue.

10. Oscar Wilde once said, "Consistency is the last refuge of the unimaginative."

Page 300:

2. Mr. Lewis's sense of propriety was bothered by Mr. Clark's rude remarks.

3. Did you see Mr. Audubon's new bird illustration?

4. My brother was just let go from his job with only two days' severance pay.

5. Jorge's computer wasn't working, so he threw it into his father's garage.

6. It's a shame that the meteor shower won't be visible from here.

7. He'd nearly reached the border when the car's engine blew.

8. He had one week's free stay at his father-in-law's hotel.

9. Staring over the rim of Sylvia's soup bowl was a cockroach.

10. The children's favorite bedtime story was the one about the man with the hatchet.

Page 301:

Answers will vary. Here are some possible ones.

2. Mr. Thomas's chance of being named chief justice seemed slim.

3. Katie thought it was strange and rude to be asked to judge her mother-in-law's cooking.

4. The baseball players' wives met them at the airport.

5. Mr. Lewis's German shepherd didn't know what to do once it had leaped over the fence.

Page 307:

2. In Langston Hughes's short story "Salvation," a boy ironically loses his faith while participating in church services.

3. Robert Frost's poem "The Road Not Taken" is one of his most well known works.

4. Before Bud read his copy of the magazine <u>Wired</u>, he decided to eat dinner.

5. The movie <u>The Wizard of Oz</u> mixes both black-and-white and color photography.

Page 309:

2. Michelle Obama received a signed copy of Toni Morrison's latest novel <u>A Mercy</u>.

3. Born in Lorain, Ohio, Ms. Morrison has been on the cover of many magazines, including <u>Time</u>.

4. Uncle Elvis was playing Bruce Springsteen's song "Born in the U.S.A." when I told him John Updike had died.

5. A number of men and women from Boise, Idaho, participated in Operation Desert Storm and are now continuing to fight in the war in Iraq.

6. During the Christmas holidays, one can see beautiful decorations in Santa Fe and Albuquerque.

7. In California, the Native American tribes are having a legal battle with the state government over gambling.

8. At the Barnes and Noble bookstore, I found the film of Shakespeare's play <u>Macbeth</u>.

9. Charlie showed Marisa his collection of <u>T.V. Guide</u> magazines.

10. The Mervyn's store on Oak Street is closing at the beginning of summer.

Page 311:

2. One never knows when all five members of Jim's jazz band will show up; it could be at 9:00 or at 12:45.

3. For the retirement party, Charlie brought 15 pastries, Woz brought 1 Clark Bar, Barbara brought 115 pounds of fresh tuna, and Carlton brought 3 chocolate cheesecakes.

or

For the retirement party, Charlie brought fifteen pastries, Woz brought one Clark Bar, Barbara brought one hundred fifteen pounds of fresh tuna, and Carlton brought three chocolate cheesecakes.

4. The inauguration ceremony on January 20, 2009, was historically unique.

5. correct

Chapter Six

Pages 348–349:

2. drunk
3. swum
4. set
5. eaten, dug
6. lying

7. shrunk
8. drank, lay
9. sung, rose
10. led, lain

Pages 358–359:

2. conscience, an
3. accept, effect
4. among, break
5. An, disinterested
6. advice, effect
7. uninteresting, already

8. all right, eager
9. number
10. complimented, complemented
11. our, break
12. choose, braking

Pages 363–364:

2. there, fewer, than
3. principal, your
4. past, threw
5. led, lose, their
6. personal, they're
7. led, principles

8. two, too, to
9. number, fewer, than
10. preceded, lose
11. quite, quiet
12. were, where, an

Page 371:

2. received, friends
3. ceiling, sufficient
4. sleigh, quiet, relief
5. Neither, believed, weird

Page 372:

2. angriest, angrier, angrily
3. portrayed, portrays, portraying, portrayal
4. silliness, sillier, silliest
5. employer, employed, employable

Page 373:

2. requring
3. inspiring
4. lovable
5. lovely
6. managing

7. management
8. completely
9. judgment
10. noticeable

Page 374:

2. wildest
3. referred
4. proceeding
5. dimmer
6. cleaner
7. committed
8. forgettable
9. happening
10. compelled

Pages 375:

2. unnatural
3. dissatisfied
4. illegible
5. mistrial
6. immoral
7. misspell
8. irreversible
9. illicit
10. unethical

Pages 377:

2. monkeys
3. echoes
4. knives
5. matches
6. months
7. kisses
8. stereos
9. candies
10. phenomena

Pages 377–378:

2. a lot
3. athlete
4. behavior
5. brilliant
6. business
7. carefully
8. career
9. competition
10. definite
11. desperate
12. develop
13. different
14. dining
15. describe
16. doesn't
17. embarrass
18. environment
19. exaggerate
20. February
21. fascinate
22. government
23. grammar
24. height
25. immediate
26. interest
27. knowledge
28. mathematics
29. necessary
30. occasion
31. opinion
32. opportunity
33. original
34. particular
35. potato
36. perform
37. perhaps
38. probably
39. ridiculous
40. separate
41. similar
42. sincerely
43. studying
44. surprise
45. temperature
46. Thursday
47. unusual
48. writing

Page 417

2. pictures
3. names
4. noncount
5. noncount
6. planets
7. noncount
8. governments
9. years
10. noncount

Page 418

2. Chantal suffered from amnesia, so she could not remember her date of birth.
3. He is a vegetarian, so he doesn't eat meat.
4. Monica's husband falls asleep in his chair whenever they watch a movie.
5. Jealousy is what caused him to act so rudely.

Page 419

2. Tolerance is a quality admired many people.
3. Irene was surprised at the disappointment that she felt.
4. The psychiatrist in the next office specializes in treating insomnia.
5. My car does not use gasoline in its diesel engine.

Page 420

2. Cerberus is the name of the dog that won the Most Beautiful Pet contest.
3. His decision to tell the truth about his theft required courage.
4. When Bill sees a homeless person, he always offers to buy him a meal.
5. The person who owns the red Honda that I hit is shouting at me.
6. Resentment was the only personal characteristic that Marie would not give up.
7. When she was robbed for the third time, Dora decided to buy a security system.
8. The chief of police could not believe what the rookie officer had just said.
9. Last year I decided to take a vacation to the Philippines.
10. Marissa eats doughnuts every day because they give her a sense of happiness.

Pages 421–422

2. Prometheus was chained to a rock.
3. Sohini wanted to return to India because she missed her family.
4. Although we were all hungry, the fish was too spoiled to eat.
5. My brother told me it is raining in Reno tonight.
6. When Ichiro looked at his paycheck, he decided to ask for a raise.
7. My cousin's parents were very rude to me last night.
8. It is too hot to wear a long-sleeved shirt today.
9. After the party had ended, everyone left Ensenada and drove home.
10. Don Quixote attacked the windmill so that he could win the love of Dulcinea.

Pages 424

2. He had trained hard, but he did not run fast enough to win the marathon.
3. The man who was standing at the corner has taken that woman's purse.
4. The suspect said the bag of money was given to him by someone else.
5. Did your son walk all the way home?
6. Benjamin's son does not want any of his good advice.
7. Everyone who meets that man is frightened by his violent behavior.
8. My neighbor Zaira has worked hard all her life to support her children.
9. Please be quiet because I am concentrating on my homework.
10. If you want to be released, you must tell who took the money.

Pages 426–427

Answers will vary. Here are some possible sentences.

2. After two hours of discussion, we still could not figure out what to do.
3. I will look after your house while you are in Switzerland.
4. The groom was devastated when his fiancée decided to call off the wedding.
5. No matter how hard I tried, I was unable to reason with my father about my low grades.
6. Lucinda did not approve of her sister's decision to tattoo her entire back.
7. Stan was embarrassed by his messy house when Barb dropped by for a short visit.
8. Sean was furious when he learned that his son had made up the entire story.
9. I'll try on the shirt, even though I hate the color of it.
10. When the contestant objected to the question, the entire audience began to laugh at him.

Pages 428

2. his torn leather jacket
3. three huge hairy horses
4. an expensive Chinese restaurant
5. this plain plastic stapler
6. my father's favorite family tradition
7. a recent modern art exhibit
8. that old red vinyl floor
9. some dishonest used car salespersons
10. these five enormous blue beach balls

Index